Comparing
Foreign Intelligence

Brassey's Titles of Related Interest

Bittman THE KGB & SOVIET DISINFORMATION: AN INSIDER'S VIEW

Bittman THE NEW IMAGE-MAKERS: SOVIET PROPAGANDA & DISINFORMATION TODAY

Danchev A VERY SPECIAL RELATIONSHIP: FIELD MARSHAL SIR JOHN DILL AND THE ANGLO-AMERICAN ALLIANCE 1941-44

Levchenko ON THE WRONG SIDE: MY LIFE IN THE KGB

Sejna & Douglass DECISION-MAKING IN COMMUNIST COUNTRIES: AN INSIDE VIEW

Shultz & Godson DEZINFORMATSIA: ACTIVE MEASURES IN SOVIET STRATEGY
2nd Edition, Revised

Related Journal

(Free specimen copy available upon request)

Defense Analysis

Comparing Foreign Intelligence

The U.S., the USSR, the U.K. & the Third World

Edited by

Roy Godson

PERGAMON-BRASSEY'S
International Defense Publishers, Inc.

Washington · New York · London · Oxford
Beijing · Frankfurt · São Paulo · Sydney · Tokyo · Toronto

U.S.A. (Editorial)	Pergamon–Brassey's International Defense Publishers, 8000 Westpark Drive, Fourth Floor, McLean, Virginia 22102, U.S.A.
(Orders)	Pergamon Press Inc., Maxwell House, Fairview Park, Elmsford, New York 10523, U.S.A.
U.K. (Editorial)	Brassey's Defence Publishers, 24 Gray's Inn Road, London WC1X 8HR
(Orders)	Brassey's Defence Publishers, Headington Hill Hall, Oxford OX3 0BW, England
PEOPLE'S REPUBLIC OF CHINA	Pergamon Press, Room 4037, Qianmen Hotel, Beijing, People's Republic of China
FEDERAL REPUBLIC OF GERMANY	Pergamon Press, Hammerweg 6, D-6242 Kronberg, Federal Republic of Germany
BRAZIL	Pergamon Editora, Rua Eça de Queiros, 346, CEP 04011, Paraiso, São Paulo, Brazil
AUSTRALIA	Pergamon–Brassey's Defence Publishers, P.O. Box 544, Potts Point, N.S.W. 2011, Australia
JAPAN	Pergamon Press, 8th Floor, Matsuoka Central Building, 1-7-1 Nishishinjuku, Shinjuku-ku, Tokyo 160, Japan
CANADA	Pergamon Press Canada, Suite No 271, 253 College Street, Toronto, Ontario, Canada M5T 1R5

Copyright © 1988 National Strategy Information Center, Inc.

First edition 1988

Library of Congress Cataloging in Publication Data
Comparing foreign intelligence.
Contents: Introduction/Roy Godson—The study of intelligence in the USA/Kenneth G. Robertson—Historical research on the British intelligence community/Christopher Andrew—(etc.)
1. Military intelligence—Study and teaching.
2. Intelligence service—Study and teaching.
I. Godson, Roy, 1942-
UB250.C68 1988   355.3'432'07   87-32851

British Library Cataloguing in Publication Data
Comparing foreign intelligence: the U.S., U.S.S.R., U.K. and the Third World.
1. Intelligence services. Comparative studies.
I. Godson, Roy, *1942-*
327.1'2

ISBN 0-08-034702-9

Austin Community College Learning Resources Center

Printed in Great Britain by A. Wheaton & Co. Ltd., Exeter

To Frank, Dorothy, and Christine

Contents

Preface

This volume originated from discussions at faculty seminars organized by the Consortium for the Study of Intelligence and held over several summers from 1980 to 1984 at Bowdoin College in Maine. These seminars brought together scholars from a variety of disciplines and over forty universities in the United States and abroad, although a majority of the participants were political scientists from American institutions.

The early eighties was a period of increased awareness of the role of intelligence in international affairs. At that time, a great deal of information, hitherto unavailable, was coming into the public domain. Not unconnected was burgeoning academic interest in the subject, particularly in several English-speaking countries. The desire to add comparative dimensions to study of the subject was then, perhaps, a natural step in the evolution of intelligence studies.

During these years, some of the "Bowdoin alumni" went on to assist in the formation of the British Study Group on Intelligence (1984) and the Canadian Association for Security and Intelligence Studies (1984). Others organized the Intelligence Studies Section of the International Studies Association (ISA), one of the largest professional societies of social scientists in the world; all three national groups are represented on the executive committee of the ISA Section.

Appropriately, it was at the international convention of ISA held in California in 1986 that most of the essays comprising this volume were first presented. They were discussed then by Ernest May of Harvard University and Angelo Codevilla of the Hoover Institution. One suggestion emerging from that panel was the need for an assessment of the study of intelligence in the United States, which had not been considered at that meeting. As the concepts and propositions put forward in the consortium's seven-volume series on U.S. *Intelligence Requirements for the 1980's* were likely to be discussed in this assessment, Ken Robertson, a British scholar who is also not a member of the consortium, was asked to fulfill the task. He has subjected the consortium's volumes to critical analysis. Some of the points he makes regarding the series are well taken. Others, I believe, are not proven. I look forward to the next round of intelligence studies to continue the discourse.

Finally, I would like to express my appreciation to all those who have contributed to and supported these discussions over the years. Particularly, I want to thank Frank R. Barnett and Dorothy E. Nicolosi, president and vice president, respectively, of the National Strategy Information Center (NSIC). For over twenty years, NSIC has assisted in institutionalizing national security studies in American universities. The center also has encouraged research contributing to innovation in U.S. national security policy. Frank and Dorothy, along with NSIC's former director of studies, the late Professor Frank Trager of New York University, were receptive to the idea of bringing together a group of academics from universities and research centers throughout the country to promote teaching and research about intelligence, which had previously not been regarded as an academic subject. This led to the formation, under the auspices of NSIC, of the Consortium for the Study of Intelligence, which I have coordinated since its inception in 1979. The consortium sponsored not only the Bowdoin seminars but also many smaller faculty seminars on intelligence held over the past several years in the United States, Canada, and the United Kingdom.

Others who continue to play an indispensable role in the activities of the consortium and who provided major assistance in the preparation of this volume are my friends and colleagues Jill Fall and Jeff Berman, both of the Washington office of the National Strategy Information Center.

I want to also pay tribute to Christine Godson, who only coincidentally is my wife. She has played a unique role in the consortium from the beginning—counselor, editor, logistics expert, sometime referee, and, not least, a most exacting and thoughtful critic. For all this and much, much more, I thank her.

Roy Godson
January 1988

1

Introduction:
The New Study of
Intelligence

ROY GODSON

Public knowledge about intelligence has expanded dramatically in recent years. Fifteen years ago only government officials with extensive contact with intelligence knew much about the subject and its important role in government and international affairs. Although there were academic pioneers who wrote important books and articles prior to the mid-1970s, little scholarly attention had been devoted to the subject. In the following years, major studies were authored by scholars with little or no intelligence experience. Others have been written by former intelligence officers who also were academics. By the decade of the 1980s, these academics and former intelligence practitioners were joined by journalists and politicians who specialized in intelligence and have contributed to what now can be called the new field of intelligence studies.

There were many reasons for these developments: the memoirs of former practitioners; the release of information in official histories; investigations of abuses and intelligence failures; and the public policy debate about intelligence, particularly in the United States. At the same time, important international events—for example the revolution in Iran, the Soviet moves in Afghanistan, and the Falklands War—highlighted the significance of intelligence. The growing recognition of intelligence and an appreciation of its role in twentieth-century history and government led to a major increase in research and publications, grant making by foundations, and the expansion of university curricula to include courses on intelligence.

As the field has just grown, there has been no single center or school of thought, no single intellectual framework guiding research and informing teaching. It became difficult for those already involved, let alone newcomers in the field, to untangle the diverse strands of intellectual discourse, to understand what had already been achieved and how, and to determine what might usefully be studied and how best this might be accomplished.

This volume is an attempt to clarify this process. The authors survey the kinds of work that have been published, the substantive concerns in these works, and the methods used. They also try to assess the strengths and weaknesses of these approaches and suggest new concerns and methodologies for future research.

The contributors, both American and British, agree that, while much progress has been made in recent decades, the next great leap forward may well come from explicit comparative research. And these contributors, who have been at the forefront of their field in the two most prolific centers of intelligence studies, the United States and the United Kingdom, argue that while American political scientists and students of international relations (for the most part) have uncovered important concepts, principles, and analytical tools for studying intelligence, the study of U.S. intelligence itself has been too parochial. It has reflected, primarily, what has become known about the post-1940 American experience seen through the paradigms of political science and policy analysis and has not been enriched by multidisciplinary study.

The other great strand of intelligence study has been the historical approach pursued, in the main, by British scholars. While adding historical depth to the study of one major intelligence system, this approach, too, suffers from the strengths and weaknesses of the historian's discipline. It is limited also by exclusive concentration on some aspects of the British experience in the first half of the twentieth century that have been available to scholars.

The contributors argue for more systematic comparative study of the subject matter. By this is meant comparisons between different experiences of countries with intelligence in diverse political or historical contexts, i.e., comparing not only one country with another but also the same country (or countries) in different historical contexts (war versus peace, states on the offensive versus states on the defensive, and so on).

By comparative is also meant employing different disciplines to study the same phenomena. Political scientists rarely engage in historical study; historians rarely explicitly use or test the concepts, principles, or hypotheses put forward by political scientists, let alone those in other disciplines such as sociology, anthropology, psychology, and the humanities.

The authors maintain that we have begun to build a solid foundation for comparative study. We are aware that there are intelligence experiences throughout world history that are comparable; we also are aware that in diverse historical and cultural contexts there are important differences in intelligence. And we have developed an awareness of our own culture, historical context, and intelligence system. Hence, we are equipped to begin understanding other intelligence systems and their similarities and differences to our own.

The contributors did not agree on a precise definition of intelligence or foreign intelligence. They did agree, at least for purposes of this volume, to employ a fairly broad definition of intelligence—to consider it as a "full service" function consisting of collection, analysis, counterintelligence, and covert action. This is in contrast to the narrower definition used sometimes, which presents intelligence as analysis and collection of information about foreign societies.[1]

Ken Robertson, of the University of Reading (United Kingdom), maintains that the United States has been the most important center of intelligence studies. Indeed, quantitatively there is no peer. The British scholar also maintains, based on the literature he analyzes, American intelligence studies have been influential and important because of the diverse conceptual approaches and general propositions about the subject matter. However, he points out that the substantive focus and knowledge of Americans has been primarily of their own intelligence system, particularly in the post-World War II period. Moreover, these concepts and propositions have been posited, in the main, by political scientists. However creative and stimulating these may be, before these concepts and propositions are accepted as universally applicable he suggests a need for more empirical research outside the postwar American experience.

Christopher Andrew, Cambridge University, traces the evolution of intelligence studies in the United Kingdom—the historical evolution of the British intelligence community—primarily until 1945. He describes the documentary sources, particularly the official archives and the official history of intelligence during wartime, that have enabled scholars to study important aspects of British intelligence. At the same time official restrictions in the archives, particularly for the pre-1939 period, are seriously inhibiting research—and, he suggests, for little good reason. Nevertheless, Professor Andrew suggests that many of the obstacles to research can be overcome by using private archives and the archives of related U.K. ministries that have not been "weeded."

Andrew also points out that the archives of friendly or allied governments are very useful. They not only contain information on British intelligence but also lend themselves to making comparisons with the British experience. In particular, Canadian, Australian, and U.S. archives offer much promise for students of individual English-speaking countries as well as for comparative studies. However, Andrew, like Robertson, also cautions against over-reliance on the U.S. postwar experience for making generalizations about intelligence. He argues that the study of intelligence by both historians and political scientists requires more "historical depth and geographic width than it possesses at present."

The study of one intelligence system, however, would seem to begin to meet the desiderata set forth by Andrew and Robertson: the Soviet intelligence and security services. Although it is far from easy to obtain reliable information about the secret activities of closed (and, indeed, open) societies, there has been important progress in understanding Soviet intelligence. This is particularly important as intelligence and security concerns appear to play a relatively more important role in Soviet politics and society than intelligence does in Western society and because the major characteristics of the Soviet intelligence system may have been adopted by most states ruled by Communist parties throughout the world.

Dr. John Dziak, a senior U.S. intelligence analyst who also is an adjunct professor at Georgetown University, surveys the history and the literature on the Soviet system. He maintains that until recently there was a tendency for Western scholars to "mirror image," or to project onto the Soviet system the concepts or assumptions they make about Western intelligence.

Dziak puts forward new propositions about the nature of the Soviet system and how it differs from Western systems. He maintains that Soviet intelligence is characterized primarily by counterintelligence and security concerns (in contrast to those of Western intelligence). Indeed, Soviet intelligence activities abroad, he suggests, are an external manifestation of what he calls the "counterintelligence state." He also discusses his documentation; not only are important primary and secondary sources available but also generations of Soviet defectors living in the West are a major source for those seeking to understand and compare seventy years of Soviet intelligence with the practices of other states.

Another scholar, Dale Eickelman of New York University, seeking historical depth and geographic breadth, adds disciplinary breadth to intelligence studies. Eickelman, an anthropologist specializing in the Middle East, is engaged in a research project on a small strategic Arab Gulf state at a particular historical juncture. The state is Oman; the juncture, decolonization. From the late 1950s through the early 1970s, the imperial mother country, Britain, was surrendering control of the intelligence and security apparatus to a combination of Omanis and British expatriates. Eickelman is seeking not only to compare intelligence in large states with intelligence in smaller ones but also to compare states that have considerable foreign involvement in their intelligence systems with those that do not. He also seeks to assess systematically social and cultural factors or contexts that affect intelligence collection and assessment by both examining archives that have been made available to him and conducting in-depth interviews with many of the participants in Omani intelligence during that period.

Adda Bozeman's concluding essay focuses explicitly on the desirability and feasibility of comparative studies of intelligence, particularly comparisons between Western and non-Western systems. Now Professor Emeritus of International Relations at Sarah Lawrence College, she has been at the forefront of the comparative study of culture and statecraft for over a generation.

Initially, she describes the essence of comparative studies and how previous generations of Westerners went about this task in their interaction with non-Western societies. She points out that American travelers, scholars, and government officials differed in their motivation and method from their European counterparts. She maintains that until very recently there was too much emphasis in the United States on theory-building and policy analysis based only on the American experience and norms. Moreover, almost all study of foreign societies has been conducted in U.S. universities, study that is therefore untested and uninformed by the experiences of Americans and others who have lived and worked in the politics of non-Western societies.

Professor Bozeman suggests that both the concepts and methods used by Western (particularly American) political scientists all too often are inadequate to permit understanding the culture, statecraft, and intelligence of other societies. She stresses the importance of multidisciplinary studies, particularly the humanities, for understanding non-Western societies, especially those with an oral tradition, as for example in Africa. Because intelligence, both domestic and foreign, in the non-Western world is a reflection of diverse cultures, traditions, and perceptions of history, Professor Bozeman stresses also the need to study society and culture rather than the state and its institutions when seeking to understand intelligence in the non-Western world. Understanding our own intelligence and our differences with the diverse intelligence systems of the non-Western world requires restructuring our studies, but she suggests this is not an insurmountable challenge, putting foward specific propositions and methods to aid in the undertaking.

Professor Bozeman and several other contributors also believe that the field has been preoccupied by American political science and by the study of the post-World War II American experience, so that it is too early to make generalizations about intelligence throughout history. As is pointed out in the volume, however, there are several different perspectives or paradigms in the United States for the study of the subject matter. One, with which this writer is associated, has put forward general propositions about the nature or principles of intelligence. These propositions were derived from the study not only of the postwar U.S. system but also what was known in the late 1970s and early 1980s about intelligence in other societies and in other historical contexts. True, our knowledge about other societies, contexts, and, for that matter, the contribution that diverse disciplines can make to intelligence studies is rather limited. It remains to be seen how well the concepts and propositions put forward at this stage will hold up when assessed as a result of the comparative research already under way.

The essays in this volume demonstrate that our knowledge of intelligence has grown considerably in recent years. A new field or subject has come into being. The contributors focus on the substantive concerns, concepts, and methods that help distinguish it from previous and other fields of study. As with these other fields (and disciplines), there are also important ambiguities and overlaps with other subject matter. However, intelligence studies are becoming institutionalized in the study of society, politics, and statecraft.

NOTE

1.   Among the few discussions of the concept of intelligence and how it has been defined in different political systems and historical contexts, see the chapters by R. Godson and J. B. Lockhart, a former senior British intelligence official, in K. G. Robertson, ed., *British and American Approaches to Intelligence* (London: Macmillan, 1987; New York: St. Martin's Press, 1987). For an analysis of these concepts, see the chapters by K. G. Robertson and A. Bozeman in this volume.

2

The Study of Intelligence in the United States

KENNETH G. ROBERTSON

This chapter will identify American approaches to the study of intelligence that have influenced research and will assess the strengths and weaknesses of these approaches by analyzing representative works. Not all intelligence literature will be surveyed but rather only works written by Americans after the Second World War that represent a shift in perspective and, therefore, influenced research.[1] It will not consider those many works that added to our knowledge by providing new pieces of information but did not indicate any change of direction and thus merely reinforced existing trends or perspectives.

All of the works selected, despite some sharp divisions of attitude, have certain common characteristics. They all recognize that the United States requires foreign intelligence despite disagreements as to how it should be organized, the kinds of activities it ought to perform, and the values that ought to guide intelligence operations. All of the works recognize that the task of intelligence is the preservation of U.S. security, although there is often deep divergence of opinion over the nature of the threats faced and the responses required. They all recognize that there are "tensions" between intelligence and democratic values, although there is considerable disagreement over the degree to which intelligence preserves or threatens democratic values and procedures. Some writers see intelligence as preserving democracy and American values through vigorous use of the full battery of intelligence techniques within the international system to protect and further U.S. interests. Others argue that fundamental values and democracy require that intelligence be carefully monitored and constrained in case the secrecy associated with intelligence leads to sacrificing such values in the name of defeating the "enemy."

However, despite common features, there are several different approaches to the study of U.S. intelligence. This is due to three main factors: changes in U.S. foreign policy or perception of the international "climate"; the domestic political environment and particularly attitudes to the "openness" and trustworthiness of American political leaders and institutions; and those debates that surfaced from within the intelligence community itself. The first of these factors can be illustrated by the impact of such policies as those implied by the Vietnam War and détente.[2] The second, by such events as Watergate and other revelations of particular abuses that are taken to indicate that values or democracy is being "betrayed" or in some way compromised.[3] The third, by the disagreements that existed within the intelligence community over the role and importance of covert action or the significance of human intelligence gathering versus technical collection.[4]

These factors have led to the study of intelligence in the United States being not only an academic pursuit but also one linked to public policy issues. Many of those who have studied intelligence have been inspired by a desire to influence Congress and the Executive branch as well as contribute to an academic discipline. This public policy focus has had the beneficial effect of encouraging participation by those with practical intelligence experience, but it has had the less desirable impact of "politicizing" some of the issues associated with the study of intelligence. It will, for example, be argued later that the focus on contemporary debates has led some writers to distort the past.[5]

The fact that intelligence is not simply of academic interest has given U.S. intelligence studies enormous and worldwide significance. The strategic role of the United States within the Western alliance has meant that U.S. public policy debates, and U.S. attitudes on intelligence, are of interest to the international community. Just as U.S. defense policy is central to Western defense, so U.S. intelligence policy is central to Western security. This fact alone justifies the claim of a worldwide significance. But when the academic impact of U.S. intelligence studies is added to this dimension, it is clear that the United States is the most influential center of intelligence study.

One reason for this influence is the sheer quantity of information, of varying degrees of reliability, that exists concerning the U.S. intelligence community. There is a willingness by former and even current members of the intelligence community to participate in debates and to express their views in print and in interviews. Many courses now taught in American colleges are devoted to intelligence or include a substantial slice of intelligence studies. The most important reason that the United States is an influential center of intelligence studies, however, is the variety of conceptual approaches developed to study intelligence.

There are four main approaches to the study of intelligence in the United States. The first of these is a series of early works that sought to lay foundations and establish intelligence as a respectable profession with an emphasis on analysis as the key issue. The second approach and one to which all others have reacted is the "liberal," which is based upon the premise that intelligence activities create particular problems for democratic political systems and democratic values. The liberal approach directs attention toward domestic issues and tends to suspect that claims of "threat" are exaggerated. This perspective sees almost as great a danger to democracy from the existence and practices of intelligence services as from the threats they are designed to counter. The third approach is that that emerges from international relations and the role of intelligence in time of national crisis, particularly war, the "surprise" school. This overlaps with the "historical" approach, which includes works devoted to particular intelligence episodes or organizations such as the Office of Strategic Services (OSS). The final school is the "realist," which argues that effective intelligence is necessary and desirable and that the main issue is not the tension between democratic values and intelligence but how such values need to be defended from threats to national security. Here the emphasis is on developing efficient and effective intelligence practices to defend national security at home or abroad. This approach tends to focus attention on the international system and the identification of threats and opportunities as well as the intelligence requirements necessary to meet such challenges. The realists have challenged the view that prior to the traumas of the 1970s all was well with U.S. intelligence and that in the 1980s the U.S. intelligence community is adequate to meet the challenges of the future.

AN EMERGENT PROFESSION

Although there were books on aspects of military intelligence and cryptography[6] in the interwar period, it is with the development of intelligence during and after the Second World War that the serious study of intelligence began. Interest resulted from government consideration of the organization of intelligence that would follow the end of hostilities.

The major contribution to the immediate postwar debate was Sherman Kent's *Strategic Intelligence for American World Policy.*[7] Kent focused on the problem of analysis and saw the value of intelligence as lying in its capacity to analyze events of a global strategic nature. One reason for this approach was his experience in the Research and Analysis Division of the wartime OSS. Kent argued that the key to avoiding war or another Pearl Harbor would lie in the creation of a central intelligence agency with the capability of amassing hard data that would be analyzed in an objective manner. Kent was skeptical of the value of espionage as the major source of information, since it was unlikely to be "hard." Kent advocated an academic, social science approach to intelligence in which the standards of objectivity and rigor characteristic of such sciences would be applied to the problems of intelligence. In such a conception, the intelligence consumer is to be relatively passive, receiving the wisdom of the intelligence community when the processes of collection and analysis are completed. Kent states, "Its (intelligence's) job is to stand behind them (consumers) with the book open at the right page."[8] The consumer is to offer guidance to the intelligence producer, but distance must be maintained if the policymaker's role is not to be taken over by the intelligence community and if the intelligence community is to maintain its objectivity. Kent sees the main task of intelligence to be prognosis, the provision of warnings and estimates of future events.[9] However, such warnings are not to be guesses; they are to be the result of a rational and laborious process of scholarship.

One can see Kent as attempting to create a *profession* with its own aims, methods, and ethos. The profession of intelligence was to equal the best of academic research with all of the professional qualities this implies. The world of spying with its connotations of bribery and corruption was to be treated with suspicion. Covert action and counterintelligence were hardly mentioned. This model of intelligence was enormously influential, since it was the first systematic public statement on U.S. intelligence requirements following the end of hostilities with the Axis powers. Kent focused attention on the problems of analysis because this was central to achieving what he considered the main aim of intelligence—prognosis.

Roger Hilsman in his major work on intelligence, *Strategic Intelligence and National Decisions*,[10] shares Sherman Kent's stress on analysis and the suspicion of cloak and dagger activities. However, he does not share Kent's belief that worthwhile analysis can be achieved only if a certain distance is maintained between intelligence and policy. Rather, Hilsman's bias is toward policy-making in that he argues that intelligence is essentially a tool of decisionmaking, which is perhaps not surprising given his background.[11] He also regrets the lack of coordination between the various participants involved in producing and consuming intelligence.[12] Hilsman argues that analysis is inseparable from policy and that no sharp boundary can be drawn between the producer and the consumer of the intelligence product. No longer is the intelligence community to be kept at a distance from policy-making in order to avoid contamination. Rather policymakers and intelligence officers must continuously interact to ensure the intelligence product is useful and relevant. Hilsman is very critical of the emphasis of both intelligence professionals and policymakers on objective "facts."[13] In practice, he argues, such "facts" are often merely "backstopping" for a policy that has already been decided.[14] Hilsman points out that good intelligence practice involves

1) the policymaker setting the values to be protected and enhanced;

2) the articulation of the assumptions of reality made by the decisionmaker and the identification of "problems" to be solved;

3) an assessment of the means to protect and fulfill the values identified at stage one;

4) an evaluation of the alternative means to attain objectives, solving the problem;

5) a calculation of the cost of these alternatives on *other* desired values;

6) an identification of other possible objectives that may fulfill the values identified at stage one;

7) clarification of the value preferences; and

8) the making of a decision.[15]

Despite the differences between Kent and Hilsman over "objectivity," "facts," and the value of long-range forecasts, they remain fundamentally united in their stress on analysis as the most valuable and important intelligence activity.[16] This approach stresses the close links between intelligence work and academic research, the concept of intelligence as either a library or as part of a team of rational researchers. These works, and that of Platt and Petee,[17] all place the same emphasis on collection and analysis as the sole "professional" intelligence activity. This may seem odd given the importance clandestine operations achieved during the 1950s and into the 1960s, but these men were heavily influenced by their wartime experience and the Pearl Harbor syndrome, the view that it is possible with objective collection and analysis to avoid the disasters inflicted by surprise.

An exception to this is Willmoore Kendall, who wrote a review[18] of Kent's *Strategic Intelligence* in which he criticizes him for his obsession with Pearl Harbor and his failure to recognize that intelligence has a different role in time of peace than in time of war. Kendall argues that only in war does one have a clear set of strategic objectives that can guide intelligence requirements. In time of peace, the international system is too fluid and uncertain for warnings and prognosis to be of value. Kendall argues that Kent is obsessed with facts, is "grossly" empirical in his approach, and ignores the real requirement for men who can think theoretically and can postulate alternatives to place before policymakers.[19] Kendall does not believe that facts speak for themselves; rather he believes that some form of theory is always necessary to guide analysis. He is more afraid that theory will be swamped by a tide of facts than he is about the contamination of objectivity by the needs or perceptions of policymakers. Kendall does not offer any clear blueprint of intelligence, but he does state that he would like to see a small group of intelligence analysts working closely with policymakers on developing theories of international affairs. For him the real dangers in intelligence lie in the "impenetrable fog of security" behind which intelligence will hide and be left to its own devices.[20] Such debates are still alive, and they will resurface later as a key issue in the Godson series on *Intelligence Requirements for the 1980's*.

In the 1960s almost no serious work was published on intelligence requirements.[21] Rather, it was during the late 1960s that the focus of attention moved toward "domestic" concerns such as the accountability of intelligence and the ethics of intelligence activity. This shift in focus may be seen as reflecting the breakup of the foreign policy consensus.

From the 1950s through the mid-1960s, there was little dispute about the nature of threats either at home or abroad. Such threats as were recognized were considered to be understood and under control. This is the period during which Congress is reported to have been more interested in ensuring the CIA had sufficient resources to "do its job" than in investigating either the nature of its activities or whether it was doing the job most suited to America's national security requirements.[22] However, during this time there were two books worthy of note published on the theme of intervention.

Blackstock and Westerfield[23] both examine case studies of covert action operations and, although they both suffer from the lack of factual information available at the time concerning the intelligence aspect of these operations, they remain of value because they attempt to place covert action in a foreign policy context. Westerfield examines economic measures, foreign aid, information programs, and military assistance as part of the "tools" available to the U.S. government to affect other nations. This is an important reminder that covert action is not the only form of intervention. Even diplomatic efforts can be seen as a part of the process of achieving foreign policy objectives by influencing other nations.[24] Too often covert action is seen as a unique instrument for achieving foreign policy objectives or even as an alternative method of achieving foreign policy objectives. Blackstock is rightly critical of this view, arguing that covert action should not be used as a form of hidden foreign policy because it may actually contradict the official policy or the actions of other parts of the foreign policy apparatus.[25]

THE LIBERAL APPROACH TO INTELLIGENCE

The most influential figure of this school is Harry Howe Ransom. In 1970 Ransom published his study, *The Intelligence Establishment*,[26] which is based on *Central Intelligence and National Security*,[27] published in 1958. His work argues that intelligence is a necessity, but one that poses particular problems in a democratic society. The question is posed as follows:

How can a democracy best ensure that its secret intelligence establishment becomes neither a vehicle of conspiracy nor the perverter of responsible government in a democracy?[28]

There is no doubt of Ransom's contribution. He provided the first serious attempt to describe the organization of U.S. intelligence, and he also provided the first attempt to describe British intelligence. This work is now outdated, but until the mid-1970s it was the best source available on the organization of U.S. intelligence. Of more lasting value is Ransom's conception of intelligence. Ransom identifies intelligence as being of three types classified according to their purpose: strategic, tactical, and counter-intelligence.[29] He then describes the intelligence process as involving several steps: tasking, collection, evaluation and production, and dissemination.[30] Strategic intelligence is concerned with information required to establish the basis of long-term national security policy; tactical intelligence, information relevant to current operations, is often of a military nature. Finally, he recognizes that counterintelligence is not only concerned with negating the enemy's intelligence efforts but also can produce valuable positive information about his capabilities and intentions.[31] He also recognizes the importance of tasking, or what he calls the "setting of requirements," although no space is devoted to a discussion of this important issue.[32] This is unfortunate, since a crucial question is always whose requirements are to determine collection priorities. Much of the contemporary debate still concerns this basic issue of who is responsible for setting intelligence policy. However valuable Ransom's effort to conceptualize intelligence may have been, the fact is that it received little attention then or later. It was Ransom's anxieties concerning the control and morality of intelligence that emerged as the key issues of the 1970s.

The major focus of Ransom's approach remains, despite his acknowledgment of the necessity of intelligence, the "tensions" between democracy and intelligence. The major tensions, he states, are accountability, secrecy, and covert action or "intervention."[33] Little attention is paid to efficiency, effectiveness, and the need to match intelligence to national security requirements. His focus on the liberal concerns with democratic processes and values leads research toward a search for intelligence "abuses," and this has distorted the picture offered of the nature and purpose of intelligence. The "liberal" concern with issues such as accountability, secrecy, and civil rights leads research to focus on the "domestic" dimension of intelligence and to ignore or downplay the threats that intelligence services are designed to counter. Such threats are virtually ignored by Ransom. For example, when he considers domestic intelligence, he only discusses the wartime role of the FBI when it was briefly a part of the foreign intelligence community.[34] However, what is perhaps more revealing is that Ransom does not specify the strategic threats facing the United States or the opposite of this coin, its national security interests.[35]

Intelligence is seen as "safe" only when it is "processing the data." Virtually all other activities pose dangers to the democratic process.[36]

Ransom sees the United States as being passive in the face of international events with the task of intelligence being to analyze information about such events. The intelligence services are also "passive" with little attention being paid to "active" collection or to covert action. Ransom makes two revealing comments concerning covert action. The first is to state, despite admitting that "the exact details are unknown outside of the inner sanctum of the CIA," that "the compatibility of these many forms of covert political action with a more narrowly defined intelligence function is open to question."[37] The second statement concerns the CIA subsidies granted to private voluntary groups such as the National Student Association. He argues, "The form of subsidy used, and the CIA as the disbursing agency, are unacceptable for the future, for they represent a step toward a totalitarian society."[38] The implication of both of these comments is clear. Any intelligence activity except "acting as a library" is fraught with hazards, making the risk of engaging in such practices virtually unacceptable. The risks are, of course, the effects on the fabric of *American society*—the "domestic" focus. Many of these points can be reinforced by examining the most influential study based on the liberal perspective, that of the Senate Select Committee on Intelligence (1975-1976) chaired by Senator Frank Church and to which Ransom was a senior consultant.

The Church Committee provides a wealth of information, but its findings and conclusions are often adversely affected by its concern with the more sensational issues associated with intelligence such as assassination, domestic spying, intervention, and the "rogue elephant" thesis. Such issues are worthy of investigation and comment, but the U.S. intelligence community has not spent most of its energy, time, and resources dealing with poisoned cigars, overthrowing governments, or subverting the democratic process. Domestic intelligence was more properly given emphasis, since it is clear that too many government man-hours, files, and effort went into surveillance of domestic subversion when there was no clear definition of subversion or clear purpose involved in the surveillance.

The bias of the Church Committee becomes clear when one examines the brief given to it by the Senate.[39] The first five tasks given to the committee concerned illegal domestic intelligence operations, the Huston Plan, and the extent of CIA/FBI coordination as to whether such coordination contributed to actions that were "illegal, improper, inefficient, unethical, or contrary to the intent of Congress."[40] Task number six concerns the CIA and the protection of sources and methods, which again focuses attention on largely domestic and constitutional matters. Tasks seven to eleven are concerned with intelligence violations of statutes. Task twelve concerns oversight; number thirteen, intelligence legislation. Only with task fourteen is any issue of effectiveness raised, and the concern with unnecessary duplication of effort still seems to be inspired by how such duplication can give rise to abuses. The final task asks the committee to examine the extent and necessity of covert action. Nowhere, except in the list of questions quoted above in task four, is efficiency cited. Only tangentially is effectiveness mentioned; and nowhere is any mention made of foreign policy, strategic interests, threats from home or abroad, defense policy, or overall national security policy.

This "domestic" and "ethical" bias is given further evidence by the analysis of the Church Committee Report carried out by Roy Godson.[41] Godson determined the number of pages in the Church Committee Final Report devoted to particular topics. The results[42] expressed in percentage terms are as follows:

Intelligence Activity	Percentage of Pages
Clandestine collection	0.40
Counterintelligence	0.70
Analysis and collection	2.25
Other	18.9
Covert action	26.6
Rights of Americans	51.2

Despite the uncertainty as to the content of the category "Other," the picture is clear: the Church Committee considered the morality of covert action and the civil rights of Americans to be the main issues raised by U.S. intelligence activities. There was no systematic or serious study of the efficiency and effectiveness of U.S. intelligence because to carry out such a task would have required the committee to develop a coherent picture of the *purpose* of intelligence. The Church Committee and the "liberal" approach find this difficult because it entails identifying actions by other nations as hostile and certain domestic activities as "subversive." The liberal sees identifying certain activities as "threats" as dangerous because this appears to justify the very activities of which he is so suspicious.

There are also problems associated with the method of inquiry adopted by the congressional committees of investigation. The Church Committee decided at an early stage to concentrate on specific examples of intelligence practice in the belief that such examples "reflected generic problems."[43] The problem with this approach is that it depends upon a key issue of credibility; just how accurate a reflection of intelligence practice are these examples? The word *reflects* is dangerously ambivalent. It may mean that the examples "reflect" those issues that are of most "interest" to the committee, or it may refer to a frequency statement such that the examples are selected to represent the most common type of activity. It is all too easy to select one's examples to "reflect" what will interest the *New York Times* or the *Washington Post* rather than to reflect the much duller average work of the intelligence community. Unfortunately, although perhaps inevitably, the sensational is all too often seen as the best reflector of generic problems.

In a key passage on the historical background to the committee's work, a statement is made indicating the general tenor of the report: "... the growth of intelligence abuses reflects a more general failure of our basic institutions."[44] Not only were abuses seen as the product of the intelligence community but also as reflecting the morality and legitimacy of government institutions. Indeed, it can almost be described as a search for the "national character" carried out via an inquiry into intelligence practices.

The Senate was not the only investigating committee of Congress; there was also a House Select Committee on Intelligence chaired by Congressman Otis Pike.[45] Unfortunately, this committee's experience was much sadder. Its report was never officially published, although a draft was leaked to *The Village Voice*.[46] The House Committee had been plagued by politics, leaks, and controversy with the Executive branch. Its style was "oppositionist," and this severely damaged its relationship with the intelligence community and the White House, thus hindering its access to information.[47] The unofficial version of its report released to the press contains an "81-page" complaint about "obstruction," which indicates the difficulty in relying on its findings.[48] The approach of the Pike Committee was to undertake an analysis of six "intelligence failures" that were a "representative spectrum."[49] The problem with representative failures is no different from representative examples; how can one know whether such instances reflect or represent anything other than the interests of the committee or its staff members? The Pike Committee also echoes the Church Committee's concern with "sloppy" covert action operations and with domestic intelligence abuses. There is no indication in the leaked draft report that the committee gave any consideration to the role of intelligence in U.S. national security policy or how reform might better enable the intelligence community to perform its tasks. The lessons are that intelligence is costly, unethical, illegal, and bungling.[50]

In sum, despite the fact that the work of the congressional committees, particularly that of the Senate, produced a great deal of valuable information, there are great difficulties in judging their conclusions and in judging how representative are the examples selected for detailed investigation. The Church Committee produced not an analysis of U.S. intelligence or an objective history of U.S. intelligence but rather a record of intelligence reflecting the concerns and issues of a particular period of U.S. political history. However, just as the Church Committee can be criticized for failing to provide the foreign policy and domestic political context within which to place the intelligence record, so one must also recognize the domestic climate of opinion that gave rise to the congressional investigations. The series of press and other leaks had understandably focused on the sensational aspects, and it is not surprising that this influenced the committee. However, it remains unfortunate that the climate of opinion distorted the work of the committees.

This discussion of the Church Committee naturally leads into the study of domestic intelligence, since this was really its main concern. The works on domestic intelligence fall into two categories: historical studies of the FBI and legal analysis of the issues associated with domestic intelligence. An example of the former is the work of Athan Theoharis.[51] He is undoubtedly one of the foremost historians of the FBI and has made major contributions to our knowledge. The major regret is that his work is motivated by a single obsession, which tends to bias his conclusions. His obsession is that all of the FBI's domestic intelligence activities are either without lawful foundation or presidential approval.[52] This is a search for the illegitimate ancestry of FBI domestic intelligence activities, and it is unfortunate that such a "genealogical" issue should be given priority. The question of whether the FBI had lawful authority for its activities is an important question. But without some understanding of the *context*, particularly the perception of threat, it is difficult to see this search for roots as anything other than a search to prove that FBI domestic intelligence activities are "illegitimate." This search for "ancestry" is also found in the writings of former intelligence officers. The conclusion they wish to reach is the exact opposite of Theoharis's, that the CIA is the product of legitimate and honorable ancestry. But the search is equally irrelevant to the key issues. The main issue associated with intelligence, either domestic or foreign, ought not to focus on whether the CIA is a direct descendant of the OSS or whether Hoover was given instructions by a particular president but on the nature of threats from home and abroad and the type of intelligence service required to respond to those threats.

Theoharis, in his study *Spying on Americans*,[53] has not a single reference in the index to the Soviet Union or its intelligence services; and the Communist party is only referred to as a victim of FBI covert action, COINTELPRO, and of the House Committee on UnAmerican Activities (HUAC).[54] There is no analysis of the degree to which the Communist party is a different type of party to others in the United States or the extent to which it has acted as a vehicle of Soviet activities including espionage. The absence of such an analysis reduces the value of the work, since it indicates that the aim of the history is to criticize rather than assess. Another factor requiring further research is the organizational or bureaucratic determinants of FBI activity. Despite the work of John Eliff, Stanford Unger, Theoharis, and several other authors,[55] there has still been insufficient research of a historical nature into FBI records. This is not an easy task since the FBI records in the National Archives are not complete; but it is one that remains to be attempted.

Frank Donner is another who has written extensively on domestic intelligence.[56] He has used the Church Committee, historical materials, and the resources of the American Civil Liberties Union (ACLU) to write an account of "political surveillance." However, the bias of Donner is so blatant that it makes it difficult to accept his conclusions. He argues that the history of domestic intelligence "reflects the power of a myth system in which intelligence rescues a permanently endangered national security from the never-ending machinations of subversion."[57] Note not merely a myth, but a myth *system*! Nowhere does Donner consider whether any of the threats that gave rise to surveillance were real; all are dismissed as exaggerated or imaginary. Donner's work is a form of revenge on McCarthyism and all of the evils associated with it. This is a morality tale as much as history where J. Edgar Hoover is equated with Stalin.[58]

A more useful approach is the Constitutional school, two representatives of which are Richard Morgan and John Eliff.[59] Eliff was the leader of the Church Committee task force on the FBI, and Morgan teaches constitutional law at Bowdoin College. Both of these authors argue that the Constitution can provide a basis by which to judge whether particular intelligence practices ought to be performed, or ought not to be performed, by the U.S. government. The focus of attention is, therefore, on examining the restraints the Constitution places on intelligence work and discovering those areas in which the government has a free hand. This approach operates on the premise that intelligence policy and requirements must take *second place* to the domestic principles of the Constitution. The assumption of this school is that, once one has identified a principle of the Constitution that has been or may be interpreted by the Supreme Court as prohibiting certain forms of intelligence activity, there can be no case made for their continuation. This implies that the Constitution is a much more rigid and precise document than some have argued,[60] and that, when faced with a choice between national security and the Constitution, it is always the former that must be sacrificed to the latter and never the other way round. The experience of the United States in time of war would indicate that the balance of risk is not always so easy to make.

Furthermore, analysis of the relationship between the Constitution and intelligence focuses attention on the domestic sphere and the "rights of Americans." This leads both authors to develop a set of principles for judging the legitimacy of U.S. intelligence activities that depend upon distinguishing between "foreign" threats, groups, and links and those that are solely or primarily domestic in nature.[61] However, this distinction is often artificial, since the degree of threat or the seriousness of the threat can hardly depend simply upon whether foreigners are involved. Does a threat become serious just because foreigners are involved or a domestic threat from Nazi groups become less serious because it is purely domestic? Both Morgan and Eliff argue that domestic intelligence is bound to be different from foreign intelligence because there exists a body of case law, statute, and constitutional interpretation against which to judge domestic intelligence activities. This legal framework makes the task of judging the "legitimacy" of domestic intelligence activity easier than in the case of foreign intelligence because international law is much more vague.[62] In the former case, one has at least some established standards against which to judge "ethical issues" that are not simply a matter of individual opinion but that reflect accumulated wisdom. There is, of course, still room for debate over the exact meaning of statutes or the Constitution, but it is much less than when judging the "morality" of covert action or intervention.

Three issues emerge from the work of Theoharis, Donner, Morgan, Eliff, and the Church Committee. The first concerns the extent of the political and personal abuse of FBI powers by presidents and Director Hoover; the second, the extent of illegal harassment of political radicals; the third, the use of illegal techniques of intelligence collection (surveillance). The solution offered is to bring the FBI under more direct and continuous control by the Justice Department and to issue clearer guidelines and rules including a "charter."[63] However, such an approach is premised on the assumption that the internal threats the United States faces are well defined and the requirement necessary to counter such threats understood and in place.

In fact, the opposite is the case. There exists substantial disagreement as to whether there are any serious internal threats to U.S. security and little agreement as to the requirements to match those threats. Consideration of FBI guidelines that do not address this question is inadequate. This is as true whether one believes that there are no threats or whether one believes the threats to be serious. Scholars can help, but it is the responsibility of the political institutions to offer a conception of the threats and the measures necessary to respond.

So far there has been little serious work on the nature of internal threats and how these can be linked to intelligence requirements for domestic intelligence.[64] The scholarly study of "subversion," treason, hostile intelligence activity, technological espionage, disinformation, terrorism, and the protection of classified information is essential if one is to begin to discuss the past and future of "domestic intelligence" in a manner that recognizes the key fact that past and future intelligence activity depends not only on civil liberties but also on the nature of the challenges to security.

One recent approach that does attempt to tackle these issues is the sixth volume on *Domestic Intelligence* in the Consortium for the Study of Intelligence series.[65] A key debate to emerge from this volume is that concerning the "standard" required before an FBI investigation can be opened or a file maintained on a person or an organization. The argument is that the "criminal standard" has become the de facto law of the United States whatever the Constitution or statutes may say.[66] The criminal standard requires that no investigation or file be opened unless there are reasonable grounds to believe that a criminal action has taken or is about to take place. John Eliff argued that the FBI be guided by a criminal standard "plus" in his study, and Richard Morgan argued for a rhetoric or advocacy "plus" standard in his, i.e., that the proposed target has advocated violating the law.[67] The argument centers on two issues: one is the protection of constitutional rights, particularly the First Amendment's concern with free expression and association; and the other, the effect of such measures on the activities of the FBI. Both arguments refer to the effect of perception, as well as reality, on constraining activity both of individuals and the government. Guidelines may be as likely to chill FBI investigations as FBI investigations are to chill discussion in radical organizations.

However, this issue is of less importance than the one raised by de Graffenreid in his comment on the paper by Rommerstein.[68] The issue is the purpose of collecting information on domestic threats. Having collected information, what is to be done with it and what action is to be taken?[69] The debate on abuse has focused attention on the investigators, the FBI, to the staggering neglect of what one does with the information when collected. What is the point of intelligence collection if it is never analyzed or acted upon? If the only purpose in collecting information is to prosecute offenders in a court of law, then there can be no reason for collecting information *except* if one believes a criminal act has been or is about to be committed. This means that without some other purpose for investigation than the prosecution of criminal activity the criminal standard becomes by default the only justification for investigation. This simple truth seems to have been forgotten in a welter of argument about the law and the Constitution.

Unless one recognizes that domestic intelligence has at least one other purpose apart from prosecution, then the criminal standard is the only possible rationale for collection. The most obvious such "other purpose" is a goal similar to that underlying foreign intelligence collection, namely, to assist the policymaker in recognizing the dangers challenging the security of the United States, correctly assessing the seriousness and dimensions of this challenge, and developing policies and actions to meet it. However, this can only be done if there exists an analytical system and a mechanism for advising the president that matches the best that foreign intelligence can produce. The United States has patently not had either of these requirements, and it is this fact more than any other that is cause for concern.[70]

This is not to make an ideological point that the United States is threatened by sinister forces. It is to argue that without analysis and dissemination of the domestic intelligence product there is no rationale for collection whatever the nature of the threat. Much more research needs to be undertaken into the use that presidents and policymakers have made of information collected by the FBI at various periods of history and how this link between policy-making and domestic intelligence can be organized so as to insure that collection is not left to the whims and fancies of a director of the FBI, his staff, or to the values of a particular president. It is essential that a system equivalent to the National Security Council be constructed for domestic intelligence, if public confidence is to be won—whatever the standard employed for the investigation of *criminal* conduct.

Other issues to emerge from this volume are the nature of the threats facing the United States and the degree to which law and the Constitution actually constrain the United States's ability to respond to such threats. Angelo Codevilla attempts to change the focus of collection and analysis of domestic threats away from "subversion" and toward "technological transfer" or industrial espionage.[71] However, one might ask whether this is really a radical shift of focus, since it still implies that domestic intelligence, if it is to be uncontroversial, must be linked to foreign nationals and states. This is actually a very traditional approach to domestic security, since it depends upon "linkage," the involvement of foreign powers, in order to justify domestic intelligence. For example, attitudes toward the U.S. Communist party have been colored by the view that it is not a truly domestic political party but is actually an agent of a foreign power, the Soviet Union. The paper by Allen Weinstein provides an overview of this aspect of the nature of domestic security.[72] The discussion of the constitutional constraints on domestic intelligence concludes that, although such constraints do exist, they do not incapacitate the United States in dealing with domestic threats to national security.[73] It is clear, however, that the premise remains as outlined above: if the Constitution prohibits certain activities, then nothing can be done to respond to threats. To shift the focus of research requires further work on the interaction among domestic threats, whether indigenous or linked to foreign powers; the activities of U.S. intelligence; and the evolving legal concepts of search and seizure, privacy, and free speech.

In conclusion, the liberal approach has been enormously influential because it has focused attention on an issue of immediate concern to many Americans—their rights and liberties. However, this approach has directed attention toward domestic concerns and has avoided the key issue of identifying the national security interests of the United States and the type of intelligence service necessary to protect those interests. One cannot know what constraints to apply to intelligence until one has clearly identified the threats that one faces.

SURPRISE AND THE LESSONS OF HISTORY

One of the most influential approaches to the study of intelligence in the United States is that based on the concept of "surprise." This approach focuses on the role of intelligence in times of international crisis. In particular, it asks the question of how intelligence can assist in crisis management and whether adequate, let alone complete, information can provide the key to successful crisis management. If it can be shown that "failure" is not the product of inadequate or incomplete information, then the role of intelligence is reduced in significance. This approach poses a central question: How important is intelligence in avoiding war or defeat in war? This school of thought has directed research toward an examination of the circumstances in which war occurs and the role of intelligence collection and analysis in providing warning of attack. This issue has attracted scholars not only for historical reasons, particularly the Pearl Harbor syndrome, but also because war between major powers may lead to nuclear attack.

The most influential study of "surprise" was that carried out in 1962 by Roberta Wohlstetter on the attack at Pearl Harbor.[74] Wohlstetter not only added new conceptual dimensions to the study of intelligence but also brought together primary sources, secondary works, and her conceptual tools to demonstrate that lessons could be learned. Wohlstetter's major contribution was the concept of "noise." This concept moved the debate away from merely focusing on the gaps in intelligence collection to a new focus on the problems in correctly reading the information collected. "Noise" refers to the density (number) of signals, ambiguities in signals, contradictory messages, and useless or irrelevant signals that cloud or fog the relevant signals.[75] Perhaps the key lesson of this study is that intelligence is not *the* key. There are no magic formulas; one must live with uncertainty. This is a valuable point that can bear repetition, since both the critics of intelligence and some of its more ardent supporters would seem to believe that it is the cause of all misery or all happiness. She points out that there is many a slip between collection and action, not least the bureaucratic blocks to the flow of intelligence information. Wohlstetter has generated an enormous body of literature in this area.[76]

Richard Betts of the Brookings Institution argues that surprise is inevitable.[77] He means that intelligence warnings are of secondary importance in understanding surprise and that political and psychological factors are primary.[78] A key factor underlying the persuasiveness of Betts's conclusions is the comparative and historical work that he has carried out.

Although Michael Handel[79] has suggested that studies of surprise may soon be reaching the point of diminishing returns, there is still room for further comparative studies of "surprise," whether diplomatic, military, or even technologically innovative. Other examples of comparative studies devoted to warning and intelligence policy are those edited by Ernest May and by Robert Pfaltzgraff, Uri Ra'anan, and Warren Milberg.[80] Although these volumes include contributions from scholars from a variety of countries and backgrounds, they show the strength of the attempt to link intelligence with military and political decisions. This trend—the attempt to show the influence of intelligence on decisions—is one that is likely to continue. This is so for two main reasons. The first is greater access to public documents, especially those concerning the Second World War. The second is the spread of interest in intelligence among scholars in related disciplines such as military history. An increasing trend is likely to be the application of intelligence concepts by a variety of specialists in fields such as diplomatic history, arms control, foreign policy, international relations, and criminology.

A related body of literature, although one which has no single conceptual approach, is the historical study of particular intelligence organizations or episodes. Representatives of the historical school include Bradley Smith and Thomas Troy.[81] Troy's work on the OSS was written as an "official" history for the CIA, and it attempts to prove the claim that there was continuity between the OSS and the CIA and that "Wild" Bill Donovan was the major influence on the nature and organization of postwar U.S. intelligence.[82] This thesis is challenged by Smith, who argues that there were several influences on the creation of the Central Intelligence Agency.[83] Among these influences were the British intelligence professionals who collaborated with Americans during and after the Second World War; the image or "myth" of the OSS that Donovan propagated; and the international situation, particularly fear of the Soviet Union. This debate, continuity of reality or continuity of myth, has echoes of the earlier debate over the legitimacy/illegitimacy of the FBI. The origins of American intelligence organizations are likely to continue as a topic of inquiry.

THE REALISTS

The Godson series on *Intelligence Requirements for the 1980's*[84] will occupy most of this section, but I will begin by examining other representatives of the "realist" approach. A major representative of this school is Ray Cline, with his volume *Secrets, Spies, and Scholars*.[85] This was the first example of a former senior intelligence officer reacting to the climate of the 1970s by attempting to "set the record straight." The main idea running throughout Cline's work is that the "central" concept of Central Intelligence needs to be made even clearer than it already is with the Director of Central Intelligence (DCI) being elevated to Cabinet status and through the creation of a new "genuine" central intelligence system to better serve the president.[86] Here the debates initiated by Kent, Hilsman, and Kendall some forty years before have reemerged. Cline believes that a new central structure would not only give the DCI the authority to act as the president's central adviser on foreign intelligence but would also give the DCI a key role in tasking collection and approving proposals for covert action.[87] Such a system involves dismantling the present CIA, with analysis and tasking being moved to a new and separate organization to be known as the Central Institute of Foreign Affairs Research, and with the clandestine services (collection) being moved into a separate agency to be known as the Clandestine Services Staff.[88] Covert action is to be reduced, if not abandoned, with no "permanent organization for covert action."[89] The logic behind Cline's proposals is clear. He argues that analysis must be linked to policy with intelligence playing a larger part in policy-making at the highest level to ensure that intelligence is properly used. He has accepted the view that the current status of the DCI is not matched with actual authority and has accepted the view that the parceling of intelligence that has emerged over the years fails to provide a truly central, coordinated, and efficient system. However, seeing the rationale for his scheme does not make it workable. The interests of the Department of Defense and the State Department will ensure, as they did in 1947, that no truly central system will emerge.

Furthermore, to separate analysis from collection and covert action from everything seems to create as many problems as it solves. In particular it is clear that all of these activities create opportunities for the more effective operation of the others. Opportunities for covert action emerge from clandestine collection, and it can be argued that analysis removed from collection may not permit proper understanding of the significance and reliability of the data being analyzed. However, other intelligence systems do operate on the principle that analysis should be separate from intelligence collection and more closely linked to the requirements of the Foreign Service. The intelligence system of the United Kingdom is one such example. Whether this is desirable in the United States is debatable given the nature of the relationship between the president and the CIA. Cline seems to be arguing that a "truly" central service will better serve the president, but this could only be achieved if there was a "truly" central mechanism of foreign policy-making. The role of the National Security Adviser in the White House and his relationship to the State Department would indicate that presidents have been uncertain as to whether the State Department alone meets their requirements. Without the centralization of the whole system of defense and foreign policy-making, something that appears unlikely, there can be little justification for further centralizing intelligence.

Cline is a "realist" in that he seeks to have an effective intelligence service, but he is also a reformer who has been influenced by the events of the 1960s and 1970s. It is clear that Cline sees the Directorate of Operations as having been too powerful and too inclined to engage in covert actions that were unclear in purpose and lacking in "deniability." But his solution, to break up the CIA into various parts and then create two new services with only a vague capacity for covert action, seems no more satisfactory. The key issue is the *political* process of decisionmaking; and improvement in this does not depend upon a bureaucratic rearrangement of intelligence but in scrutiny of the roles of the president, his staff, the National Security Council, the cabinet, and Congress.

Although many former intelligence professionals have written books on intelligence,[90] few have developed the kind of blueprint for change described by Cline. Most of the memoirs are valuable as sources of information on intelligence organization, activities, and ethos. However, one aspect of these memoirs worthy of note is that not all intelligence professionals seek to reject liberal criticisms or justify the past. Indeed, some such as Philip Agee, Frank Snepp, and James Stockwell are deeply criticial of aspects of U.S. intelligence policy.[91] Agee has gone so far as to call for the destruction of all U.S. intelligence capacity: "If put at the service of those we once oppressed, our knowledge of how the CIA really works could keep the CIA from ever really working again."[92] Other intelligence professionals have written memoirs describing their experience in intelligence in a more favorable light. One example is the work of Cord Meyer.[93] Meyer portrays a picture of U.S. intelligence that is almost the opposite of that portrayed by the critics. His experience was that the CIA was among the more liberal agencies in Washington, despite its continuing struggle with the Soviet Union. Meyer describes the "reality" of the challenges that he considers America has faced in the last thirty years and the response of U.S. intelligence. The memoirs of former intelligence officers are one of the few places where the interaction between challenge and response is discussed.

One of the other useful functions performed by such autobiographies and biographies is that they show the debates and divisions that occurred within the CIA itself. Two examples are the memoirs of William Colby[94] and the study of Richard Helms written by Thomas Powers, *The Man Who Kept the Secrets.*[95] Powers's book, with its strong criticism of covert action, shows what can be done with a notepad and secondary sources. Powers had the advantage over many of those who wrote their own memoirs of taking the time to crosscheck what various participants in the intelligence community said about a particular incident. This is invaluable in giving additional credibility to what he writes. Few other intelligence authors have taken the time or trouble to call on their friends and colleagues to check their version of events against the authors' memory. This makes it difficult to know what is reliable and what is unreliable in their memoirs. This is especially acute when they write of things in which they did not directly participate.

The main interest in these books is the focus on politics within the CIA. They discuss the wisdom of the action taken in the 1970s to reduce personnel, to compile the "family jewels," and to "cooperate" with congressional committees. Helms was deeply skeptical of Colby's policy of lifting the "cloak of secrecy" to prevent the agency from being "crippled."[96] Helms believed that an attitude of mea culpa would not convince the American people that, after repentance, all would be sweetness and light. Rather, Helms feared that the process of catharsis would be a wrecking strategy.[97] Can one now make a judgment as to whose analysis of the likely results of telling the "bad secrets" to preserve the "good" was correct? I doubt it—the main reason being that we do not have sufficient information to judge the true impact of that period on the effectiveness and efficiency of the CIA.

One of the few sources we have on this is the memoir of a post-Church DCI, Stansfield Turner's *Secrecy and Democracy*.[98] Turner paints a picture of a secret intelligence service "adapting" to oversight and new ground rules. One consequence, argues Turner, of the existence of permanent intelligence committees was that the CIA now had "spokesmen" on the Hill who could "defend" as well as criticize.[99] Turner believes that oversight is valuable for preserving the trust of the people, although this is not a view shared by all intelligence professionals. Another interesting dimension to Turner's book is the issue of management, a much neglected topic in discussions of the CIA.[100] Better management may help to solve many of the problems that concern critics without requiring either extensive reorganization or relying solely on *external* review.

The final section is devoted to one of the most influential approaches to intelligence, that based on the concept of intelligence requirements developed by Roy Godson and the Consortium for the Study of Intelligence. The series of seven volumes, *Intelligence Requirements for the 1980's*, has contributed more to a shift in the nature of the intelligence debate in the United States than any other publication.

This series of books argues that the United States requires a full-service intelligence capacity to meet the challenges to national security. A full-service intelligence capacity refers to an integration of the four "elements" of intelligence—collection, analysis, covert action, and counterintelligence—with policy. The argument is that an efficient and effective intelligence service is one in which *all* of these functions are coordinated and fully developed.[101] The series is critical of the idea that one can assess, reform, or constrain any one of these without this affecting the others. Intelligence is taken to be an "active" agency of government and not merely the passive recipient of information or of world events. A volume is devoted to each of these elements, which attempts to define its nature by a priori argument and by refining the conceptualization against the intelligence practice of the United States and other nations such as the Soviet Union. However, this mixture of a priori conceptualization and testing of the concepts against practice does pose problems, which will be discussed later. Another objective of the series is to formulate "intelligence policy," the means and ends of U.S. intelligence, which will meet current and future U.S. national security requirements. This combination of academic analysis and policy analysis also causes tensions, which will be reviewed later.

It is clear that this approach, stressing the interdependence between the major intelligence activities, is a radical departure from the debates offered by the Church Committee and other liberal scholars. First, it implies that one cannot develop "rules" for one aspect of intelligence in isolation from the others. For example, one cannot legislate for counterintelligence without examining the effect of such rules on the reliability of the intelligence being collected. The second change is that it redirects research away from the domestic sphere toward the international system. Third, the series is concerned with analyzing the extent to which the threats facing the United States require the development, or maintenance, of a particular type of intelligence capacity and organization to respond to these challenges, particularly from the Soviet Union. Maintenance of national independence and the strength to achieve this task are taken as key democratic values without which other freedoms are endangered, and intelligence is taken as an essential means to maintain these values.

A key issue raised by any claim to have developed a new conceptualization of intelligence is not simply the content of the concepts but the nature of the approach to the whole problem of how the task of conceptualizing intelligence ought to proceed. Therefore, before discussing the content of the elements, what is contained in the "boxes," it is essential to consider the strategy adopted in the series and the criteria necessary for judging its success.

If it is claimed that intelligence involves assessing and responding to threats to the national interest by collecting information, analyzing the information, acting upon it (covert action), and checking the secret efforts of others to influence events (counterintelligence), then one must have some basis for judging whether these activities are the key components of intelligence and whether there are four and only four such components. Is the idea that intelligence consists of four elements useful and, if so, useful for what? It may be that this concept of intelligence is the most useful in assisting a president to decide upon the organization of intelligence, or it may be the most useful for engaging in comparative analysis. Any uncertainty in the purpose of the conceptualization is likely to produce uncertainty as to the appropriate criteria for judging its value.

What is an "element"? Nowhere in the series is this question addressed. There are three possible meanings. It may refer to certain functions that must be performed if intelligence is to be worthwhile, effective, "good." That is, it may refer to elements (functions) that must be performed if the attainment of national security objectives is not to be impaired. However, for this interpretation to be accepted, to arrive at a conclusion, one would require evidence from a variety of states with different national security interests and intelligence experiences. Although some valuable comparative work is undertaken in each of the volumes,[102] it may well be too early to reach a definitive answer that these intelligence activities are *more* important or significant than others.

Second, the choice of "elements" may simply reflect the division of labor characteristic of intelligence systems. The selection of elements may simply reflect the fact that all or most intelligence services have divisions or specialist branches devoted to each of these tasks. Here again, one would require much more historical evidence than is provided that all intelligence services have organized themselves in a common pattern despite obvious differences in terminology.

The final interpretation is that such elements reflect a "frequency" count so that an "element" describes the most common type of activity performed by intelligence services. An intelligence element may mean nothing more than that certain activities are performed by most intelligence services most of the time. This is to make a frequency statement about *most* intelligence services and the activities *most* frequently performed by them. This can hardly have been the method used to derive the elements of intelligence, since they were announced in the very first volume. Only after extensive comparative and historical research could any such frequency count be undertaken. In the mid-1970s, no such task could have been contemplated, since the comparative and historical work necessary to perform such a task had only begun.

Given these possible interpretations, it is clear that only the first is a plausible candidate. An element of intelligence refers to an intelligence activity whose absence will impair the ability of the state to fulfill its national security requirements. However, there remains the question of whether one can deduce such requirements a priori. The claim that one can derive the elements of intelligence from the definition of intelligence risks being either circular or culture bound. Intelligence is defined in *The Elements of Intelligence* (revised edition) as

> in the American context intelligence connotes information needed or desired by the Government in pursuance of its national interests. It includes the process of obtaining, evaluating, protecting and eventually exploiting the same information. But that is not all. Intelligence encompasses the defense of U.S. institutions from penetration and harm by hostile intelligence services. ... Intelligence is at once knowledge, organization, and process. Its four major disciplines (analysis, collection, counterintelligence and covert action) are interdependent.[103]

If one defines intelligence as being activities such as the collection and use of information, then it will be true by definition that these activities will be found to be "elements" of intelligence. In this sense, intelligence does not have elements. It is *defined* as being the sum of its parts; collection, covert action, analysis, and counterintelligence are not "elements" of intelligence but what intelligence is.

Another problem concerns the extent to which the concept of intelligence is culture bound. The phrase "in the American context intelligence connotes" raises the question of what intelligence would connote in other contexts and how this would affect the elements of intelligence. This phrase may be interpreted as simply an empirical statement, a statement of fact, that only in the United States are all these activities performed by the intelligence community. Or it may have the much more radical meaning that in a different tradition there would be a different conception of intelligence and, therefore, a different set of "elements." Whatever the case, it is unfortunate that such ambiguities exist, since they make it difficult for the reader to judge exactly what is being claimed. However, it should be stressed that this attempt to define and describe is new, radical, and something largely avoided by other writers. The series does point the way forward by encouraging historical and comparative work on different intelligence traditions in order to test and refine the concepts.

The series, then, does have a coherent theme: there are four elements to intelligence that must be not only treated in their own right but also coordinated as parts of a system if one is to meet the intelligence requirements of a modern nation. The coherence is provided by the theme of intelligence requirements, a concept not fully developed until the seventh and final volume, but that Godson summarizes in the first volume as consisting of the assessment of past performance, the identification of U.S. strategic "needs," and use of such needs to identify the necessary intelligence structures and practices.[104] In the final volume, such requirements are more clearly spelled out as involving the development of intelligence policy in three dimensions: a policy for intelligence covering such matters as organization, finance, personnel, recruitment, standards of performance, and accountability; improving the link between intelligence capacity and performance and the *needs* of policymakers; and the use of intelligence as an instrument of policy.[105] All of these depend upon the state possessing an overall national security policy that can structure decisions in these three areas.

The series, however, shows that there exist many, and sometimes deep, disagreements over the strategic interests of the United States and that such disagreements lie behind many of the debates over intelligence issues. It is clear that participants have differing conceptions of the Soviet Union and, for example, its capacity for deception, which affects the discussion on the value of technological collection versus espionage.[106] It is also clear that participants have differing views over the foreign policy implications of covert action. Some would see covert methods as legitimate to "aid friends" but not to destabilize unfriendly governments. Others argue that the United States is living in such a hostile environment that anything goes (or just about), since the only option open if the Soviets keep "winning" is nuclear war.[107] Such debates on the effectiveness, long-term success, and morality of covert action are bound to display differences of interpretation as to the "true" nature of U.S. strategic interests. *Must* one hold the Soviets from expanding into country X even if this means funding guerrillas? Are the oil resources of country Y so significant that we are entitled to interfere in its domestic politics by funding a political party favorable to our interest? Such questions as these can only be answered if all parties—for example, the intelligence planners, the operatives, the State Department, and the president—are aware of the interests at stake in order to make a risk assessment in its true sense. Without a clear foreign policy, risk assessment is likely to be interpreted as meaning only the probability of getting caught! The nature of strategic interests has emerged from the series as one of the key issues to be addressed in any future discussion of intelligence requirements, since it is clear that such requirements cannot be arrived at until one has a clear national security policy.

However, the key issue remains whether the series has correctly identified the four elements of intelligence. As stated earlier, such an approach faces a diversity of intelligence practice, organization, and values that make the imposition of a single conceptual order appear, a priori, problematic. For example, counterintelligence is one of the four elements; but the participants do not agree on its nature, its definition. This raises the key issue of whether one can state that an element of intelligence has been identified before agreement has been reached on its boundaries, shape, and content. Can one have an element of intelligence if one does not know what is meant by it? One must surely have agreement as to the central core of meaning even if there are differences at the boundary. Volume three defines counter-intelligence (CI) in the following way:

> At a minimum, however, CI can be defined as the identification and neutralization of the threat posed by foreign intelligence services, and the manipulation of these services for the manipulator's benefit.[108]

And yet, despite the fact that CI is defined above as specifically referring to the activities of foreign intelligence services, the volume devoted to CI has essays that take CI to include at least one of the following: terrorism, personnel security, physical security, and the denial of secret information.[109] The concept of security, a rival term, would include domestic threats, threats from non-state actors, defensive measures such as locks, and criminal penalties for releasing certain categories of information as well as countering hostile intelligence services. Does "security" entail counterintelligence, or does "counterintelligence" entail security? Which is the fairest of them all?

A similar problem occurs with the concept of clandestine collection. Here the issue concerns the relative importance of open as opposed to closed sources. Does clandestine collection include collecting the daily issue of *Pravda*? Not if one defines intelligence collection as collection by "clandestine or special means."[110] This emphasis on clandestine methods of collection is particularly ironic in the light of the extract from Cord Meyer's *Facing Reality* that is included as an appendix to the volume on CI. In this extract, Meyer states that "(the) continuous flow of worldwide *public* information ... does in fact comprise approximately 90 percent of what we need to know ..."[111] (emphasis added). The importance of open sources is further given emphasis by the official British inquiry, chaired by Lord Franks, on the Falkland Islands Affair that concluded that insufficient attention had been paid to Argentinian newspapers in arriving at conclusions on Argentinian intentions.[112] It is true that neither Meyer nor the Franks Committee would wish to downplay the importance of clandestine sources; both recognize they are vital. But it is unfortunate that intelligence should be *defined* as involving clandestine collection so as to appear to exclude open sources. It may be argued that this definitional problem is relatively unimportant unless it affects research, but that it does have such a consequence is evidenced by the fact that the volume on collection pays no attention to many of the problems associated with collection from open sources. There is too little discussion of the reliability of open sources and how the information from these can be integrated into that from closed sources. More attention could have been paid to problems of analyzing open source information and to the problem of how states have used open sources to mislead or deceive opponents. This highlights the important point that one's conception of intelligence can affect discussion of intelligence requirements.

To conclude this discussion, three main issues are raised by the strategy. First, that the elements of intelligence are derived not from empirical study but from the meaning of intelligence. Second, that this "deductive" approach leaves the precise meaning of the elements open to a range of interpretation, which makes it difficult to test the claim that four intelligence activities are of a special status. Third, that the conception of intelligence offered does lead certain intelligence problems and requirements to be given prominence and others to be relatively neglected.

A somewhat different problem arises with the series' discussion of analysis. Disagreement exists over the degree to which it is possible or desirable to have "objective" collection and "objective" analysis of that information. Some writers seek to show that analysis can only be worthwhile if it is guided by the needs of policymakers, while other writers seek to show that past policies have led to the distortion of intelligence assessments. Frank Barnett, president of the National Strategy Information Center, provides in his foreword to volume two the following marvelous summary of the dilemma facing all analysts:

> If the analyst is right he is likely to be scorned. Of course, he is often wrong (or partially wrong); and then he is the convenient whipping-boy for Ministers or chiefs-of-state whose policies are already so muddled they were bound to fail, with or without good intelligence. Therefore, to deliberately overstate the cynic's case, one is tempted to assert that the truly "successful" analyst is he who subtly tailors his assessment to what the political traffic will bear and cloaks even that analysis in such ambiguity that, in the case of scandal, he can escape through administrative cracks to a more prestigious job.[113]

The problems of analysis are perhaps the most difficult and complex facing any intelligence service. One can conceive of ways of obtaining other people's secrets, even if only by indirect means such as by studying radio traffic patterns; but how is one to prevent preconceptions so clouding one's judgment that even the best information is misinterpreted or "not seen"?

The volume on analysis answers this question by advocating five changes.[114] Two are concerned with making improvements to the organization of analysis and with recruitment and management. The more interesting three fall under two further headings: theory versus empiricism and producers versus consumers. The use of the word "versus" may raise some eyebrows; but its use will, hopefully, be clear later. A problem faced by a major power such as the United States is that there are apparently no limits to the quantity or quality of information that it seeks. This is a key issue in the volume on intelligence and policy and appears in the volume on collection under the heading of "tasking," or the assignment of intelligence priorities. It covers such issues as how much of the intelligence technology, manpower, and effort should be devoted to Europe and how much to Africa. What kinds of information do U.S. policymakers require to make what sort of decisions? How much effort should be devoted to recruiting human agents and how much to new technology? How great a danger is the possibility of deception (partly a CI problem)?

Such questions can be all too easily avoided by simply asking one's intelligence service to collect information on everything and anything, but this answer is not only wasteful of resources but also makes the task of the analyst virtually impossible. He becomes so swamped with information that the task of analysis becomes hit and miss, depending upon what struck the attention of various intelligence officers at various points in the filtering process. Michael Handel refers to this problem in his essay on *Avoiding Surprise*.[115] However, it is also quite clear that we do not know how much information is enough. Indeed, without a clear statement of the decision to be made and the options open, it is impossible to even begin to provide an answer. However, the lack of clarity in the policy-making or decision-making system is often the very reason why analysis failures occur. The policymakers' perceptions bias their priorities, which affects the collection process and then doubly feeds into the analysis process. And finally, as Barnett pointed out above, the policymaker does not listen unless it conforms to his prejudices! Perhaps the cynic is right after all, although surely one can seek improvements if not perfection.

Two essays in volume seven illustrate these points well. One is the essay by Kenneth de Graffenreid (then a special assistant to the president on intelligence matters) and the other by Mark Schneider (director of Strategic Arms Control Policy, Office of Assistant Secretary of Defense).[116] In his essay, de Graffenreid complains that too rarely has intelligence collection been geared to the requirements of policymakers and too often has reflected the desire of the professional to amass as much information as possible in the hope that this will make for better decisionmaking. This produces the problem that information and analysis that are not geared to the concerns of the policymakers will be ignored. He states:

> (Traditionalists) conceive of intelligence as basically "objective" information and analysis and neglect the connection between policy and intelligence activities (other than collection), process and organization. While understanding that intelligence products can be useful for policy-making, proponents of this view place a premium on a substantial degree of separation between the intelligence community and the policymaker. They characterize the relationship between the intelligence community and the policymaker as similar to that between the librarian and reader. Librarians, or curators, and not readers, determine what should be in the collection of books; likewise, the intelligence community determines what information should be available to the president.[117]

This would seem to be a clear and definite answer to the cynic; intelligence is to be driven by policy whether collection or analysis. "Users" are to decide what information (books) they need. However, if one turns to the essay by Schneider, the opposite problem is displayed.[118] Schneider complains that the policy of détente failed to provide the president of the United States with accurate and objective assessments of Soviet capacity. He shows that the errors made were not simply, or even mainly, a product of CIA or Defense Intelligence Agency (DIA) biases or a lack of responsiveness to policymakers. He shows they were the result of the consensus on the strategic doctrine of Mutually Assured Destruction (MAD), the belief that the Soviets were "only" seeking nuclear parity and the policy of détente. Here was a situation in which a policy colored both the type of information collected and the analysis of that information to produce a faulty intelligence product. The fact that intelligence is guided by policy is no guarantee that the intelligence product will be "good" intelligence.

The dilemma that intelligence tasked by policymakers may be colored by prejudices, or that intelligence unconnected to policy will lie gathering dust, remains unsolved. However, is this an "intelligence" problem? The issue may be put in a way that makes it clear it is not, or not only so; one cannot formulate intelligence requirements until politicians formulate policies.

There is no doubt that the series has redirected the focus of attention and research away from the rather narrow concerns of the Church Committee era. The series has shown that questions of efficiency and effectiveness are as important in protecting the rights of Americans as are constraints. It has directed research to new areas of inquiry by focusing on the threats faced by the United States and on the international context within which national security objectives should be considered. It has formulated a useful, even if not final, answer to the problem of conceptualizing intelligence by examining the experience of both the United States and other countries. It has sought to argue that intelligence is a vital component in the security structure designed to preserve democratic values and not simply or mainly to thwart a threat to such values. It has developed a series of requirements and policies that can assist in the development of intelligence policies. The series has provided an agenda for debate, which was previously absent, by providing the first systematic study of the wide range of intelligence activities. This among other things separates it from the "professionals," "liberals," and the surprise approach.

The series has succeeded in providing a clear statement of a principle that many did not accept in the mid-1970s: intelligence is both necessary and desirable in any democratic society. This is no mean achievement when one considers the number of doubting Thomases there were in the time of Senator Church.

CONCLUSION

In the 1980s and heading onto the 1990s, one can see that the growth of intelligence studies has been affected by the particular climate of opinion in the mid-1970s that culminated in the Church Committee Report. It was not until after the Vietnam War, the Watergate Affair, fear of the "Imperial Presidency,"[119] and the reaction they produced that intelligence became a central focus of concern. The reasons why intelligence became a focus of public disquiet are complex and many, but the main such reason I would argue is that intelligence was seen as an aspect of "secret" government that was held responsible for several humiliations and policy disasters. The inquest on these disasters took the form of a public inquiry into the role of the intelligence community, since this was convenient for politicians and critics alike. The intelligence community was the hidden hand, the "inner conspiracy," that had led America astray. Here was a scapegoat for the ills of government, which had acted without authority and in secret to pervert American ideals and institutions.[120] To state that the actual record hardly justifies the odium received by the intelligence community may not be accepted in all quarters even today; but to anyone who has read "both" sides, the record is clear. There were errors and abuses, but these were not and never have been the sole or even "average" activities of the U.S. intelligence community. Insofar as such operations occurred, they were often the product of a lack of clear policies on the part of those supposedly responsible—presidents, attorneys general, committees of Congress—and not simply, or even mainly, of zealots in the intelligence community.

It is also clear that American anxieties concerning intelligence did not begin with the Church Committee. The origins of both the FBI, or more accurately the Bureau of Investigation, and the CIA were associated with fears concerning the creation of a spy system that was claimed to be alien to American values.[121] Indeed, the new factor is that there are now some commentators who see intelligence as necessary and desirable in peace as well as war. However, certain "anxieties" are fairly constant.

Intelligence is inherently a secret activity; therefore, there are anxieties over who is in control of intelligence. Congress is bound to be concerned as to whether giving the executive control over secret money, men, and operations does not shift the balance of power in favor of the executive and away from Congress. This is particularly acute within the American political system because of the uncertainty as to who has legitimate claim to be the "tribune of the people." The people rule, but they rule through elected representatives, congressmen, and the president, who cannot be *publicly* accountable for secret intelligence. The uncertainties over control and accountability underlie one of the key issues raised by Senator Church, the accusation that the CIA had been a "rogue elephant."[122] This is the claim that the CIA had not been adequately controlled by anyone, a devastating accusation within a political culture of rule by the people.

Another anxiety is associated with the morality of secret operations. The secrecy associated with intelligence raises doubts as to the values that underlie intelligence activities. Many of the "liberal" commentators argue[123] that the United States ought to be a society committed to human rights, to the preservation and extension of democracy at home and abroad, and to individualism and the privacy associated with it. All such values are seen as threatened by secret intelligence. What makes such anxieties more acute is that the conflict between values and secret intelligence may be irreconcilable, so that one is forced to trade off effective intelligence against basic human rights. This is not the place to enter into the debate as to whether this is true, but many commentators have argued that it is so.[124]

A third anxiety concerns the relationship between secret intelligence and truthfulness in government. The preceding years had seen important changes in the form of the Freedom of Information Act (FOIA) and the Privacy Act,[125] which were premised on the ideals of openness and honesty in government. Secret intelligence seems to be a sphere that either jeopardizes or severely constrains such ideals. Intelligence activities are often exempt from the normal FOIA provisions under the heading of "national security" or "law enforcement."

Finally, secret intelligence may be feared because it may give to those in power an ability to influence their political future in a way that distorts the democratic political process. This can take the form of spying on opponents or spreading false stories in the newspapers.[126] If secret powers are seen as having the potential to distort a key part of the democratic process, the election of representatives, it is hardly surprising that such powers are a cause for concern.

Such anxieties reflect a strong liberal tradition in the United States that is valuable in alerting the public to the dangers of the excessive concentration of power in any one branch of government; but it is not the only tradition. There is also the tradition that focuses on international relations, the threat of the Soviet Union, and the dangers of surprise attack. The study of intelligence needs to call upon all of these traditions and not simply one that was dominant in the 1970s.

This survey of the American study of intelligence has identified several strengths and weaknesses. The main weakness is that intelligence studies began from the view that intelligence posed particular problems for democratic institutions and values. The fact that there are such issues to be discussed does not mean that the focus on this aspect was beneficial to research. It led to a neglect of the reasons why intelligence services exist at all, that is, to protect the national security of the state. An example, discussed earlier, of how this focus on abuse of "rights" affected intelligence is the debate over the criminal standard. Intelligence ought not to be seen as merely a preliminary to prosecution but as a tool of policy-making. The understanding of domestic intelligence has been distorted because of the failure to recognize this truth. The abuses of domestic intelligence were not simply the product of "overzealous" operatives but of the failure of the political system to determine the goals of collection and to analyze the information collected.

In the case of foreign intelligence it is also unfortunate that so much attention has been devoted to the domestic aspects of this activity and to the moral issues associated with American foreign policy. Again, there are issues to be discussed, but the key debate must be concerned with identifying the challenges faced by the United States and developing an intelligence policy capable of responding to those challenges. There are authors who have addressed this issue, most of them referred to above. But there are many who have written about the CIA without such a recognition.

The main strength of U.S. intelligence studies lies in the conceptual tools that it has provided, particularly those of the "surprise" and "realist" schools. The chic value of the "movable conscience" has declined; and ethics are now seen to be a part, but only a part, of the debate. Effective and efficient intelligence is also seen as desirable. Concepts such as warning, surprise, intelligence requirements, intelligence management, and intelligence policy all show that there exist approaches to intelligence that will help ensure that the next decade will lead to progress in the understanding of a vital and indispensable part of all democratic societies, the intelligence service.

NOTES

1. This means that those works written by non-American authors such as Ronald Lewin's study of *Magic* or works written prior to 1945 such as Herbert Yardley's *Black Chamber* are excluded.
2. Such policies generated debate over a) the morality of covert action and intervention that were a major focus of concern for the Church Committee and b) the reliability of CIA estimates of the Soviet strategic threat. See pages 14-17 of this chapter.

3. This concern with intelligence abuse is the major focus of the "liberal" approach. See page 13 of this chapter.

4. Such debates can be found in the series edited by Roy Godson on *Intelligence Requirements for the 1980s: Elements of Intelligence* (1979, revised 1983); *Analysis and Estimates* (1980); *Counterintelligence* (1980); *Covert Action* (1981); *Clandestine Collection* (1982); *Domestic Intelligence* (1986); and *Intelligence and Policy* (1986). Volumes 1-5 are published and distributed by the National Strategy Information Center, Washington, D.C. Volumes 6 and 7 are published and distributed by Lexington Books, Lexington, Mass.

5. See the comments on Theoharis and Donner for examples, pages 17-18 of this chapter.

6. Examples of such works are Herbert Yardley, *The American Black Chamber* (New York: Ballantine, 1931); Lieutenant General Hunter Liggett and Wesley W. Stout, *A. E. F., Ten Years Ago in France* (New York: Dodd, Mead & Co., 1928); T. M. Johnson, *Our Secret War* (Indianapolis: The Bobbs-Merrill Co., 1929); Helen F. Gaines, *Cryptanalysis* (New York: Dover Publications, 1939); General L. C. Baker, *History of the U.S. Intelligence Service* (Philadelphia, Pa.: King and Baird, 1967); Henry Merritt Wriston, *Executive Agents in American Foreign Relations* (Gloucester, Mass.: Peter Smith Publishers, 1929).

7. Sherman Kent, *Strategic Intelligence for American World Policy* (Princeton, N. J.: Princeton University Press, 1949).

8. Ibid., p. 182.

9. Ibid., pp. 60-61.

10. Roger Hilsman, *Strategic Intelligence and National Decisions* (Glencoe, Ill.: The Free Press, 1956).

11. Roger Hilsman was a director of the State Department's Bureau of Intelligence and Research. In 1963 he was appointed assistant secretary of state for Far Eastern Affairs, a post that he resigned in January 1964 due to his disagreement with the Johnson administration's policies in Vietnam.

12. Hilsman, *Strategic Intelligence*, p. 161 and see also pp. 121-22.

13. Hilsman, *Strategic Intelligence*, p. 113. "... (Most) of the intelligence men interviewed seemed to agree with the position shared by both the operators (policymakers) and the administrators (intelligence bosses), and in reaching that position they seemed to put the same emphasis on the role of facts and the fear of bias."

14. Ibid., pp. 43-46.

15. Ibid., chap. xviii.

16. Roger Hilsman in A. C. Mauer, M. D. Tunstall and J. M. Keagle, eds., *Intelligence: Policy and Process* (Boulder, Colo.: Westview Press, 1985), p. 19. "The first part of this chapter, which deals with indeterminacy, attempts to distinguish between intelligence as factual information on the one hand, and intelligence as interpretation and forecasting on the other. It concludes that the *real* problem of intelligence is one of interpretation and forecasting" (emphasis added).

17. Brigadier General Platt, *National Character in Action: Intelligence Factors in Foreign Relations* (New Brunswick, N.J.: Rutgers University Press, 1961). George S. Petee, *The Future of American Secret Intelligence* (Washington, D.C.: Infantry Journal Press, 1946).

18. Willmoore Kendall, "The Functions of Intelligence," *World Politics* 1 (July 1949).

19. Ibid., p. 550.

20. Ibid., p. 545-46.

21. U.S. Congress, Commission on Organization of the Executive Branch of Government, chaired by Hon. Herbert Hoover, *Intelligence Activities*, 84th Cong., 1st sess., June 1955. U.S. Congress, Senate Committee on Government Operations, Subcommittee on National Policy Machinery, chaired by Senator Henry Jackson, *Intelligence and National Security*, 86th Cong., 2nd sess., (Washington, D.C.: GPO, 1961).

22. Loch Johnson, *A Season of Inquiry: The Senate Intelligence Investigation* (Lexington, Ky.: University of Kentucky Press, 1985), pp. 6-9.

23. Paul Blackstock, *The Strategy of Subversion: Manipulating the Politics of Other Nations* (Chicago, Ill.: Quadrangle Books, 1964). H. Bradford Westerfield, *The Instruments of America's Foreign Policy* (New York: Thomas Y. Crowell, 1963).

24. Westerfield, *The Instruments*, part 5, "Overt and Covert Intervention."

25. Blackstock, *Strategy of Subversion*, pp. 184-90. He argues that this did happen in the Bay of Pigs invasion.
26. Harry Howe Ransom, *The Intelligence Establishment* (Cambridge, Mass.: Harvard University Press, 1970).
27. Harry Howe Ransom, *Central Intelligence and National Security* (Cambridge, Mass: Harvard University Press, 1958).
28. Ibid., p. xiv; all references are to the 1970 edition.
29. Ibid., pp. 13-14.
30. Ibid., pp. 15-47.
31. Ibid., p. 14.
32. Ibid., p. 15.
33. Ibid., chap. 10, "The CIA Problem."
34. Ibid., pp. 143-45.
35. Ibid., pp. 3-7. Ransom merely illustrates a few of the national security problems.
36. Ibid., pp. 37-40. It is revealing that Ransom waxes quite lyrical about CIA data-handling, indexing, and information processing. This is the only CIA activity that Ransom describes without raising the question of "risks." The reason for this is that it is "library" work, essentially academic in nature, and therefore "safe."
37. Ibid., p. 94.
38. Ibid., p. 244.
39. U.S. Congress, Senate Select Committee to Study Governmental Operations with Respect to Intelligence Activities, chaired by Senator Frank Church, *Final Report*, Book 1, 94th Cong., 2nd sess., 1976, pp. 2-4.
40. Ibid., p. 2.
41. Ernest Lefever and Roy Godson, *The CIA and the American Ethic* (Washington, D.C.: Ethics and Public Policy Center, 1979), chap. 2.
42. Ibid., p. 49. Percentages adapted from Lefever and Godson.
43. U.S. Congress, Senate Select Committee to Study Governmental Operations with Respect to Intelligence Activities, chaired by Senator Frank Church, *Final Report*, Book 1, 94th Cong., 2nd sess., 1976, p. 5.
44. Ibid., book 1, p. 10.
45. U.S. Congress, House Select Committee on Intelligence, chaired by Congressman Otis Pike, *U.S. Intelligence Agencies and Activities, Hearings*, 94th Cong., 1st sess., 1975 (Washington, D.C.: GPO, 1975).
46. A version of the Pike Committee Report was leaked and published in *The Village Voice*, February 16, 1976, and February 23, 1976.
47. The controversy surrounding the Pike Committee is described in J. L. Freeman, "Investigating the Executive Intelligence: the Fate of the Pike Committee," *Capitol Studies* (Fall 1977) and in Loch Johnson, *A Season of Inquiry*, pp. 180-91.
48. Aaron Latham, in his introduction to the publication of the leaked version of the Pike Committee Report, describes section one, the Committee's complaints of executive obstruction, as occupying 81 pages, *The Village Voice*, February 16, 1976. However, section one, when published the following week in *The Village Voice*, February 23, 1976, occupies 9 pages of newsprint.
49. The Pike Committee Report as in *The Village Voice*, February 16, 1976, p. 76.
50. The Pike Report, as in *The Village Voice*, February 16, 1976, has sections devoted to Intelligence Costs, Performance Failures, The Risks of Covert Action, and Domestic Intelligence Abuses.
51. The works of Athan Theoharis on this issue include: *Spying on Americans: Political Surveillance from Hoover to the Huston Plan* (Philadelphia, Pa.: Temple University Press, 1978); "The FBI's Stretching of Presidential Directives, 1936-1953," *Political Science Quarterly* 91, no. 4 (1976-77); "The Truman Administration and the Decline of Civil Liberties," *Journal of American History* 64, no. 4 (March 1978): 1010-30.
52. Theoharis, *Spying on Americans*, p. xi. For example, Theoharis describes his three main questions as being: "First, what was the nature of the relationship between the presidency

and the intelligence community—and did presidents and attorneys general effectively oversee the internal security bureaucracy? Second, did executive branch officials establish the limits within which internal security bureaucrats operated and ensure compliance either with their orders or the law? Third, what contributed to the expansion of presidential powers as well as to the increased authority and the independent initiatives of the intelligence agencies?"

53. Ibid., index.

54. Ibid., pp. 135-39 and pp. 161-68.

55. John Eliff, *Crime, Dissent and the Attorney General* (Beverly Hills: Sage Publications, 1971) and *The Reform of FBI Intelligence Operations* (Princeton: Princeton University Press, 1979); Sanford Ungar, *FBI* (Boston: Little, Brown and Company, 1975); Athan Theoharis, "FBI Files, The National Archives and the Issue of Access," *Government Publications Review* 9 (1982); Tony Poveda, "The Rise and Fall of the FBI," *Contemporary Crises* 6, no. 2 (1982) and his "The FBI and Domestic Intelligence," *Crime and Delinquency* (April 28, 1982); David Williams, "The Bureau of Investigation and its Critics, 1919-1921," *The Journal of American History* 68, no. 3 (December 1981); David Martin, "Investigating the FBI," *Policy Review* 18 (Fall 1981).

56. Frank Donner's works on the FBI include: "How J. Edgar Hoover Created his Intelligence Powers," *Civil Liberties Review* 3, no. 6 (1977); "Hoover's Legacy," *The Nation* 218 (June 1, 1974); *The Age of Surveillance: The Aims and Methods of America's Political Intelligence System* (New York: Vintage Books, 1981).

57. Donner, *The Age of Surveillance*, p. xxii.

58. Ibid., p. 125.

59. Richard Morgan, *Domestic Intelligence: Monitoring Dissent in America* (Austin, Texas: University of Texas Press, 1980). John Eliff, *Reform of FBI*.

60. See, for example, the comment by Hadley Arkes (Professor of Jurisprudence at Amherst College) in Roy Godson, ed., *Intelligence Requirements for the 1980's: Domestic Intelligence* (Lexington, Mass.: Lexington Books, 1986) and the review of this and other constitutional issues by John S. Warner, *National Security and the First Amendment* (McLean, Va.: Association of Former Intelligence Officers, 1984).

61. Morgan, when discussing the threats that America faces, devotes several pages to only one such threat, namely terrorism, because terrorism is closely linked to two factors that provide the most commonly accepted justifications for monitoring "dissent": violence and foreign involvement. See Morgan, *Domestic Intelligence*, pp. 133-43.

62. A well-known critic of intelligence from the perspective of international law is Richard Falk. See his article in *Proceedings of the American Society for International Law* 69 (April 1975) and his "President Gerald Ford, CIA Covert Operations and the Studies of International Law," *American Journal of International Law* 69, no. 2 (April 1975). For other views see Scott Breckenridge, "Clandestine Intelligence—International Law," *International Studies Notes* 9, no. 2 (1982) and Alona Evans and J. F. Murphy, eds., *Aspects of International Law* (Lexington, Mass.: Lexington Books, 1978).

63. See Morgan, *Domestic Intelligence*, pp. 157-59; John Oseth, *Regulating U.S. Intelligence Operations* (Lexington, Ky.: University of Kentucky Press, 1985), pp. 144-49; and Angelo Codevilla, "Reforms and Proposals for Reform" in Roy Godson, ed., *Intelligence Requirements for the 1980's: Elements of Intelligence*, rev. ed. (Washington, D.C.: National Strategy Information Center, 1983). For the congressional hearings see: U.S. Congress, Senate Select Committee on Intelligence, *National Intelligence Act of 1980, Hearings on S. 2284*, 96th Cong., 2nd sess., 1980; U.S. Congress, House Permanent Select Committee on Intelligence, *Intelligence Oversight Act of 1980*, H. Rept. 96-1153, 96th Cong., 2nd sess., 1980; U.S. Congress, Senate Select Committee on Intelligence, *Hearings on the Intelligence Reform Act of 1981*, 97th Cong., 1st sess., 1981.

64. Such work that has been done is largely historical in nature, dealing with the "Red Scare" and "McCarthyism." For an exception, see Angelo Codevilla, "What is Domestic Security?" in Godson, ed., *Domestic Intelligence*.

65. Godson, *Domestic Intelligence*.

66. See Peter Lupsha, "Intelligence Requirements, Political Climate and Reform," in Godson, ed., *Domestic Intelligence*.

67. John Eliff, *The Reform of the FBI*, pp. 119-20. Richard Morgan, *Domestic Intelligence*, p. 146.

68. Kenneth de Graffenreid's comment in Godson, ed., *Domestic Intelligence*, pp. 133-35.

69. Ibid., p. 133. de Graffenreid expresses this point well in the following quotation: My basic premise is that the purpose of intelligence information is to inform or affect policy. For the policymaker, information must relate and lead to decisions. Information collected or analyzed has little meaning if it is not used in the context of a policy decision.

70. The introduction in Godson, ed., *Domestic Intelligence*, p. 9, forcefully states that "there is no 'Director of Domestic Intelligence' to coordinate collection tasking and analysis. There is no national budget for domestic intelligence. There is no overall national examination of domestic intelligence needs and capabilities."

71. Codevilla in Godson, ed., *Domestic Intelligence*, pp. 32-43.

72. Weinstein in Godson, ed., *Domestic Intelligence*, pp. 13-27.

73. "... Properly understood, the limits imposed by the Constitution as presently interpreted do not preclude an effective, albeit carefully controlled, domestic intelligence effort." Morgan, *Domestic Intelligence*, p. 68.

74. Roberta Wohlstetter, *Pearl Harbor, Warning and Decision* (Stanford, Calif.: Stanford University Press, 1962).

75. Ibid., p. 169.

76. The literature on "surprise" is linked to the related problems of deception, perception, crisis management, and intelligence failure. On surprise see Klaus Knorr and Patrick Morgan, *Strategic Military Surprise* (New York: National Strategy Information Center, 1983); R. L. Pfaltzgraff, U. Ra'anan, and W. Milberg, eds., *Intelligence Policy and National Security* (Hamden, Conn.: Archon, 1981), parts 5 and 6; Michael Handel, "Surprise and Change in International Politics," *International Security* (Spring 1980); Robert Axelrod, "The Rational Timing of Surprise," *World Politics* (1972); "Forum on Intelligence and Crisis Forecasting," *Orbis* (Winter 1983); and Richard Betts, see endnote 77 below.

77. Richard Betts, "Analysis, War and Decision—Why Intelligence Failures are Inevitable," *World Politics* 31, no. 1 (1978); "Surprise Despite Warning—Why Attacks Succeed," *Political Science Quarterly* 95, no. 4 (1980-81); *Surprise Attack* (Washington, D.C.: The Brookings Institution, 1982).

78. "The historical cases discussed in the first part of the book show that warning is a secondary element in the problem of surprise and that political and psychological impediments are primary." Betts, *Surprise Attack*, p. 286.

79. Michael Handel, "The Study of Intelligence," *Orbis* 26, no. 4 (Winter 1983): 819.

80. Ernest May, ed., *Knowing One's Enemies: Intelligence Assessment Before the Two World Wars* (Princeton, N.J.: Princeton University Press, 1984); R. L. Pfaltzgraff et al., eds., *Intelligence Policy and National Security.*

81. Bradley F. Smith, *The Shadow Warriors: OSS and the Origins of the CIA* (New York: Basic Books, 1983); Thomas Troy, *Donnovan and the CIA: A History of the Establishment of the Central Intelligence Agency* (Frederick, Md.: University Publications of America, 1981).

82. Troy, *Donnovan and the CIA*, p. vii. Troy states his thesis as follows: "The thesis of this volume is that there is a 'missing link' and that the CIA historically and substantively embodies Donnovan's creative conception of a central intelligence organization." See also chaps. 9 and 16 of the volume for summaries of his argument.

83. Smith, *The Shadow Warriors*, chap. 9. Smith identifies several factors as important in understanding the origins of the CIA. These are the efforts of the former head of the OSS, William Donnovan, but also the British, members of the military and foreign policy branches of government, other members of the OSS who were in important bureaucratic positions, the political climate, and the attitudes of President Truman.

84. Roy Godson, ed., *Intelligence Requirements for the 1980's: Elements of Intelligence* (1979, revised 1983); *Analysis and Estimates* (1980); *Counterintelligence* (1980); *Covert Action* (1981); *Clandestine Collection* (1982); *Domestic Intelligence* (1986); *Intelligence and Policy* (1986).

85. Ray Cline, *Secrets, Spies, and Scholars* (Washington, D.C.: Acropolis Books, 1976). For revisions and updating, see Cline's *The CIA: Reality vs. Myth* (Washington, D.C.: Acropolis Books, 1982).

86. Cline, *Secrets, Spies, and Scholars*, chaps. 1 and 6 best illustrate this concern with "coordination."

87. Ibid., pp. 265-68.

88. Cline, *Secrets, Spies, and Scholars*. It seems odd to give the more "open" function of analysis a cryptic title, *Foreign Affairs Research*, and the more clandestine function of collection an open title of *Clandestine Services Staff*. Perhaps Cline hopes to mislead opponents by this reversal of what one would expect!

89. Ibid., p. 267.

90. Other "memoirs" worthy of note but not referred to in this chapter include: T. Shackley, *The Third Option* (New York: The Reader's Digest Press, 1981); M. Copeland, *The Real Spy World* (London: Weidenfeld and Nicolson, 1974); D. S. Blaufarb, *The Counterinsurgency Era: U.S. Doctrine and Performance, 1950 to the Present* (New York: The Free Press, 1977); D. A. Philips, *The Night Watch* (New York: Atheneum, 1977); P. de Silva, *Sub Rosa: The CIA and the Uses of Intelligence* (New York: Times Books, 1978); L. Kirkpatrick, *The Real CIA* (New York: Macmillan, 1968); V. Marchetti and John D. Marks, *The CIA and the Cult of Intelligence* (New York: Dell, 1975); R. W. McGee, *Deadly Deceits* (New York: Sheridan Square Publications, 1983); M. Beck, *Secret Contenders* (New York: Sheridan Square Publications, 1984).

91. For example, the works of Philip Agee, *Inside the Company: CIA Diary* (New York: Stonehill, 1975); Frank Snepp, *Decent Interval* (New York: Vintage Books, 1978); and James Stockwell, *In Search of Enemies* (New York: W. W. Norton, 1978), are not sympathetic to the policies that directed U.S. intelligence or to many of the activities that U.S. intelligence carried out.

92. Philip Agee, "Introduction—Where Myths Lead to Murder," in P. Agee and L. Wolff, eds., *Dirty Work: The CIA in Western Europe* (Secaucus, N.J.: Lyle Stuart, 1978), p. 23.

93. Cord Meyer, *Facing Reality: From World Federalism to the CIA* (New York: Harper and Row, 1980).

94. William Colby with Peter Forbarth, *Honorable Men: My Life in the CIA* (New York: Simon and Schuster, 1978).

95. Thomas Powers, *The Man Who Kept the Secrets: Richard Helms and the CIA* (New York: Knopf, 1979).

96. Ibid., pp. 13-14 and Colby, *Honorable Men*, p. 310.

97. Powers, *The Man Who Kept*, p. 3.

98. Stansfield Turner, *Secrecy and Democracy* (Boston: Houghton Mifflin, 1985).

99. Ibid., p. 150.

100. Ibid., part 4. For further discussion of managing intelligence, see A. C. Maurer et al., *Intelligence: Policy and Process*; Jeffrey Richelson, *The U.S. Intelligence Community* (Cambridge, Mass.: Ballinger, 1985), chaps. 13-15; Pfaltzgraff et al., eds., *Intelligence Policy and National Security*, part 8.

101. See the introduction by Godson in *Elements of Intelligence*, rev. ed.

102. Godson, ed., *Intelligence Requirements*. The comparative essays in the series include Adda B. Bozeman and Donald Jameson in *Covert Action*; Robert Chapman and Amrom Katz in *Clandestine Collection*; John Dziak, Schlomo Gazit, Michael Handel, and Herbert Rommerstein in *Counterintelligence*; and Angelo Codevilla in *Analysis and Estimates*.

103. Godson, ed., *Elements of Intelligence*, rev. ed., p. 5.

104. Godson, ed., *Elements of Intelligence* (1979), p. 4.

105. See the introduction in Godson, ed., *Intelligence and Policy*, and the excellent essay by de Graffenreid.

106. See the comments, discussion, and paper by Amrom Katz in Godson, ed., *Clandestine Collection*.

107. See the essays by Tovar and Schackley in Godson, ed., *Covert Action*.

108. Godson, ed., *Counterintelligence*, p. 1.

109. The list is taken from essays by Smith, p. 214; Pratt, p. 229; de Graffenreid, p. 263; and Gazit and Handel, p. 128, in Godson, ed., *Counterintelligence*.

110. Godson, ed., *Clandestine Collection*, p. 1.

111. Godson, ed., *Clandestine Collection*, p. 200. The extract in appendix 1 of this volume is from Meyer, *Facing Reality*.

112. Lord Franks, *Falkland Islands Review* (London: HMSO, 1983), paras. 158, 232, 316.

113. Godson, ed., *Analysis and Estimates*, p. vii.

114. Ibid., p. 4.

115. Michael Handel, "Avoiding Political and Technological Surprise in the 1980's," in Godson, ed., *Analysis and Estimates*.

116. Kenneth de Graffenreid, "Intelligence and the Oval Office," and Mark Schneider, "Intelligence in the Formation of Defense Policy," in Godson, ed., *Intelligence and Policy*.

117. de Graffenreid in Godson, ed., *Intelligence and Policy*, p. 14.

118. Schneider in Godson, ed., *Intelligence and Policy*, pp. 56-57, states that "modern American defense intelligence ... reflected the conventional wisdom that ... the United States and the Soviet Union had entered into an inherently stable, inherently equal relationship that was in the interest of both to preserve."

119. Arthur M. Schlesinger, *The Imperial Presidency* (Boston: Houghton Mifflin, 1973).

120. S. P. Huntington, "American Ideals versus American Institutions," *Political Science Quarterly* 97, no. 1 (Spring 1982) and his *American Politics: The Promise of Disharmony* (Cambridge, Mass.: Harvard University Press, 1981).

121. For a discussion of the ethics of intelligence and some of the anxieties that intelligence has aroused, see K. G. Robertson, "The Politics of Secret Intelligence" in K. G. Robertson, ed., *British and American Approaches to Intelligence* (London: Macmillan, 1987).

122. Loch Johnson describes Senator Frank Church, chairman of the Senate Select Committee on Intelligence, as a believer in the "rogue elephant thesis," although no clear attributable source for Senator Church having used this phrase exists. See Johnson, *A Season of Inquiry*, pp. 57-61.

123. A plethora of examples can be found in Howard Frazier, ed., *Uncloaking the CIA* (New York: The Free Press, 1978).

124. One example is the graphic image used in the introduction to M. H. Halperin, J. J. Berman, R. L. Borosage, and C. M. Marwick, *The Lawless State: The Crimes of the U.S. Intelligence Agencies* (New York: Penguin Books, 1976), p. 5: "Using secret intelligence to defend a constitutional republic is akin to the ancient medical practice of employing leeches to take blood from feverish patients."

125. The Freedom of Information Act, title 5, section 552, was amended in October 1984 to allow exemption for all "operational files," those concerning intelligence sources and methods. The Intelligence Identities Protection Act (1982) also reflected a new climate of opinion on the need for secrecy in intelligence.

126. Such anxieties are expressed in Donner, *The Age of Surveillance*, chap. 7, and in the Introduction to Halperin et al., *The Lawless State*.

3

Historical Research on the British Intelligence Community

CHRISTOPHER ANDREW

One of the main problems confronting all researchers on intelligence is that their subject still remains at least partly taboo. British taboos are, by tradition, bigger and better than their American counterparts; nowhere is this truer than in the field of intelligence. Sir Michael Howard, regius professor of modern history at Oxford University, explains British policy thus:

> In Britain the activities of the intelligence and security services have always been regarded in much the same light as intra-marital sex. Everyone knows that it goes on and is quite content that it should, but to speak, write, or ask questions about it is regarded as exceedingly bad form. So far as official government policy is concerned, the British security and intelligence services, MI5 and MI6, do not exist. Enemy agents are found under gooseberry bushes, and our own intelligence is brought by the storks. Government records bearing on intelligence activities are either industriously "weeded," or kept indefinitely closed.[1]

British intelligence taboos not merely lead the Western world, in some respects they even exceed those in the Soviet Union, which in 1987 ran a competition with prizes for the best books, films, and television programs to celebrate the seventieth anniversary of the KGB. In the USSR the head of the KGB, Viktor Chebrikov, is a prominent public figure (and, of course, a member of the Politburo). Whitehall still insists, however, that the name of the head of the Secret Intelligence Service (better known as MI6, or SIS) is too secret to mention. When the writer Compton Mackenzie was prosecuted under the Official Secrets Act in 1932, his alleged offenses included revealing the name of the first head of MI6, Sir Mansfield Cumming. Mackenzie protested that Cumming had died nine years before,

43

and that seems to have been regarded by the court as a mitigating factor. But the prosecution claimed that Mackenzie had revealed certain personal details about Cumming that might interest potential enemies—for example, that he had a wooden leg and a chin like "the cutwater of a battleship." For this and other revelations of British intelligence work in the First World War, Mackenzie was fined £100 with costs. To revenge himself and pay his costs, he wrote the brilliant satire of official secrecy *Water on the Brain*.[2]

Former intelligence officers during the Second World War also have commonly been threatened with prosecution when they have attempted to publish their memoirs. Sir John Masterman, author of the classic account of wartime deception *The Double Cross System* (significantly first published in 1972 not in Britain but the United States), is believed to have escaped prosecution only because the foreign secretary at the time was his friend and former pupil Sir Alec Douglas-Home.[3] In 1982 the greatest surviving codebreaker of Bletchley Park, Gordon Welchman, was subjected to similar menaces after the publication of his wartime memoirs, *The Hut Six Story*. By now an American citizen, Welchman was visited by the FBI (acting, he was told, at the request of MI5), had his security clearance at the Mitre Corporation withdrawn, and lived for the remaining three years of his life under the threat of prosecution.[4]

The records of the intelligence services themselves remain completely taboo. The government refuses to set any date, however distant, for the release of any of the files, however old, of MI5, MI6, GCHQ (Government Communications Headquarters—Britain's NSA) and its interwar predecessor GC & CS (Government Code and Cypher School). Indeed, Whitehall continues to maintain that all these files are so sensitive that it may never be possible to release a single one.

One example of the rigidity with which it sticks to this principle concerns the diaries of Sir Mansfield Cumming, which are traditionally kept in the office of the head of MI6. The diaries are said to contain entertaining entries about Sir Mansfield's disguises, which are sometimes used to amuse new recruits. For some time Sir Mansfield's family has been seeking access to his diaries but has been told by the Foreign Office that not a single line of the diaries, even for the period before the First World War, can be declassified either now or for the foreseeable future.

Whitehall's extraordinary tenacity in guarding ancient secrets derives from its traditional though irrational conviction that the only options are all or nothing, total secrecy or total disclosure. Austen Chamberlain told the Commons in 1924:

> It is of the essence of a Secret Service that it must be secret, and if you once begin disclosure it is perfectly obvious to me as to hon. members opposite that there is no longer any Secret Service and that you must do without it.[5]

Successive prime ministers up to and including Mrs. Thatcher have remained in broad agreement.

The main obstacles to historical research on the British intelligence community are thus the generally discredited Official Secrets Acts[6] and the overclassification of even the most ancient "sensitive" material. Research will continue to be difficult until the introduction of official secrets legislation and a system of classification based on the present needs of national security rather than on antiquated taboos. Both are overdue.

A sensible system has already been devised for advising on the release of old intelligence files presently withheld from the Public Record Office despite the "thirty year rule" on most official documents. Unhappily it has yet to be implemented. In 1981 an official committee of inquiry into the public records, chaired by the former ambassador to Moscow Sir Duncan Wilson, recommended that a subcommittee of the present Advisory Council on Public Records, probably composed of privy counselors with experience of the intelligence community, should advise on access to intelligence and other "sensitive" files. In March 1982 the government rejected that proposal on the grounds that no retired minister or official, however eminent, can possess a sufficiently "intimate knowledge of current policies and developments" to grasp the continuing importance of intelligence material contained in files over thirty years old. Four months later, in July 1982, the government effectively demolished its own argument by appointing just such an eminent retired official, Lord Franks, to head a committee of privy counselors to inquire into the origins of the Falklands conflict. The committee was given unrestricted access to intelligence files and personnel; and the government accepted both its findings on the Falklands and its recommendations for changes in the Joint Intelligence Organization. The government cannot credibly argue that a committee of privy counselors is competent to form a judgment on the intelligence services in the 1980s yet incompetent to advise on the release of intelligence records at least thirty years older. It does, however, argue just that. Its arguments were considered and demolished in hearings of the all-party Commons Select Committee on Education, Science, and the Arts in 1982-83.[7] Sadly, the 1983 election intervened before the committee (subsequently disbanded) could issue its report.

THE SLOW DECLINE OF OFFICIAL SECRECY

Whitehall is, however, now fighting a losing battle in its attempt to make intelligence history almost unresearchable. The first major breach in the wall of Whitehall secrecy came with the publication in 1966 of the official history *SOE in France: An Account of the Work of the British Special Operations Executive 1940-1944* by M. R. D. Foot. SOE was not covered by the traditional taboos that protect the peacetime intelligence community because it was a purely wartime organization concerned only with covert action and was dissolved in 1946. But Foot's book revealed how SOE had taken over the work of "Section D" of MI6 in 1940 and continued to have sometimes bitter demarcation disputes with it. SOE occupies a rather contradictory position in the Whitehall system of overclassification. Its files remain completely closed, but there is an SOE "historical adviser" (whose identity is officially secret) at the Ministry of Defence who responds helpfully to specific inquiries. And, as David Stafford shows in *Britain and European Resistance 1940-1945: A Survey of the Special Operations Executive with Documents* (1980), many SOE documents have found their way into Foreign Office and other files at the Public Record Office. "Indeed," writes Stafford, "the removal of SOE material has been so imperfectly and arbitrarily done, with no apparent criterion underlying it, that one can only marvel at the collective mind responsible for it."[8]

The first serious assault on the traditional taboos that protect the secret intelligence services themselves from historians came in 1973 with the revelation of the "Ultra Secret." The success of the codebreakers at Bletchley Park in decrypting the German "Enigma" machine ciphers had too large an influence on the Second World War for the secret to be preserved indefinitely as Whitehall wished. The suppression for almost forty years following the war of a secret shared by, among others, the 10,000 employees of Bletchley Park represents in itself a minor miracle of official secrecy in a democratic society. Following the publication in 1973 by General Gustave Bertrand of the French side of the story, *Enigma ou la plus grande énigme de la guerre 1939-1945* (a book that attracted curiously little attention in France at the time of publication), it became impossible to contain the secret any longer.

Academic historians at first appeared nonplussed at the prospect of researching so sensational and undocumented a subject. For the next five years, the lead was taken by more adventurous nonacademic historians and by wartime intelligence officers (the two categories sometimes overlapping): F. W. Winterbotham, Anthony Cave Brown, Patrick Beesly, David Kahn, R. V. Jones, Brian Johnson, Ronald Lewin, Ewen Montagu, and Peter Calvocoressi.[9] The first major work on Ultra by an academic historian was Sir F. H. Hinsley's magisterial official history, *British Intelligence in the Second World War*, whose first volume was published, after a long rearguard action by the leading Whitehall champions of official secrecy, in 1979.

The publication of the official history, combined with the release to the Public Record Office of some but by no means all of the wartime intercepts issued to service ministries and commanders in the field, has acted as both a stimulus and a deterrent to further academic research. Sir Harry Hinsley has had unrestricted access to files of the secret intelligence community that are, he tells us in his preface, "unlikely ever to be opened." Most scholars are understandably wary of devoting a major research effort to a subject on which they are denied access to documents available to others. Further research on Ultra since this publication of the official history, therefore, has been conducted chiefly by those with access to additional Polish source material (Marian Rejewski, Christopher Kasparek, Richard Voytak, Josef Garlinski, Wladyslaw Kozaczuk, and Jean Stengers), by former cryptanalysts at Bletchley Park (Gordon Welchman, Ralph Bennett, and Christopher Morris), and by other experts in cryptography (notably Alan Hodges, author of *Alan Turing: The Enigma*, and a number of contributors to *Cryptologia*).[10]

It is believed within Whitehall that Mrs. Thatcher was opposed to the decision taken by the Callaghan government to publish Sir F. H. Hinsley's official history but concluded after taking office that there was little point in banning subsequent volumes once the first had been published. For several years, however, she has resisted publication of the official history of wartime deception operations written by Sir Michael Howard and commissioned at the same time as Hinsley's history. Publication of Howard's volume and of a wartime history of MI5 by its former deputy director general, Anthony Simkins, was still under consideration in 1987.

Those in Whitehall who resisted the publication of Sir Harry Hinsley's official history during the 1970s argued that it was bound to prove the thin end of the wedge—that the Ultra secret would alert scholars to the role of British intelligence services in peacetime. Their fears will doubtless one day be fulfilled. Thus far, however, even the revelation of the wartime Ultra secret has done surprisingly little to attract the attention of British historians and political scientists either to other forms of intelligence or even to cryptanalysis in other periods. Biographies of major British statesmen and studies of British foreign policy still commonly treat intelligence as either unresearchable or not worth researching. No study of Clement Attlee so far published mentions his remarkable relationship with MI5; he was, however, the first British prime minister to pay regular visits to MI5 headquarters where he took part in discussions on Communist "subversion." Even Martin Gilbert's massive and, for the most part, impressive biography of Winston Churchill, despite its numerous references to Ultra, contains some striking intelligence gaps. None of the seven volumes so far published includes a single reference to Britain's longest-serving intelligence chief, Sir Vernon Kell, director general of MI5 from its founding in 1909 to 1940. Kell had a remarkable relationship with Churchill, spanning the full length of his career; and Churchill was intimately involved with the early years of MI5, initially as a keen supporter of Kell. Yet only a month after becoming prime minister in 1940, Churchill ordered Kell's dismissal.[11]

A wide variety of British nonacademic authors have tried to fill the void left by academic historians in the history of intelligence before the Second

World War. Their books are all too frequently either unreliable or uncheckable (or both). Some, like the television series "Reilly, Ace of Spies," shown to large audiences on both sides of the Atlantic, are largely fantasy. Even the most prolific and resourceful nonacademic British writer on intelligence history, "Nigel West" (who under his real name, Rupert Allason, became Conservative MP for Torbay in 1987), includes scarcely a single source reference in most of his books on MI5, MI6, and the Special Branch—even when he quotes from documents in the Public Record Office.[12] The errors noted by reviewers in his first editions demonstrate that the reader cannot reasonably be expected to take on trust everything he cannot check.

Even the most glaring errors in unreferenced histories of British intelligence have a depressing habit of reappearing in their successors. "Nigel West"'s claim in the first (though not the second) edition of his book *MI5* (published in 1981) that the prime minister in 1921 was Ramsay MacDonald (and not, as usually believed, Lloyd George) duly reappears in Anthony Masters's biography of the MI5 officer Maxwell Knight, *The Man Who Was M*, published in 1984. Even as good a book as Thomas G. Fergusson's *British Military Intelligence, 1870-1914*, also published in 1984, repeats the myth derived from Richard Deacon's *A History of the British Secret Service* (on which Colonel Fergusson acknowledges in his preface that he has, unwisely, "relied") that the Secret Intelligence Service, in reality not founded until 1909, already existed in Victorian Britain.

SOURCES FOR INTELLIGENCE HISTORY

One of the aims of the author's reseach and that of other members of the British Study Group on Intelligence[13] is to show that scholars have in the past overestimated the archival obstacles to the writing of British intelligence history. When I first began in the mid-1970s to write articles on British and French intelligence, I did not expect to find enough reliable source material to write a book. By the time I began writing *Her Majesty's Secret Service: The Making of the British Intelligence Community*[14] in the early 1980s, the main problem had become the sheer amount of material. Though there are, of course, enormous gaps in the archives, historians of the Dark Ages and analysts of Soviet politics frequently have to cope with even larger gaps. What is available is too important to be ignored. *Her Majesty's Secret Service* seeks to demonstrate that enough reliable source material has now either been officially released or escaped official censorship to make possible detailed study of the development of the British intelligence services at least until the end of the Second World War, analysis of some of their major successes and failures, and an assessment of the use made of their intelligence.

By and large the British official archives are most revealing at the junction between the secret intelligence community and the overt government bureaucracy. The complexities of the interface between overt government bureaucracies and unavowable secret agencies have produced an unusually confusing archive for both official censors and researchers. These same complexities have allowed through the net of official censorship many documents that Whitehall never intended to release.

Thus, though all SIS files remain closed (in principle forever), some of those of the passport control organization that provided cover for most SIS stations between the wars are available. These provide, inter alia, both the names and salaries of SIS station chiefs. Similarly, the files on the overt side of GC and CS operations (the security of British communications) reveal a good deal about the personnel and organization of its secret work. Foreign Office files contain much evidence on the intelligence supplied by SIS; those of the Special Branch, War Office, and Home Office are even more revealing about MI5.[15] Wesley Wark's excellent monograph, *The Ultimate Enemy: British Intelligence and Nazi Germany, 1933-1939* (1985), shows how much about the intelligence assessment can be learned from the files of the service ministries. Documents "weeded" from the archive of one government department are frequently discovered in the files of another. While working on SOE, David Stafford found that "material removed from the minutes and memoranda of the Chiefs of Staff has in many cases not been removed from the papers of the Joint Planning Staff, thus rendering the weeding exercise pointless."[16]

The precedent set by the revelation of the Ultra secret is, very gradually, increasing the flow of intelligence documents to the archives. Following the release of some World War II intercepts, the government was reluctantly obliged to release similar material for World War I. But it has, so far, illogically refused to release diplomatic intercepts for the interwar period despite the fact that some have already slipped through the net. Officially, therefore, French intercepts of the early 1920s remain much more highly classified than German intercepts of the early 1940s. When asked to explain this anomaly in 1983, the secretary of the cabinet, Sir Robert Armstrong, replied that the government regards peacetime intelligence documents as more secret than more recent wartime intelligence documents—an eccentric policy clearly derived from ancient taboos rather than the current needs of national security.

Such anomalies in present government policy have begun to erode official attempts to keep classified the entire intelligence archive. The journal *Intelligence and National Security*, which began publication in 1986, included in its first issue a short history of GC & CS between the wars that was written in 1944 by its former head A. G. Denniston and gives the first official summary published so far of the successes and failures of British interwar signals intelligence. The original document remains hidden in the archives of GCHQ and is a good example of the overclassification of ancient secrets in the much-abused name of national security. A decade ago the government would probably have sought an injunction to prevent its publication. Nowadays, though unwilling to release such documents itself, Whitehall is also reluctant to risk the public ridicule of defending such ancient secrets in the courts. Its reluctance is bound to encourage the revelation of other forbidden intelligence documents. The second issue of *Intelligence and National Security* published a fascinating memorandum by the vice-chief of the wartime SIS, Valentine Vivian, complaining about the machinations of his arch-rival, the assistant chief, Claude Dansey. This is another document of the kind that the government claims officially should never be revealed but cannot bring itself to ban. The continued publication of such harmless but officially "sensitive" documents makes a modest contribution to subverting the present overclassification of intelligence archives.

The anomalies in government policy also make it embarrassed to enforce its own rules on private archives. In principle Whitehall is entitled to prohibit public access to any intelligence document, however old, in private papers as well as the Public Record Office. Until the 1980s it frequently did so. Files in the papers of Viscount Templewood, the British foreign secretary, held in the Cambridge University Library and that deal with his intelligence activities in Russia *before* the Bolshevik Revolution are still banned by government order. But while Whitehall keeps this and other equally eccentric restrictions in force, it can no longer bring itself to behave with similar eccentricity toward new acquisitions by private archives. When the diaries of Sir Alexander Cadogan, permanent undersecretary at the Foreign Office during the Second World War, were published in 1971, the Foreign Office refused to allow the publication of many entries dealing with intelligence activities. However, the full version of the diaries, including the forbidden entries, is now available in the Churchill College Archive Centre at Cambridge.

Foreign archives sometimes offer a further means of circumventing the restrictions imposed by Whitehall on British official archives. Thanks to Anglo-American intelligence collaboration in the First World War and the special relationship that developed during the second, the National Archives in Washington contain important British intelligence documents still unavailable in Britain (though many others have been withheld to avoid offending Whitehall). Among First World War material in the National Archives is the MI5 handbook on "Preventive Intelligence," still withheld indefinitely from the Public Record Office.[17] Second World War intelligence documents include a number of Joint Intelligence Committee assessments, all still officially classified in Britain.[18] The largest British intelligence archive in the National Archives are the files of the Special Branch of the Shanghai Municipal Police, the British-run security agency active until 1941 in the Shanghai International Settlement.[19] Its records include hundreds of intelligence reports on the Chinese Communist Party and its link with Comintern. The whole archive fell into the hands of the Nationalist Chinese Government, which passed it on to the CIA just before the Communist capture of Shanghai in 1949. The CIA, in turn, released the files to the National Archives in the early 1980s.

The main immediate priority for intelligence historians, however, concerns oral rather than written records. Each year retired intelligence officers die, taking with them irreplaceable memories of the interwar and Second World War British intelligence services. There are still a handful with unique recollections of intelligence work in the First World War. In the United States, the NSA has a well-established program for recording the recollections of retired American cryptanalysts and others, but no such program exists in Britain. Indeed, Whitehall seems positively anxious to discourage anything of the kind. All retired intelligence officers have instructions to refer all requests for information on any aspect of their careers, however long ago, to their former services. Such requests are usually refused.

Whitehall is, however, increasingly confused in its attitude to revelations by retired intelligence officers. One striking example of its confusion concerns the article by Gordon Welchman, "From Polish Bomba to British Bombe," published in the first issue of *Intelligence and National Security*. The article, which goes only to 1940, involves no credible threat to national security. Indeed, at Gordon Welchman's request it was cleared before publication by the Defence, Press, and Broadcasting Committee (better known as the "D Notice" Committee) at the Ministry of Defence that advises the British media on "sensitive" subjects. Scarcely had the article been cleared by the "D Notice" Committee, however, than Mr. Welchman received a letter shortly before his death from the director-general of GCHQ, Sir Peter Marychurch, accusing him of causing "direct damage to security" and setting "a disastrous example to others." The most distinguished surviving cyptanalyst at Bletchley Park, Sir Stuart Milner-Barry, former head of Hut 6 who went on to become undersecretary at the treasury and ceremonial officer in the Civil Service Department, has described Sir Peter's letter as "a prime example of the lengths to which GCHQ's paranoia about the preservation of ancient secrets will carry them."[20]

A better publicized case of official confusion about intelligence history concerned the attempts by Her Majesty's Government to prevent publication of *Spycatcher*, Peter Wright's memoirs of his twenty-five years in MI5 from 1951 to 1976. Since Wright had retired to Tasmania and was thus well beyond the reach of the British Official Secrets Act, Her Majesty's Government brought a civil action against him in Australia, accusing him of breach of his duty of confidentiality to the Crown. The trial in the New South Wales Supreme Court late in 1986 revealed a series of anomalies in the British case. The government had, it emerged, known that Wright had been the principal source for, and had shared in the royalties of, Chapman Pincher's book *Their Trade is Treachery* published in 1981 but had made no attempt to prevent its publication. The British counsel, Theo Symos QC, strove without much success to persuade the judge that there was a fundamental distinction between an intelligence officer publishing classified information under his own name and supplying the same information for publication by another author. As the defense was quick to point out, the government had made no attempt to ban a television interview in 1984 (repeated during the trial) in which Wright reminisced at some length about his years in MI5.

It became increasingly clear in the course of the trial that Her Majesty's Government's attempt to defend an important issue of principle—its power to prevent unauthorized disclosures by retired intelligence officers—was seriously prejudiced not merely by the inconsistency with which that principle had been applied but also by Whitehall's exaggerated definition of the level of secrecy required by the needs of national security. The cabinet secretary, Sir Robert Armstrong, maintained in evidence that even intelligence records as far back as the 1911 Agadir crisis "should not be made available." Theo Symos insisted that the principle of non-disclosure applied even to such trivia as whether an MI5 officer liked baked beans. In a judgment delivered in March 1987 in the New South Wales Supreme Court, Mr. Justice Powell found in favor of Peter Wright and awarded him costs.[21] Though the British government announced its intention to appeal, most observers have concluded, like Dr. Ray Cline, former deputy director of the CIA and president of the National Intelligence Study Center, that the case "will make rigorous application of the British system of controls over intelligence publications difficult in the future."[22] In July 1987, Peter Wright's *Spycatcher* was published in the United States by Viking/Penguin and became an instant best seller.

Despite all the material that has escaped official censorship, the continued overclassification of ancient secrets inevitably sets limits to scholarly historical research. The problems are greatest at the level of day-to-day analysis of the supply, assessment, and use of intelligence. For example, enough evidence is now available to indicate the general influence of intercepted Soviet communications on British policy during the decade after the Bolshevik Revolution and to study their impact on the negotiation of the Anglo-Soviet trade agreement of 1921 and the breach of Anglo-Soviet diplomatic relations in 1927.[23] Not until the complete run of Soviet intercepts (or as many as survive) is available, however, will it be possible to assess their influence with the precision of Professor Hinsley's analysis of German intercepts during the Second World War. It is even harder to assess the influence of French intercepts on interwar British policy. We now know that no French diplomatic code or cipher system defeated GC & GS until 1935, but almost no French intercepts have so far been discovered later than 1924. The archives of the intelligence services up to 1945 doubtless contain far more gaps than those of the Whitehall ministries. But their eventual, probably gradual, release will one day transform historical study of the intelligence community.

Perhaps the most fruitful field at present for detailed research on the operational role of British intelligence in the twentieth century is the First World War, principally because official censorship is less rigid for wartime than for peacetime records. Curiously, we know less about British intelligence in the First World War than in the second, largely because of the lack of an official history. We badly need, for example, a detailed analysis of the early development of photographic reconnaissance, which began during the First World War and led half a century later to the age of the spy satellite. The photographic map constructed by the Royal Flying Corps during the First World War of "Hun-land," the territory immediately behind the enemy lines in the British sector of the Western Front, has yet to be analyzed in detail. Research in progress by Nicholas Hiley and John Ferris is uncovering other important new material on British cryptanalysis, espionage, and counterintelligence in the First World War.[24]

Scholarly research on the development of the British intelligence community since 1945 is substantially more difficult than research on the previous half century. Far fewer intelligence documents have leaked into the Public Record Office from the Cold War period than for any earlier period in the twentieth century. There are, of course, some exceptions. The fact that Guy Burgess and Donald Maclean worked for the British diplomatic service as well as for the KGB until their defection in 1951 makes it possible to deduce from Foreign Office files much of what they betrayed to the Soviet Union. The research of Christopher Catherwood has shown that, though a low-ranking diplomat of outrageous personal habits, Guy Burgess had access to reports from some of the most sensitive British and American intelligence agencies. Donald Maclean's value to the KGB probably reached its peak in December 1950, when as head of the Foreign Office American desk, he helped brief Clement Attlee for the Washington summit with President Truman on Korea. When Maclean's 1950 papers were declassified, his successor on the American desk, Robert Cecil, concluded that within the Foreign Office he "had access to almost any kind of information he wanted to see."[25]

In general, however, because of the paucity of declassified intelligence material, the main sources for British intelligence operations during the Cold War are the recollections of those concerned with them and evidence from the United States. The most interesting, though not the most reliable, memoirs of a British intelligence officer during the Cold War are those of Kim Philby, *My Silent War* (1968). Most retired intelligence officers willing to discuss their careers, however, do so unattributably. It is inevitably far more difficult to evaluate the reliability of works that depend on unattributable evidence, particularly in so controversial an area as intelligence, than of works that identify their sources. The studies of postwar British intelligence by "Nigel West" and Chapman Pincher, the two authors who have made most use of unattributable interviews, have therefore to be treated with some caution.[26] "West"'s and Pincher's sources, though providing new information, differ on such essentials as whether Sir Roger Hollis, director-general of MI5 from 1956 to 1965, was or was not a Soviet mole. Pincher concludes that he was; "West," that he was not. In 1987 "West" advanced the equally implausible theory that the mole was Hollis's deputy, Graham Mitchell.[27]

Because of the close cooperation between the CIA and MI6 in covert action during the Cold War, American archives and memoirs are frequently more informative about MI6 operations than their British counterparts. Nicholas Bethell's study of covert action in Albania, *The Great Betrayal* (1984), is a good example of what can be pieced together from American sources, the recollections of intelligence officers, and the scanty material in the Public Record Office. Reliable evidence on MI6 covert action during the Cold War is, however, only a fraction of that available on CIA operations.[28]

Rather more is available on British intelligence operations during decolonization. Anthony Short's *The Communist Insurrection in Malaya, 1948-1968* (1975)[29] is based on "full access" to the secret records of the Malayan government (though these do not appear to record the direct involvement of Sir Percy Sillitoe, Sir Dick White, and other senior MI5 officers during the Malayan emergency). The Suez crisis of 1956 presents particular problems of source material. MI6 is said to have devised a plan to assassinate President Nasser, but how close the plan came to implementation and how far it had the personal blessing of the prime minister, Anthony Eden, remain obscure. Hugh Greene, then director-general of the BBC, once observed to Lord Normanbrook, the BBC chairman who had been cabinet secretary during the Suez crisis, that "one day presumably the whole truth would emerge." "Damned good care has been taken," replied Normanbrook, "to see that the whole truth never does emerge."[30]

The most difficult period for research on British intelligence is, inevitably, the most recent. There is no parallel in Britain to the congressional inquiries of the mid-1970s that revealed so much about the CIA. However, the steady decline of the "D Notice" system (by which the media formerly accepted a remarkable degree of self-censorship on intelligence matters), a series of government defeats or pyrrhic victories in official secrets trials, and revelations of security lapses past and present (among them those associated with Anthony Blunt and Michael Bettaney of MI5 and Geoffrey Prime of GCHQ) have gradually increased the volume of reliable information about the current British intelligence community to at least a trickle. The Falklands conflict, partly because it produced the Franks inquiry, generated far more material on British intelligence (ably analyzed by Lawrence Freedman)[31] than any other recent international crisis. The journalist Duncan Campbell has shown how much can be deduced about the Anglo-American signals intelligence (SIGINT) network from technical and service journals and other overt sources. At the ABC Official Secrets Trial in 1978 when Campbell was one of the defendants, the chief witness from GCHQ, Colonel H. A. Johnstone, bewildered by repeated evidence that much intelligence that he had believed to be top secret could be obtained from unclassified publications, finally confessed, "To be frank, I am not certain what is secret and what is not."[32] Jeffrey Richelson and Desmond Ball provide in *The Ties that Bind: Intelligence Co-operation between the UKUSA Countries* (1985) details of no less than 447 UKUSA (the United Kingdom, the United States, Canada, Australia, and New Zealand) SIGINT facilities and stations.

All studies of current and recent British intelligence operations suffer, however, from two obvious insuperable handicaps. Though it is absurd to suppose that the revelations of wartime or prewar operations could nowadays put British security at risk, contemporary operations usually deserve the protection of official secrets legislation. We neither know nor should we know, for example, the extent of GCHQ's recent operational success, though we may suspect it to be large. (Its director told GCHQ staff after the Falklands conflict that so much praise had never been accorded by Whitehall.) Second, even when infomation on recent operations is available, it is rarely possible to judge how much more remains to be discovered. Contemporary analyses inevitably tend to place too much emphasis on what is known and make too little allowance for what is not—just as American studies may well be frequently guilty of underestimating the influence of the NSA because it produces so much less accessible evidence of its activities than does the CIA. By the time Kim Philby fled to Moscow in 1963, much of the damage done by the moles and atom spies had become public knowledge, but the successes of British codebreakers against Soviet codes *forty years before* had still to be revealed. Until the mid-1970s, British histories of the Second World War commonly contained references to a variety of human intelligence (humint) operations but failed to refer at all to sigint operations at Bletchley Park. Some recent studies of British intelligence may appear equally unbalanced in a generation's time.

THE UKUSA INTELLIGENCE NETWORK

One of the main present priorities for historical research on the British intelligence community within the constraints imposed by the over-classification of source material concerns its links with other intelligence communities, notably those in the United States and the Commonwealth, that led to today's UKUSA network. The study by Jeffrey T. Richelson and Desmond Ball, *The Ties that Bind: Intelligence Cooperation between the UKUSA Countries*, makes a valuable pioneering contribution to this research. But much more remains to be done.

The distant origins of this remarkable intelligence alliance go back to the Fenian bombing campaigns in British cities a century ago, when the Special Irish Branch in London depended on intelligence from both Canada and the United States. Surveillance of the Indian diaspora before the First World War in areas as far apart as Britain and British Columbia marked a new stage in the forging of an imperial intelligence network. Analyses of the alleged responsibility of Vancouver Sikhs for the Air India 747 disaster in 1985 omitted to mention that before the First World War Vancouver Sikhs were already one of the main targets of surveillance by British imperial intelligence. Shortly after the outbreak of war, a Vancouver Sikh assassinated the Canadian security officer in charge of their surveillance.[33] The First World War both greatly extended the imperial intelligence network and established the beginnings of an intelligence "special relationship" between Britain and the United States. Historians of that "special relationship" during the Second World War commonly overlook its origins in the first. Franklin Roosevelt's willingness to begin the special relationship even before Pearl Harbor reflects at least in part his admiration for Britain's "wonderful intelligence service" in the First World War.[34]

Since the 1976 publication of William Stevenson's rather romanticized account of Sir William Stephenson's role as wartime head of British Security Coordination (BSC) in New York, *A Man Called Intrepid*, the Anglo-American intelligence alliance during the Second World War has been somewhat sensationalized in a number of popular histories. Important though Stephenson's role was, he was never a global spymaster; his responsibilities were limited to North and South America. The time has come for a more sober assessment of BSC's achievements than is provided by *A Man Called Intrepid*. For all the sensationalism that it has evoked, however, the wartime Anglo-American intelligence alliance was, despite the inevitable strains that beset all alliances, unprecedented in both its scope and intimacy. As Thomas Parrish's *The Ultra Americans* (1986)[35] demonstrates, that intimacy was even more striking in sigint than in humint. Postwar Anglo-American collaboration, particularly in sigint, remains a much more difficult field of research.

Further promising areas for research include the growth of Britain's links with the main intelligence communities of the Empire and Commonwealth. Like American archives, some Commonwealth archives have been less heavily censored than those in Britain and sometimes contain copies of British intelligence documents unavailable in the Public Record Office. Richard Popplewell has discovered much new material on intelligence collaboration between Britain and the Indian Raj among the files of the India Office Library and Records. Peter St. John, Reginald Whitaker, Robert

Keyserlingk, Lawrence Aronsen, and Wesley Wark draw on Canadian archives in their articles on Canadian intelligence during the Second World War and Cold War.[36] David Stafford's *Camp X* (1987)[37] provides an interesting case study of the Canadian contribution to wartime intelligence collaboration: the training of British, American, and Canadian agents at a secret location on Lake Ontario. James Littleton's *Target Nation* (1986)[38] considers critically some of the issues raised by Canada's postwar membership in the UKUSA alliance.

Britain's most important Commonwealth intelligence connection over the last half century has been with Australia. The Australian Security Intelligence Organization (ASIO) was founded in 1949 largely as a result of British pressure. Frank Cain's *The Origins of Political Surveillance in Australia* (1983)[39] traces British influence on Australian counterintelligence back to the founding of the Counter-Espionage Bureau in 1916. Robert Manne's *The Petrov Affair* (1987)[40] discusses collaboration between ASIO and MI5 during the events surrounding the well-publicized defection of Vladimir and Evdokia Petrov in 1954. British influence on the development of the Defence Signals Directorate (DSD, Australia's NSA) and the Australian Secret Intelligence Service (ASIS) has been equally important. The first two heads of the Defence Signals Bureau (the postwar predecessor of DSD) were both British. For two years after the formation of ASIS in 1952, its officers abroad operated as members of British stations. For the next generation ASIS is said to have referred to MI6 London headquarters as "Head Office." The memoirs of the former head of Australian scientific intelligence, R. H. Mathams, *Sub Rosa* (1982),[41] provide important insights into Australian intelligence collaboration with Britain and the United States during the quarter century up to 1979. The series of reports on Australian intelligence agencies since 1976 by Royal Commissions chaired by Mr. Justice Hope, though generally informative, are predictably discreet on the question of cooperation with allies. The research of Desmond Ball and a number of leaked intelligence reports have, however, revealed rather more about the recent history of that cooperation than Canberra, London, and Washington intended to become public.[42]

The history of the British intelligence community and of its links with the intelligence communities of other English-speaking states has important implications even for political scientists working mainly on American material. Much work by political scientists on intelligence is based at present on a dangerously narrow data base. Because there is so much more reliable evidence since the Second World War on U.S. intelligence than on any other major intelligence community, there is an inevitable over-concentration by political scientists on recent American experience. Intelligence studies in the United States thus sometimes tend to become the American experience writ large. Any attempt to derive general truths about the nature of intelligence from an incomplete knowledge of little more than a generation of American intelligence experience is, however, a hazardous enterprise.

Over-concentration on the American experience affects even such important general analyses as Walter Laqueur's *World of Secrets: The Uses and Limits of Intelligence* (1985). Laqueur's problem is that the rest of the world has yet to surrender a sufficient number of its secrets to make possible a truly global analysis of the "uses and limits of intelligence." Apart from the United States, the only "open societies" whose intelligence communities he considers (all in the space of thirty pages) are the British, German, and Israeli; and his brief analysis of British intelligence is marred by a series of errors.[43] At present it is difficult to be certain how much of the "uses and limits" of American intelligence apply equally to other intelligence communities.

"Mirror-imagery" (the tendency to project one's own assumptions onto other societies) is a case in point. This is clearly not uniquely an American problem. The Foreign Office, like the State Department, appears to have been reluctant to credit intelligence pointing to the invasion of Czechoslovakia in 1968 because, judged by Western standards, an invasion would damage Soviet interests. "Mirror-imaging" also helps to explain how the Israelis were taken by surprise in the Yom Kippur War. But comparative research may (or may not) reveal that European intelligence services, though their resources do not compare with those of the United States, find it easier to take account of cultural differences of perception. Because of its sheer size and power, the United States suffers from what Laqueur aptly describes as the "parochialism of bigness" and may be unusually prone to project its own standards and values on the outside world. In the days of the British Empire, Britain sometimes had much the same problem.

British intelligence, too, cannot be fully understood in isolation from the experience of other intelligence communities. The study of intelligence by both historians and political scientists requires far more historical depth and geographic width than it possesses at present. For intelligence studies to assume their rightful place within the framework of international studies, they have first to become truly international.

═══

SUPPLEMENT: THE "D NOTICE" COMMITTEE, GCHQ AND GORDON WELCHMAN

A Case Study in the Eccentricities of British Official Secrecy

One of the consequences of keeping so many antiquated secrets is growing confusion within Whitehall over which of them any longer have any bearing on national security. A bizarre recent case in point, illustrated by the three letters reproduced in this supplement, concerns the article by the late Gordon Welchman, "From Polish Bomba to British Bombe: The Birth of Ultra," published in the first issue of *Intelligence and National Security*.* On July 8, 1985, the contents of this article were cleared by the Defence, Press, and Broadcasting Committee (better known as the "D Notice" Committee) at the Ministry of Defence that advises the media on articles with a possible bearing on national security. Four days later the director of GCHQ, Sir Peter Marychurch, wrote a personal letter to Gordon Welchman, accusing him of causing "direct damage to security" and setting a "disastrous" precedent. In accordance with Mr. Welchman's wishes, shortly before his death in October 1985 a copy of Sir Peter's letter was supplied to *The Guardian*, which published an extract from it on October 15. The reaction of many of Mr. Welchman's friends and former colleagues is reflected in a letter from Sir Stuart Milner-Barry published in *The Guardian* on October 29.

London, 8 July 1985

Dear Doctor Andrew,

May I refer to your letter dated 15 May 1985 enclosing Mr. Gordon Welchman's article, and to our telephone conversations on 26 June and 3 July 1985.

I am writing to confirm my verbal statement to you in the second conversation that no deletions need be made to the article on D Notice grounds.

Yours sincerely,

P R KAY
Major General
Acting Secretary,
Defence, Press and
Broadcasting Committee,
Ministry of Defence.

---

* Gordon Welchman, "From Polish Bomba to British Bombe: The Birth of Ultra," *Intelligence and National Security* 1, no. 1 (January 1986): 71-110.

Cheltenham, 12 July 1985

Dear Mr. Welchman,

It has come to my notice that Dr. Christopher Andrew is proposing to publish an article of yours in a journal called *Intelligence and National Security*. The article, entitled 'From Polish Bomba to British Bombe: The Birth of Ultra', appears to have been conceived as a corrective addendum to your book published in 1982, *The Hut Six Story*.

2. Dr. Andrew has submitted this article to the Secretary of the Defence Press and Broadcasting Committee for consideration under the D Notice system, stating that he does this at your request. I understand the Secretary to have replied that there are no deletions which he can usefully suggest and that the proper course was for you to submit any proposed publication to your former department, in accordance with your obligations under the Official Secrets Acts and with the guidelines issued by the Foreign Secretary in 1978 (endorsed by the Prime Minister in 1979) of which a copy is attached to this letter.

3. I can only endorse the Secretary's response. It was (as I believe you know) a great shock to my predecessor and to the US authorities when you published your book in 1982, without consulting us and in defiance of undertakings which thousands of others have faithfully observed; I am disappointed to find you following a similar path again in 1985. These words may seem somewhat harsh, but I ask you to consider not only the direct damage to security but also the knock-on effect of your actions: each time a person like yourself, of obviously deep knowledge and high repute, publishes inside information about the inner secrets of our work, there is more temptation and more excuse for others to follow suit. The ultimate result must be as obvious to you as it is to me. We do not expect outsiders to show any great sense of repsponsibility in what they publish, but you can perhaps understand that it is a bitter blow to us, as well as a disastrous example to others, when valued ex-colleagues decide to let us down.

Yours sincerely,

(Sir) PETER MARYCHURCH.

Director, GCHQ

Enclosure:

Extract from *Hansard* 941, no. 36 (12 January 1978).

Dr. Owen (the Foreign Secretary), pursuant to his reply (Official Report, December 16, 1977; Vol. 941, c481), gave the following information:

The release of Enigma/Ultra records to the Public Record Office has understandably caused those who worked on or used this material and who have maintained the undertakings of reticence which they gave at the time to ask where they now stand.

Amongst the records of the war-time Service Intelligence Directorates which the Government, in accordance with the provisions of the Public Records Act, have released to the Public Record Office are those based on intercepted radio messages of the enemy armed forces which no longer require security protection. The availability of the records which have been released in this way will enable a better historical judgement to be made of the part that intelligence played in the conduct of the war. Those who gave the undertakings of reticence to which I have referred are now absolved from them to the limited extent that they may now disclose the fact that they worked on or used material based on intercepted radio messages of the enemy armed forces. They may, for example, acknowledge having worked as interceptors, cypher breakers, distributors or users of this material, and may reveal what they know of the use made of it in the conduct of the war.

Other information, including details of the methods by which this material was obtained, has not been made available to the Public Record Office, the records in question having been retained with the approval of the Lord Chancellor in accordance with the relevant provisions of the Public Records Act. It remains subject to the undertakings and to the Official Secrets Acts and may not be disclosed. Those in any doubt should, therefore, satisfy themselves beforehand that any disclosure which they have it in mind to make does not go beyond information contained in the records released to the Public Record Office.

Those who worked on or used material based on these intercepted messages and who contemplate any book, article, lecture or other form of publication drawing on information obtained in the course of their official duties remain under the normal obligation to consult their former departments — now Foreign and Commonwealth Office or Ministry of Defence as appropriate.

As the Prime Minister told the Hon. Member for Melton (Mr. Latham) on 30 November, the preparation of an Official History of Intelligence in World War II is well advanced. If it is published the principles governing the extent of permitted disclosure embodied in the guidance above will apply also in relation to the Official History.

From *The Guardian*, November 29, 1985:

Sir,

As one of Gordon Welchman's oldest friends and colleagues from Hut Six, I feel bound to record an emphatic protest at the slur cast on his memory by the letter from Sir Peter Marychurch, quoted in your issue of October 15 as having been sent to Welchman within a few months of his death.

Even had there been substance in Sir Peter's complaint, he might, I should have thought, have refrained from writing to a man of Welchman's distinction, 20 years his senior, in terms more appropriate to the rebuke of an erring subordinate.

But, in fact, the complaint is, as Dr. Christopher Andrew has pointed out, a prime example of the lengths to which GCHQ's paranoia about the preservation of ancient secrets will carry them. To talk of 'direct damage to security' in the context of Welchman's article in *Intelligence and National Security* is surely absurd.

The secrets of the Enigma and how it was broken are of fascinating interest historically, and it is a sad pity that the authorities still prevent the story being properly told. But to suppose that the battles which we had to wage before the birth of the first electronic computer (which must seem to present-day cryptanalysts rather like fighting with bows and arrows) could be relevant to security now is just not credible. That this was the view of the D-notice committee is indicated by their letter to Dr. Andrew, which stated simply that 'no deletions need to be made to the article on D-notice grounds'.

It is worth remembering that the secret of Ultra was kept for 30 years, and might well have been kept, so far as the members of Hut Six were concerned, for another 30, if others had not revealed it. To suggest that the first head of this organisation (and a man who of all the remarkable group assembled at Bletchley Park made possibly the biggest contribution to the success of the whole operation) could be guilty of doing anything to endanger national security does indeed, as Dr Andrew has said, reveal a nasty attitude.

Yours very truly,

(Sir) Stuart Milner-Barry

NOTES

1. An abbreviated version of Sir Michael Howard's comments appeared in the *New York Times Book Review*, February 16, 1986, p. 6.

2. Compton Mackenzie, *My Life and Times: Octave Five* (London: Chatto and Windus, 1966), pp. 86-88.

3. *New York Times Book Review*, February 16, 1986, p. 6.

4. Information from the late Gordon Welchman.

5. House of Commons, *Parliamentary Debates*, December 15, 1924, col. 674.

6. D. G. T. Williams, *Not in the Public Interest* (London: Hutchinson, 1965) and David Hooper, *Official Secrets: the Use and Abuse of the Act* (London: Secker and Warburg, 1987).

7. House of Commons, Education, Science, and Arts Committee (Session 1982-83), *Public Records: Minutes of Evidence*.

8. David Stafford, *Britain and European Resistance 1940-1945* (London: Macmillan, 1980), p. xii. Other recent work on SOE includes M. R. D. Foot, *SOE: The Special Operations Executive* (London: BBC., 1984); Charles Cruickshank, *SOE in the Far East* (New York: Oxford University Press, 1983), and *SOE in Scandinavia* (New York: Oxford University Press, 1986).

9. See the bibliography appended to Gordon Welchman, "From Polish Bomba to British Bombe: The Birth of Ultra," *Intelligence and National Security* 1, no. 1 (January 1986): 71-110.

10. Ibid.

11. Christopher Andrew, "Churchill and Intelligence," *Intelligence and National Security* 3, no. 3 (July 1988).

12. "Nigel West," *MI5: British Security Service Operations 1909-1945* (New York: Stein and Day, 1982), and *MI6: British Secret Intelligence Service Operations 1909-1945* (New York: Random House, 1983); Rupert Allason, *The Branch* (London: Secker and Warburg, 1983). "West"'s most recent volume, *GCHQ: The Secret Wireless War 1900-86* (London: Weidenfeld and Nicolson, 1986) contains some (though insufficient) source references on the period up to 1945. For his work on post-1945 intelligence, see below.

13. Essays by some members of the group appear in Christopher Andrew and David Dilks, eds., *The Missing Dimension: Governments and Intelligence Communities in the Twentieth Century* (Urbana, Ill.: University of Illinois Press, 1984); K. G. Robertson, ed., *British and American Approaches to Intelligence* (London: Macmillan, 1987); and Christopher Andrew and Jeremy Noakes, eds., *Intelligence and International Relations 1900-1945* (Exeter, England: Exeter University Press, 1987).

14. Christopher Andrew, *Her Majesty's Secret Service: The Making of the British Intelligence Community* (New York: Viking, 1986). Published in London as *Secret Service: The Making of the British Intelligence Community* (London: Heinemann, 1985).

15. The source references to *Her Majesty's Secret Service* contain numerous examples.

16. Stafford, *Britain and European Resistance 1940-1945*, p. xii.

17. U.S. National Archives Record Group (RG) 165, 11013-21.

18. See, e.g., the British JIC reports filed with American JIC papers in RG 165, ABC Russia 336, box 250.

19. RG 263, SMP files.

20. See supplement.

21. Hooper, *Official Secrets*, appendix 7; and Richard V. Hall, *A Spy's Revenge* (Ringwood, Australia, Victoria and Harmondsworth: Penguin Books, 1987).

22. *Foreign Intelligence Literary Scene* 6, no. 1 (1987).

23. Andrew, *Her Majesty's Secret Service*, chaps. 9 and 10.

24. See, inter alia, Nicholas Hiley, "British Security in Wartime: The Rise and Fall of P.M.S. 2, 1915-17," *Intelligence and National Security* 1, no. 3 (September 1986); and John Ferris, "Whitehall's Black Chamber: British Cryptology and the Government Code and Cipher School, 1919-29," *Intelligence and National Security* 2, no. 1 (January 1987).

25. Peter Hennessy and Kathleen Townsend, "The Documentary Spoor of Burgess and Maclean," *Intelligence and National Security* 2, no. 2 (May 1987).

26. "Nigel West," *A Matter of Trust: MI5 1945-72* (Briarcliff Manor, N.Y.: Stein and Day, 1982); *GCHQ.* Chapman Pincher, *Inside Story* (New York: Stein and Day, 1978), *Their*

Trade is Treachery (London: Sidgwick and Jackson Ltd., 1981), and *Too Secret Too Long* (New York: St. Martin's Press, 1984).

27. "Nigel West," *Molehunt* (London: Weidenfeld & Nicolson, 1987).

28. See, e.g., John Prados, *Presidents' Secret Wars: CIA and Pentagon Covert Operations Since World War II* (New York: W. Morrow, 1986).

29. Anthony Short, *The Communist Insurrection in Malaya* (London: Muller, 1975).

30. *The Guardian*, October 30, 1986.

31. Lawrence Freedman, "Intelligence and the Falklands," *Intelligence and National Security* I, no. 3 (September 1986): 309-335.

32. See, e.g., Duncan Campbell, *The Unsinkable Aircraft Carrier: American Military Power in Britain*, rev. paperback ed., (London: Grafton Books, 1986); Crispin Aubrey, *Who's Watching You?* (Harmondsworth, U.K.: Penguin Books, 1981).

33. See the article by Richard Popplewell in Andrew and Noakes, eds., *Intelligence and International Relations*.

34. Andrew, *Her Majesty's Secret Service*, p. 466.

35. Thomas Parrish, *The Ultra Americans* (Briarcliff Manor, N.Y.: Stein and Day, 1986).

36. See Peter St. John, *Conflict Quarterly* 4, no. 4 (1984); Reginald Whitaker, "Origins of the Canadian Government's Internal Security System, 1946-1952," *Canadian Historical Review* 65, no. 2 (June 1984); Robert Keyserlingk, "'Agents Within the Gates': The Search for Nazi Subversives in Canada during World War II," *Canadian Historical Review* 66, no. 2 (June 1985); Lawrence Aronsen, "Some Aspects of Surveillance: 'Peace, Order and Good Government' during the Cold War: The Origins and Organization of Canada's Internal Security Program," *Intelligence and National Security* 1, no. 3 (September 1986); and Wesley Wark, *Journal of Contemporary History* (forthcoming, 1987).

37. David Stafford, *Camp X* (New York: Viking, 1987).

38. James Littleton, *Target Nation* (Toronto: Lester and Orpen Dennys, 1986).

39. Frank Cain, *The Origins of Political Surveillance* (Sydney and London: Angus and Robertson, 1983).

40. Robert Manne, *The Petrov Affair* (Sydney and Oxford: Pergamon Press, 1987).

41. R. H. Matthams, *Sub Rosa* (Sydney and London: Allen and Unwin, 1982).

42. Ball and Richelson, *Ties That Bind: Intelligence Co-operation Between the UKUSA Countries* (Winchester, Mass.: Allen & Unwin, Inc., 1986); and Brian Toohey and Marion Wilkinson, *The Book of Leaks* (Sydney and London: Angus and Robertson, 1987).

43. See the author's review in *London Review of Books*, April 3, 1986. Despite errors, Laqueur's study is essential reading.

4

The Study of the Soviet Intelligence and Security System

JOHN J. DZIAK

The serious study of foreign intelligence and security systems is a recent development in nongovernment circles in the West and as such still has a limited literature, whether theoretical or operational. Much research and writing to date has tended to fix upon Western systems, if for no other reason (and a good one at that) than accessibility of data due to the publicity generated by investigations, oversight, leaks, and assorted controversies. Also, autocratic, dictatorial, and despotic systems are difficult to access on this subject, to say the least. The down side to this is twofold: (1) there is an excessive amount of generalization and mirror-imaging of Western intelligence and security systems with the result that (2) the unique historical, ideological, and political ethos of a non-Western system is forced to fit the Western paradigm.

This writer proposes that the twentieth century offers some unique examples of intelligence and security systems that seem to be the impelling drive of the political system they appear to serve. Put another way, certain political systems display an overarching concern with "enemies," internal and external, to the extent that security and the extirpation of real or presumed threats thereto are the premier enterprises of such systems— and are among the few state enterprises that work with a modicum of efficiency and success.

The fixation with enemies and threats to the security of the state involves a very heavy internal commitment of state resources and the creation of a state security service that penetrates and permeates all societal institutions, including the military, but not necessarily including the claimant to monopoly power, usually a self-proclaimed "revolutionary" party. This security service is the principal guardian of the party; the two together constitute a permanent counterintelligence enterprise to which all other major political, social, and economic questions are subordinated. Indeed, the commonweal is not the principal objective of such an amalgam of ensconced power and the security screen; self-perpetuation is.

I would label such a system the counterintelligence state. In such a system, foreign activities are an external variant of this security imperative. Hence, foreign intelligence in some respects takes on the dimensions of external counterintelligence. The security service and foreign intelligence tend to be the same organ of the state.

Clearly throughout its history, the Soviet Union and the various surrogates and satellites it has spawned fit this label. Western security and foreign intelligence services are poor models for analyzing these counterintelligence states. These states must be examined on their terms and in the context of their political traditions. This brief study attempts to probe the Soviet intelligence and security system from the dimension of the counterintelligence state.

THE NATURE OF THE SYSTEM: THE COUNTERINTELLIGENCE STATE

It would be appropriate first to establish why this writer sees the USSR as a counterintelligence state. Soviet state security began as an integral feature of the party-state virtually from the inception of the Bolshevik regime. The very structure of this party-state, as well as its statecraft and harsh internal regimen, bear all the hallmarks of a preeminent security service or what has already been labeled the counterintelligence state. No matter how one defines a totalitarian, or totalist, system, one comes to a police state; and the USSR is the longest-lived, pervasive police state of the twentieth century[1]—one may even argue the most massive in history. But unlike the police states of authoritarian dictatorships or even that of Nazi Germany, which lasted only twelve years and where security and intelligence powers were surprisingly diffuse for most of that period, Soviet state security was and is almost conterminous with the party.

There is more than mere sloganeering involved when the KGB is touted as the "shield and sword" of the party. Party and state security are intermeshed in an operational amalgam that is too frequently misperceived by observers from a pluralist political tradition where institutional boundaries define power relationships and where security and intelligence services are subject to rigid constitutional or traditional restraints.

Prior to the appearance of the Soviet party-state, history offered few, if any, precedents of a millenarian, security-focused system. One might argue that the generic "Oriental" or "Asiatic despotisms" studied by such disparate students of social history as Karl Marx, Max Weber, and Karl Wittfogel presented compelling analogies for such a system.[2] However, certain key ingredients, such as a dominant ubiquitous ideology or a continuously institutionalized secret police, were lacking in those despotisms both in scope and intensity. Certainly intrusive claims on the totality of human existence, common to the Soviet state, were not characteristic of those despotisms.

The Bolshevik victory created a party-state structure that equated domestic opposition (and later, even apathy) with treason, declared whole classes of people as foreordained by history to destruction, and arrogated to itself a mandate to execute history's will on an international scale. Such sweeping claims were seriously held and meant to be acted upon. In a sense a secular theocracy was born in which a priesthood (the party), served by a combined holy office and temple guard (the *Cheka*), sought to act its will: the imposition of its ideas and the extirpation of those actually or potentially opposed. Such a system is pathological about enemies and makes the search for them and their discovery and elimination an overriding state objective. Police and counterintelligence operations, such as arrest, investigation, penetration, provocation, deception, entrapment, denunciation, and censorship, with coincident informants, spy mania, dossiers, and so on, soon distinguish the behavior of the whole state structure, not just of the security organs. Domestic society is the first object of these operations; the millenarian imperative then carries them into the international system.

The military above all is subject to special scrutiny in this security system. From the creation of the Red Army in 1918 to the Soviet armed forces of the late-twentieth century, state security has had the exclusive mandate for military counterintelligence (another argument against applying a Western paradigm). The Special Departments (OOs) were formed by Dzerzhinskiy's *Cheka*—with the strong support and concurrence of Red Army Chief Leon Trotsky—to facilitate a special, punitive means of penetration to ensure party control of the military gun. No Bonapartism, or threat of a military takeover, here! These means included a covert network of informants and hostage-taking of families to guarantee the loyalty of the so-called "military specialists," former Tsarist officers recruited to captain the new Red Army. While hostage-taking is no longer needed, the KGB's OOs still suffuse the Soviet armed forces under the overall direction of the KGB's Third Chief Directorate. The savaging of the Soviet officer corps by state security in the late 1930s, with little or no evidence of either guilt or attempts at self-defense by the victim, is a tribute to the mindset, yet workability, of the counterintelligence state.

Thus, the discovery and elimination of perceived conspiracies and enemies characterized the motives and behavior of the counterintelligence state.

Hence, it is this writer's belief that the USSR is the foremost example of a counterintelligence state.

Historically, conspiracy was central to the formation of the Soviet system and the party's monopolistic position therein. The long years spent underground prior to the Bolshevik coup in October 1917 involved not only covert provocational and counterprovocational duels with the Tsar's security service, the *Okhrana*, but intense struggle with the Mensheviks and even with elements within the Bolshevik faction of the Russian Social Democratic Labor Party (RSDLP).

The tradition of *Okhrana* penetration and provocation within the revolutionary parties had gone to bizarre lengths. Witness the case of Yevno Azef, a police spy who took part in the establishment of the Socialist Revolutionary Party (SR) for the Russian Empire and who also was a founding member of the Battle Organization, the terrorist section of the SR; or that of the Tsarist *Okhrana* police agent Roman Malinovsky, colleague of Lenin, member of the Bolshevik Central Committee, and chairman of the Bolshevik faction of the Fourth Imperial Duma of which he was a deputy. Zinoviev's lament was not without foundation:

> At that time ... there was not a single organization in the areas into which a provocateur had not wormed himself, and everyone trailed each other around, one member fearing and not trusting the next.[3]

The case of Roman Malinovsky is a particularly intriguing and bizarre example of police provocation and penetration. When Vladimir Burtsev—an SR writer who was a self-styled, one-man security service against the *Okhrana* (and later the *Cheka*)—warned Lenin that one of his confidants, Jacob Zhitomirsky, was an agent-provocateur, Lenin sent Malinovsky, of all people, to investigate the matter with Burtsev. And Malinovsky himself was a police spy! Lenin protected Malinovsky almost to the end, hurling venomous charges of "malicious slanderers" at the Mensheviks Julius Martov and Theodore Dan who in 1914 demanded a nonfactional Social Democratic Party investigation of Malinovsky. Even when Bukharin had earlier voiced his suspicions of Malinovsky to Lenin, Lenin and Zinoviev offered a spirited defense of the man. Malinovsky, it is said, told Lenin before World War I of his earlier criminal past (which led him to his police connections) to which Lenin allegedly replied, "For Bolsheviks such things are of no importance."[4]

In 1917 Lenin was called to testify on Malinovsky before the Extraordinary Commission of the Provisional Government, which was probing *Okhrana* operations and provocations. He emphatically exonerated Malinovsky on the grounds that everything he did benefited the Bolshevik faction, which gained far more than the *Okhrana*.[5] This was an interesting claim insofar as the *Okhrana* all along had intended to help the Bolsheviks through their use of Malinovsky to ensure continuation of the split between Bolsheviks and Mensheviks, thereby preventing unification of the revolutionary movement. And this was precisely the complaint of the Mensheviks—and some Bolsheviks—as early as 1913 when they raised the charges against Malinovsky in the first place.

When Malinovsky returned to Russia in November 1918, he noisily demanded his own arrest and that he be brought to see Lenin. He was granted his first wish, but Lenin remained strangely silent, refusing to see him. Had Lenin finally grasped the truth, and was he too embarrassed to persist in Malinovsky's defense in the face of the evidence? Or had Lenin known all along, in effect making common cause with the police in the interest of a "higher" objective that required furtherance of the split with the Mensheviks and ultimately, as events turned out, an exclusive Bolshevik victory? And if he knew, did Lenin cynically drop Malinovsky at the end; or was he prevented from protecting him by Bolsheviks who had been the "victims" of Malinovsky's denunciations, e.g., Stalin, Sverdlov, Krylenko?

Krylenko, the prosecutor at Malinovsky's trial, was also suspected of both *Okhrana* and German intelligence connections during World War I.[6] The man who had acceded to Malinovsky's request for arrest was Zinoviev, who with Lenin had defended him against Bukharin's charges years before.

Why was Malinovsky executed so quickly, within hours of his trial, after even the prosecution sought to prove that his activities redounded more to the party than to the *Okhrana* and after all knew of his highly acclaimed Bolshevising work among Russian prisoners in German prison camps during the war? Why was Beletsky, the director of the Department of Police to whom Malinovsky reported, also shot so quickly after Malinovsky's execution?

Malinovsky's behavior in returning to Russia in 1918, fully aware of his notoriety, itself raises questions. Most police agents whose covers were blown or threatened fled to other countries, frequently with a respectable bonus from the *Okhrana*. Was Malinovsky's bravado driven by a stricken conscience, or did he expect a deserved exoneration and welcome from a Bolshevik leadership whose double agent he really was? Did a thoroughly cynical triumvirate of Lenin, Zinoviev, and Krylenko sacrifice him in the interest of hiding a very criminal episode in Bolshevik history that could threaten the legitimacy of their revolution?

And what was the role of Stalin in Malinovsky's trial and execution? Little seems to have surfaced on this point; yet as we shall see, it would likely have been in Stalin's direct interest to have Malinovsky silenced forever. The trial itself was the last bizarre episode of the Malinovsky affair and bore an eerie similarity to those notorious theatrical productions of the 1930s, Stalin's purge trials. The more one probes the Malinovsky business, the more frangible does Bolshevik historiography actually become.

An intriguing characteristic of Malinovsky and other police provocateurs, unique to the Russian milieu, is that such men tended to confuse their double roles, obscuring their true loyalties and thereby staining the reputations both of their police sponsors and the revolutionary groups they penetrated and served. They contributed in a major way to furthering the split in the Social Democratic Party whose Menshevik faction already feared the joint threat of *Okhrana* provocations and the despotic predilections inherent in Lenin's unitary organizational schemes.

It should be remembered that well before the Malinovsky controversies the non-Bolshevik left had voiced strong fears over future revolutionary developments should the Social Democrats succumb to Lenin's insistence on his recipe for the future. At the 1906 Stockholm Congress of the Social Democrats, Plekhanov's and others' fears of a despotic restoration forced a grudging Lenin to offer up a set of "protective" guarantees calculated to inhibit the degeneration of their revolution. These guarantees were (1) that socialist revolutions would occur in the West, which even Lenin admitted he could not call forth of his own volition; and (2) the promise that there would be no standing army and no bureaucracy, accomplished through the "complete democratization ... of the whole system of the state."[7] And as late as March 8, 1918, at the Seventh Party Congress, Lenin broadened the institutional prohibition to include the police: "Soviet power is a new type of state in which there is no bureaucracy, no standing army, no police."[8]

Already within a few short months of the Bolshevik coup of November 1917, Plekhanov's fears were realized, guarantees notwithstanding: on December 20, 1917, a far more pervasive and virulent form of the *Okhrana* was reinstituted as the *Cheka*; a massive and arbitrary party-state bureaucracy quickly emerged, evoking bitter disillusionment manifested by the Kronshtadt uprising and Workers' Opposition; "democratization of the state" was terminated with the forced dissolution of the democratically elected Constituent Assembly in January 1918; and a standing Red Army based on conscription followed in April. In short order then, not only did a despotic restoration occur but also it bore repressive similarities more akin to the older pre-Petrine tradition of Muscovy, Ivan the Terrible, and his *Oprichnina*, than it did to the relatively ineffectual *Okhrana* and the weakened autocracy it inadequately served. Russia of 1917 simply was not the autocratic system of ages past. The Tsar's powers were attrited significantly throughout the last of the nineteenth century and the years prior to World War I; hence, the resemblance of Bolshevik despotism was not to the fragile edifice under Nicholas II but to the arbitrary powers of Ivan the Terrible.

Still another element of conspiracy involved the German efforts to knock Imperial Russia out of the war. These ranged from penetration of the Tsarist government to support for national separatist and revolutionary elements. A complex skein of German espionage and political action, obscured by intelligence legends and missing or destroyed records, may have become intermeshed with revolutionary intrigues of the Bolsheviks and provocational manipulations of the *Okhrana*.

One such confluence might well have included the Tsarist General Mikhail D. Bonch-Bruevich, brother of the Bolshevik revolutionary and Lenin's associate Vladimir D. Bonch-Bruevich. In 1916 General Bonch-Bruevich had duties comprising both intelligence and counterintelligence, first at General Headquarters and then at the Northern Front. He had developed a reputation as a spy hunter and figured prominently in the arrest, trial, and execution in 1915 of an alleged German spy, one Colonel S. N. Myasoedov. The case was a shocking miscarriage of justice. As one respected historian notes, Myasoedov became a scapegoat for military failures and the victim of intrigues by Generals Bonch-Bruevich and Batyushin,[9] both of whom exercised major military counterintelligence and intelligence responsibilities. Both generals were strongly suspected of having been agents of the Central Powers,[10] although Batyushin is believed to have been responsible for the blackmail and recruitment of the homosexual Colonel Alfred Redl of the Austro-Hungarian General Staff—an unlikely accomplishment for a German or Austrian agent.

General Bonch-Bruevich's rendering of the Myasoedov affair is notoriously specious and self-serving,[11] not surprising given the man's record both during World War I and after. Bonch-Bruevich maintained the reputation of a liberal yet remained in close contact with his Bolshevik brother. Historian George Katkov suggests a German-Bolshevik collusive link whereby

> secret information from the armies of the Northern Front reached Lenin in Switzerland at the time when M. Bonch-Bruevich was Chief of Staff to the commander of this front, General Ruzsky. Some secret documents signed "Bonch-Bruevich" and "Ruzsky" were published in Switzerland by Lenin and Zinovyev in the Bolshevik magazine *Sbornik Sotsial-Demokrata*. This material was probably sent to Lenin via the German-controlled intelligence agency run by Alexander Keskula.[12]

Such linkage no doubt extended beyond espionage and into the realm of political action-cum-political sabotage. Bonch-Bruevich is alleged to have been one of those responsible for the poor conduct of military planning and operations.[13] He was also connected to those Tsarist generals who helped engineer the abdication of Nicholas II.

Several months after the October 1917 Bolshevik coup, General Bonch-Bruevich became director of the Supreme Military Soviet, "entrusted with the direction of all military operations with the unconditional subordination of all military institutions and personnel...."[14] His brother, M. D. Bonch-Bruevich, headed the Soviet regime's first security organ known originally as the Committee for Combating Pogroms and then becoming the Investigation Commission, which actually preceded the *Cheka* and for a while operated in parallel with it. He also organized and implemented the government's move from Petrograd to Moscow under extreme conditions of secrecy buttressed by a superb deception plan.

Thus, the two brothers moved with great dispatch to the highest positions of military-security affairs in the months following the Bolshevik putsch. Few Tsarist officers of such seniority were accorded such high Soviet rank so speedily and readily. General Bonch-Bruevich's wartime activities, the amazing speed of his Bolshevization, his attainment of high Soviet rank (he is listed as a lieutenant general as of 1944), and his phenomenal longevity despite his Tsarist service (neither he nor his brother were touched by the blood purges of the 1930s, and both died of natural causes in the middle-to-late 1950s), suggest much more than just a long streak of good fortune. Was General Bonch-Bruevich serving the German General Staff on behalf of the Bolsheviks while a Tsarist officer? One of Lenin's biographers, Stephan Possony, strongly suspects just such a cross connection.[15] It would have been in keeping with the convoluted, conspiratorial traditions of the Bolshevik party and the determined German political action program aimed at bringing down the Russian Empire.

Before leaving the business of police agents and provocateurs and their formative influence on the character of the new Soviet counterintelligence state, it is worth a brief revisit to an enduring controversy that has its roots in this period. Both before and after 1917, there were persistent suspicions and rumors that Stalin also had been an *Okhrana* police agent. A trail of compromises and arrests of Stalin's associates—not dissimilar to events in the Malinovsky case—seemed to follow Stalin's activities until he supposedly was fingered by Malinovsky in February 1913 and exiled to Siberia. Indeed, Stalin's arrest could have been the unanticipated result of his failed attempt to compromise Malinovsky.[16] The reminiscences of a former *Okhrana* officer, one Nikolai Vladimirovich Veselago, have both Malinovsky and Stalin reporting on Lenin as well as on each other. Stalin, according to this account, was not aware that Malinovsky was also a penetration agent,[17] although the compromising of Malinovsky may have been a provocation by Stalin to supplant the man in his premier double role as police agent and Bolshevik luminary in the duma. Later, there were also claims in Bolshevik circles of Lavrenty Beria's dubious activities in the Caucasus prior to Bolshevik consolidation of control there. These ranged from criminal involvements to serving the secret police forces of various political regimes.[18]

To be sure, the proposition of Stalin as an *Okhrana* police agent is controversial and the evidence incomplete, yet insistent and persistent. The implications, though, for the nature of the Soviet system and the development of state security would be profound and highly unsettling to several generations of Soviet leaders. Clearly it was in the interests of Stalin and his successors that a scandal far greater than Malinovsky's never surface. Therefore, any careful study of Soviet state security should at the very least take note of this controversy, its implications, and the sources involved.

What are some of the more notable of these sources? In addition to the recollection of the former Tsarist police officer cited above, there were many hints and charges from within the Soviet Union, some of which are aired but not accepted by Roy Medvedev in his 1971 work *Let History Judge*.[19] Medvedev's arguments against the evidence are themselves ambivalent and contradictory. As an example, he argues that Stalin would have or should have eliminated such people as Beria and his henchman General Bogdan Z. Kobulov, who were aware of Stalin's alleged *Okhrana* links, as Stalin had done with others who knew the secret. Yet, earlier, Medvedev had answered his own objection by acknowledging that Stalin relied on the likes of Yezhov, Beria, and even Vyshinsky because he knew they were compromised by their own murky political pasts.[20] Medvedev seems unwittingly to make a case for a criminal conspiracy as the pedigree of the Soviet system. But his methodology is somewhat inconsistent. He readily accepts as valid those sources that condemn Vyshinsky's and Beria's pre-Bolshevik past. Yet similar evidence against Stalin is treated as hyperbole or hearsay and cavalierly dismissed. Something is wrong here.

Finally, at the very beginning of the Soviet regime, a study was begun under the Provisional Government but published in 1918 under the Bolsheviks that continues to intrigue researchers. It identified twelve secret agents of the *Okhrana* who had penetrated the Social Democrats: the first eleven names including Malinovsky's were spelled out, but the last one was identified only by his Communist party *klichka*, or sobriquet, of "Vasili."[21] "Vasili" indeed had been one of Stalin's party pseudonyms used in numerous party communications. Medvedev cites the same source listing the twelve agents but gives no indication that he was privy to the "Vasili" connection.[22] His historiography, in its efforts to keep the Bolshevik coup cleanly Leninist, does not come to grips with its shabby past.

Another important source in the charges against Stalin, and one difficult to write off, is General Alexander Orlov, former NKVD (People's Commissariat of Internal Affairs) *rezident* in Spain during the civil war. Orlov claimed that the accidental discovery of Stalin's *Okhrana* file by the NKVD was a key factor in the purges and even precipitated a stillborn coup in 1937 by military and NKVD elements.[23] Orlov's charge appeared in the same year as Isaac Don Levine's *Stalin's Great Secret* (1956), which claimed that a 1913 internal *Okhrana* classified document identified Stalin as an agent of the St. Petersburg *Okhrana* office.[24] Both the book and the document provoked a storm of controversy, many claiming that Levine relied on a forgery.

This document, or *Okhrana* memorandum (called the "Eremin letter" after its alleged author), while most certainly a forgery, does bear a compelling air of authenticity. Despite its obvious errors, it was a far cry from such decipherable fabrications as, for instance, the Litvinov diaries attributed to Grigory Bessedovskiy.[25] Edward Ellis Smith, who carefully probed Stalin's pre-1917 years, concludes "that the letter was produced by someone (not a novice at operational intelligence matters) who had knowledge of Stalin's *Okhrana* dossier and who comprehended the interactions of the *Okhrana* and revolutionary movements. Most important, he was convinced that Stalin had been an agent of the *Okhrana.*"[26] Smith also developed a persuasive argument that Stalin's *Okhrana* past actually dated to the early 1890s in the Caucasus. He demonstated that there was a surprising congruence between official Soviet, Stalin-inspired accounts of Stalin's alleged 1903-04 exile and a belated (1911) *Okhrana* report signed by Colonel Eremin and his *Okhrana* superior! The latter were building Stalin's "legend" to protect his credibility among the people he was betraying; the Stalinist hagiographers (Beria for one) necessarily had to keep up the legend.

It might be significant that Colonel Eremin had been chief of the Tiflis Gendarme Administration, chief of the Special Section (*Osobyi Otdel*) at Department of Police Headquarters in St. Petersburg, and, finally, chief of the Gendarme Administration in Finland when he disappeared following the February 1917 Revolution. He had long been associated with running double agents in the revolutionary movement. If Eremin was not the author of the 1913 *Okhrana* document, then it must have been someone with similar authority for access to and an intimate knowledge of Stalin's early life and police and Bolshevik affairs during that period. The question remains then, it was whose forgery and to what purpose?

THE COUNTERINTELLIGENCE TRADITION ESTABLISHED

For students of Soviet state security, then, there is still a pressing question as to the roots of both the service and the system itself. However historians settle that issue, it must be stressed that the formative, underground period of the Bolshevik faction was suffused by conspiracy, counterconspiracy, and factional hostility pursued by Lenin with a vengeance.

And this long-term conspiracy suddenly and unexpectedly come to power certainly would not be inclined to assume the attributes of the proto-democratic government it just drove out. While superficially it may have had more in common with the *Okhrana* and an older Tsarist tradition, the new Bolshevik regime certainly had no repressive models to copy from the Provisional Government. Indeed, it may be argued that had the Provisional Government employed a modest but true security service in democracy's defense the "inevitable" Bolshevik victory might well have gone the way of failed coups, or putschs, by other self-appointed agents of history.

The new system tipped its hand early as to its intent and direction. Within one-and-one-half months of its seizure of power, the government created a secret police that has since become an export commodity for repressive revolutionary regimes and movements throughout the world. The Council of People's Commissars (*Sovnarkom*) on December 20, 1917, issued the protocol creating the *Cheka*, or All-Russian Extraordinary Commission to Combat Counterrevolution and Sabotage.[27] Shortly thereafter the People's Commissar of Justice I. Z. Shteinberg issued his instruction on the Revolutionary Tribunals, which virtually became one with the *Cheka* and in June 1918 were granted further powers with the authority to pass death sentences.

In short order a fused police-security-judicial network enjoying extraordinary (read "extralegal") powers reminiscent of the sixteenth-century *Oprichnina* operated virtually at will on the body politic of the new party-state. It must be stressed that this was all the creation of Lenin and Dzerzhinskiy; it cannot be ascribed to the "cult of personality" or other fictive constructs for Stalin and Stalinism. Stalin may have epitomized the underclass thug-cum-provocateur, but it took the superior strategic vision of Lenin and the ascetic determination of the once seminarian Dzerzhinskiy to create and hone a bureaucratic terror machine constrained only by a party vested with deity-like omniscience.

The bloody mindedness of both men set an operational style for the *Cheka* requiring little adjustment to fit Stalin's brutal temperament. Missive upon missive issued from Lenin's pen urging the *Cheka* to beat and shoot remorselessly. Dzerzhinskiy got down to the following basic principles in a candid interview with a Russian correspondent in 1918:

> The (society and the press) think of the struggle with counter-revolution and speculation on the level of normal state existence and for that reason they scream of courts, of guarantees, of inquiry, of investigation, etc.... We represent in ourselves organized terror—this must be said very clearly....
> Of course, we may make mistakes, but up till now there have been no mistakes. This is proved by the minutes of our meetings. In almost all cases the criminals, when pressed against the wall by evidence, admit their crimes. And what argument would have more weight than the confession of the accused himself.[28]

These were the new relationships of state to society that ushered in no restraints on the former, state-directed terror, the infallibility not merely of the party but of state security as well, and the fixation with forced confession as the determinant of guilt—the legacies that made the later phenomenon of Stalinism possible.

The priorities are instructive here. Tremendous energies were poured into the internal repressive organs even though the new regime was also beset from all sides by hostile armies. For several months, the Bolsheviks equivocated in the face of these external threats until a no-nonsense approach finally cast Trotsky in the role of revolutionary drillmaster of a new conscript army. But there was no dawdling in the creation of the *Cheka* and the Revolutionary Tribunals or in defining their purposes as seen by the above interview. From the very beginning, the party was single minded and decisive when it came to protecting its monopoly of power and vesting that protection in the so-called "organs." Lenin's dictum that "a good Communist is at the same time a good Chekist" and the Chekist Moroz's observation that "there is no sphere of our life where the Cheka does not have its eagle eye" captured the spirit of the party-police amalgam and the fixation with state security.

Has almost seventy years of the Soviet state altered that fixation? One way of answering would be to examine the first mechanisms that Moscow exports to a new socialist client state, revolutionary movement, or satellite. Almost simultaneous with, or even before the arrival of military advisers and hardware, are the state security cadres whose job it is to replicate local versions of the KGB. With the socialist division of labor, of course, East Germans, Bulgarians, and Cubans often may stand in for their Soviet counterparts, but the purpose is the same.

The counterintelligence and security focus of early Soviet state security is underscored by the relative plethora of information on internal organization and operations but much less on early *Cheka* foreign operations. This counterintelligence tendency is best illustrated by Lenin's lament that "our intelligence service in the Cheka, although splendidly organized, unfortunately does not yet extend to America."[29] Two weeks later, in fact on December 20, 1920, the anniversary of the *Cheka*, Dzerzhinskiy ordered the creation of the *Inostrannyy Otdel* (INO), or Foreign Department, for conducting foreign intelligence and counterintelligence operations.[30]

This does not mean that Moscow ran no foreign operations prior to December 1920. A good deal of the mission that now belongs to the KGB's First Chief Directorate was conducted by the Comintern with which the *Cheka* was intimately associated. Dzerzhinskiy himself represented both the Russian Communist Party and the Polish Communist Party at different Comintern Congresses. High ranking Chekists were frequently dispatched on Comintern missions before and after the formation of the INO.

In addition, the Red Army as early as 1918 had an intelligence service known variously as the Third Section and Registration Directorate until 1921, when it became known as the Intelligence Directorate (RU), or Second Directorate of the Red Army General Staff. It too worked with and through the Comintern, especially after the civil war when battlefield priorities dropped off. Like all other institutions in the Soviet system, military intelligence was the subject of probing *Cheka* interest both in its tactical and strategic missions. Then and now it was monitored by a special state security counterintelligence network. Unlike Western systems, Soviet military intelligence never exercised its own counterintelligence responsibilities. Even during World War II, when the Armed Forces Counterintelligence Directorate (GUKR-NNKO-SMERSH) was titularly removed from state security, its head, Viktor Abakumov, and personnel came from the NKVD. The organizational move most likely was made to place SMERSH directly under the State Committee of Defense (GKO), of which Stalin was chief as well as commissar of defense. After the war, SMERSH was reabsorbed into state security (MBG) of which Abakumov became chief. Today, military intelligence (GRU) is subject to counterintelligence scrutiny by the Third Chief Directorate of the KGB.

Another arguable indicator of state security preeminence over military intelligence is that at critical junctures of GRU history its chiefs were drawn from state security: General Yan Berzin came to military intelligence in December 1920 direct from his post as commander of the *Cheka* Special Department (OO) of the Fifteenth Red Army, and he served as chief of Military Intelligence from 1924-35 and again in 1937; Nikolay Yezhov, NKVD chief from 1936-38, was de facto chief of military intelligence from 1937-38 at the height of the military purges; from 1958-63 former KGB Chief Ivan Serov ran the GRU; and from 1963 to the present General Petr Ivashutin, a former chief of the KGB's Third Chief Directorate (Armed Forces Counterintelligence), has been GRU head.

In a very profound sense then, foreign intelligence from the earliest years was more of an external projection of state security—external counterintelligence—than a "mere" foreign intelligence service in the mold of Western nation-states. To be sure, the emergence of the USSR as a world power after World War II altered that somewhat; and post-Stalin developments further modified that orientation. But even today the operational character of Soviet state security is so qualitatively different from its Western counterparts that approaching it analytically as just another intelligence, or even security, service will not do. "State security" connotes such an interlayering of party-KGB concerns and missions that they tend to be unintelligible when approached on the basis of Western bureaucratic or interest group models.

Swimming against fashionable academic currents, Leszek Kolakowski unabashedly—and correctly in this writer's view—insists on still identifying this system as totalitarian.[31] The upshot of the process of Stalinist totalitarianism "... was a fully state-owned society which came very close to the ideal of perfect unity, *cemented by party and police.*"[32] Two critical features of this perfect unity, the system of universal spying as the principle of government and the apparent omnipotence of ideology,[33] conceived by Lenin and honed by Stalin, are enduring pillars of the system as it approaches the twenty-first century.

Both Lenin and Dzerzhinskiy adamantly and successfully fought attempts to subordinate the *Cheka* to any governmental body, keeping it directly answerable to the party, since to them it was truly the party's "sword and shield." Even later name changes, which seemed to connote subordination to government commissariats or ministries, were more the result of arcane maneuvering on Stalin's part or the attempt to manipulate domestic and foreign perceptions than they were substantive developments. Indeed, the most recent titular change in 1978 formally dispensed with the fiction of the "KGB *under* the Council of Ministers" and simply labeled it "KGB of the USSR."

Stalin's legacy, then, must be grouped with that of Lenin and Dzerzhinskiy, since these two men presented him with an extralegal action arm unconstrained by any checks outside of the highest echelons of the party. His use of the KGB was in keeping with his and the party's conspiratorial roots and with the possibilities that such an unfettered instrument presented. State security was a bloody instrument of repression under Lenin and Dzerzhinskiy; Stalin took it to new heights. George Leggett in his excellent chronicle of the *Cheka* observed:

> The precarious and illegitimate Bolshevik regime, battling for survival in circumstances of perpetual crisis, required massive political police support.[34]

That judgment seems applicable to the Soviet system throughout its history, getting at the essence of state security.

The internal counterintelligence orientation of state security had to be modified to meet the demands and opportunities presented to Stalin by Moscow's newly won status as a world power in 1945. Intensified and aggressive foreign intelligence and covert action initiatives accompanied the Soviet presence in Central Europe and in the decisionmaking forums of the postwar international system. The death of Stalin and Khrushchev's calculated gamble of de-Stalinization, at the most, interrupted this process; it intensified following Khrushchev's defeat of the so-called "anti-party" faction.

Khrushchev faced both a dilemma and an opportunity: how to rein in state security to a position of party servant from that of party predator (to which it had degenerated under Stalin) without jeopardizing the fundamental state-security purpose of ensuring the party's monopoly of power and at the same time capitalize on the new foreign prospects for which state security was exceptionally well suited.

Part of the answer, not surprisingly, was a return to the tradition of Lenin and Dzerzhinskiy, to those halcyon days of heroic Chekists faithfully serving a wise party before everything was sullied by the alleged Stalinist aberration.[35] And thus was launched a campaign to refurbish the *Cheka*/KGB image that still continues. To a degree this was a legitimate move, for the *Cheka* had indeed been forged as the party's political cutting edge. But ignored in the new-found concern with socialist legality was the bloody extralegal mandate conferred on the *Cheka* by none other than Lenin; the gushiness produced a spate of heroic and hagiographic literature on the organs and *some* of its leaders, completely out of character for that system.

Khrushchev was undaunted by the contradiction. In late 1958 he kicked KGB Chief Serov sideways into the GRU and placed Alexander Shelepin, a party apparatchik, in the KGB chair. In 1959 Lieutenant General Nikolay Mironov was brought down from the Leningrad KGB post to run the Central Committee's Administrative Organs Department—the party overseer of the organs, the courts, the procuracy, and the military. Together with Boris Ponomarev of the Central Committee's International Department, these men were commissioned to direct the organs and other arms of the state in the new foreign initiatives under the umbrella of Khrushchev's "peaceful coexistence" policy. Within the KGB a newly institutionalized Disinformation Department under the veteran Colonel Agayant was ordered to spearhead these efforts in a pattern reminiscent of earlier successful provocational-deception schemes such as the "Trust" of the 1920s.[36] State security had come full circle.

Yuri Andropov's reign (1967-84) by no means departed from these initiatives. By the time of Agayant's death in 1968, Agayant was a general; a few years later his Disinformation Department was organizationally cited as a service (*sluzhba*). Both moves denoted official favor for successful operations. The rehabilitation of the KGB image begun under Khrushchev continued apace along with some favorable personnel moves that saw an interpenetration of KGB and party cadres reminiscent of earlier periods. A veteran observer of party-KGB interaction, Abdurakhman Avtorkhanov, folded the army into this revivified partnership, labeling it a "triangular dictatorship."[37]

However, another former insider, Peter Deriabin, while not denying such a partnership, sees the military in a less significant position while the KGB-party fusion intensifies with more and more senior party-state posts going to figures with long state-security pedigrees.[38] An even more intriguing insight offered by Deriabin is the presence of those KGB types with specific military counterintelligence backgrounds. It is no mystery, therefore, why he places the military in a lesser status in the party-KGB-military matrix.

Complementing the higher-level movement of officials are periodic shifts of even larger numbers of KGB cadres into party posts—another characteristic of the Andropov period. But lest we ascribe too much to this, it must be recalled that such transfers occurred often in the past in both directions. The recent and current shifts no doubt are related to the drawn out successions and the anticorruption efforts initiated by Andropov and continued by Gorbachev. The KGB is projected as the clean, stalwart bearer of Leninist selflessness, capable of exorcising noxious influences that had penetrated the party apparat.

And so we have the counterintelligence state, a late-twentieth-century version. It looks to its past for legitimacy and inspiration; but it is a highly selective retrospective search because it still ignores its darkest chapter, the Stalin period and the purges. And even the period that it claims as its finest hour on close examination certainly offers little in the way of pride, legitimacy, or inspiration. A manufactured, quasi-religious cult of the *Cheka* and its sainted chief Dzerzhinskiy is the best that the party and KGB could conjure up. Yet even that is threatened by the murkiness of Stalin's past and the persistent threat of the *Okhrana* scandals. Gorbachev's vaunted "openness" has come nowhere near Khrushchev's de-Stalinization. Indeed, Gorbachev has yet to come to grips with the re-Stalinizing moves of Khrushchev's successors and his own predecessors.

STATE SECURITY AND SOVIET STUDIES: AN ANALYTICAL APPROACH

First Principles

Identifying and describing the counterintelligence state as a unique phenomenon is one thing. Programmatically dissecting it is another matter altogether. On this subject it would be wise to air some propositions however disconcerting they may appear.

First, there is a serious gap in scholarship on Soviet state security notwithstanding advances in the profession and the recent appearance of more books on the subject. Robert Slusser lamented this failure in two fine articles over the last twenty years and exhorted the profession to step out smartly on this issue.[39] With the exception of some first-rate journalistic responses, little scholarly "stepping" has occurred.

Second, as the first parts of this chapter attempted to portray, we are dealing not merely with police, or intelligence, or even a secret police à la the *Okhrana*. We are confronted with the phenomenon of the counter-intelligence state, an amalgam of party and state security annealed in a tradition of conspiracy and counterconspiracy. Foreign intelligence in such a structure is in certain critical respects really external counterintelligence.

Third, elaborate Western paradigms or analytical models cannot be force-fit as frameworks for analysis. A state-security system that can eliminate tens of millions of its own citizens at the party's bidding has got to be examined on its terms. Elegant Western constructs fail to accommodate such horrific realities. A few hours with defectors and émigrés from and victims of state security will do more to verify this proposition than a thousand pages by this writer ever could.

The Persistence and Continuity of the State Security Operational Tradition

Since there is such a chasm of difference between the Soviet state-security tradition and Western intelligence and security structures and since it has been proposed above to approach the Soviet tradition on its terms, it would be well to identify critical operational "lines," or axes, of that tradition. A historical perspective must infuse this approach. The following is offered as a preliminary outline of these operational lines:[40]

1. The Counterintelligence-Active Measures Tradition[41] is a blend of internal and external counterintelligence operations embracing artifice, provocation, penetration, fabrication, diversion, deception, disinformation, agents-of-influence, combination, and so on.[42] Cases include the Lockhart Plot of 1918, the Trust Operation 1922-27, possibly the Politburo Minutes (forgeries?) of the 1920s and 1930s, the Tukhachevsky affair, Agent "Max" in World War II, the "WiN" case in postwar Poland, the biological warfare campaign of the Korean War, the anti-"Neutron Bomb" campaign, the Peace Campaign, and the anti-SDI campaign among others.

2. The "Direct Action," or "Wet Affairs," Tradition incorporates assassinations and kidnappings and support to international terrorism; the institutions—from Yezhov's Administration for Special Tasks to Andropov's Department 8; and the cases of Agabekov, Kutepov, Miller, Reiss, Sedov, Trotsky, Krivitsky (?), Bandera, Rebet, Markov, Amin, and so on.[43]

3. The Foreign Intelligence Tradition goes from the INO, Comintern, and the Red Army's RU; to the Committee for Information; to the KGB's First Chief Directorate and the General Staff's GRU.

4. The Special Operations Tradition[44] runs from the *Cheka*'s CHON (Detachments of Special Purpose) to the GRU's SPETSNAZ (Special Purpose Forces). The operations include the civil war; Kronshtadt, 1921; the Basmachi Movement, from 1918 to the early 1930s; the Green Movement, 1920-21; collectivization; the purges; the Spanish Civil War; the Winter War, 1939-40; World War II; the Ukraine and the Baltic, from the late 1940s to the early 1950s; Hungary, 1956; Czechoslovakia, 1968; Afghanistan; and the Third World.

5. The Satellite and Surrogate Tradition involves the export of state security. An example of "internal" state security is in Poland: a praetorian guard as a party alternative to a questionable military. "External" state security is exercised in East Germany and Bulgaria: reliable subcontractors in a socialist division of labor. "Internal *and* external" state security is found in Cuba, Nicaragua, Grenada, and other Third World surrogates including terrorist groups and liberation movements.[45]

The State of the Craft

Robert Slusser's scholarly pleas referenced earlier were not a blanket indictment. There indeed had been some first-rate efforts on Soviet intelligence, security, and related areas that should serve as models for the type of incisive probing required for this potentially elusive subject, although production from within the scholarly community tended to ebb in the 1960s and 1970s. On the other hand, contributions appeared from

the ranks of journalists, defectors and other former insiders, and former
U.S. intelligence officials. The following select categories of works, sources,
and commentaries provide a quick survey—not meant to be exhaustive—
into what has been accomplished and prospects for advancing our understanding of the counterintelligence state and the state security tradition:

1. **Some early "social science" and other related investigatory efforts**
   Fainsod, *Smolensk Under Soviet Rule* (1958) and *How Russia is Ruled*
      (1953, 1963)
   Bauer, Inkeles, and Kluckhohn, *How the Soviet System Works* (1956);
      Bauer, *Nine Soviet Portraits* (1955)
   Schapiro, *The Communist Party of the Soviet Union* (1960) and
      Totalitarianism (1972)
   Friedrich and Brzezinski, *Totalitarian Dictatorship and Autocracy* (1956)
   Wollin and Slusser, *The Soviet Secret Police* (1957)
   Dvinov, *Politics of the Russian Emigration* (Rand, 1955)
   Dallin, *Soviet Espionage* (1955)
   Dallin and Nikolaevsky, *Forced Labor in Soviet Russia* (1947)

2. **The historian's craft**
   Wollin and Slusser, *The Soviet Secret Police* (1957)
   Conquest, *The Great Terror* (1968 & 1973), *The Soviet Police System*
      (1968), *Inside Stalin's Secret Police* (1985), and *The Harvest of Sorrow*
      (1986)
   Leggett, *The Cheka* (1981)
   Hingley, *The Russian Secret Police* (1970)
   Erickson, *The Soviet High Command* (1962)
   May (ed.), *Knowing One's Enemies* (1984)
   Gerson, *The Secret Police in Lenin's Russia* (1976)
   Brook-Shepherd, *The Storm Petrels* (1977)
   Andrew's *Her Majesty's Secret Service* (1985) is included here because it
      offers some of the first comprehensive insights into the struggle
      between U.K. intelligence and security and Soviet state security,
      Comintern, and GRU.
   Smith, *The Young Stalin* (1967)
   Heller and Nekrich, *Utopia in Power* (1986)

3. **Contemporary "operations" analysis** includes some defectors because
   of the timeliness of their work. The quality and reliability of these
   works vary from author to author. For evaluative commentary on some
   of them, see the *Bibliography on Soviet Intelligence and Security
   Services.*[46]
   Barron, *KGB* (1974) and *KGB Today* (1983)
   Deriabin, *Watchdogs of Terror* (rev., 1984)
   Rositzke, *The KGB* (1981)
   Corson and Crowley, *The New KGB* (1985)

Pincher, *Their Trade is Treachery* (1981) and *Too Secret Too Long* (1984)
Adelman, *Terror and Communist Politics* (1984)
Boyle, *The Fourth Man* (1979)
Freemantle, *KGB* (1982)
Martin, *Wilderness of Mirrors* (1980)
Shultz & Godson, *Dezinformatsia* (1984)
Tolstoy, *Stalin's Secret War* (1981)
Weinstein, *Perjury* (1978)
Lamphere and Schachtman, *The FBI-KGB Wars* (1986)
Richelson, *Sword and Shield* (1985)
Bittman, *The KGB and Soviet Disinformation* (1985)
Hood, *Mole* (1982)
Articles, chapters, interviews, and special studies by Natalie Grant, Stanislav Levchenko, Amy Knight, Robert Moss, James Barros, Edward Epstein, John Dziak, Roy Godson, Steve Rosefielde, Robert Conquest, and others.

4. **Defector and other "insider" accounts.** Defectors and others associated with or affected by the Soviet organs of state security come the closest to primary sources, yet to an extent they are underappreciated and underutilized by scholars. Granted, there are some difficulties associated with some accounts, but on this subject *all* categories of sources present difficulties of varying magnitude. For whatever reason, human witnesses on this topic tend to be overlooked and ignored, which is unfortunate because even those of demonstrable unreliability (e.g., Bessedovskiy) are witnesses to the cause and nature of the problem they represent (again, in Bessedovskiy's case, probable Soviet-directed fabrication). Added to the literature sampled below would be the whole deposit of "camp" literature and other dissident *samizdat* that penetrate state-security barriers.

Deriabin, *The Secret World* (1959) and *Watchdogs of Terror* (rev., 1984)
Akhmedov, *In and Out of Stalin's GRU* (1984)
Agabekov, *OGPU* (1931)
Antonov-Ovseyenko, *The Time of Stalin* (1981)
Rapoport & Alexeev, *High Treason* (1985)
Bittman, *The Deception Game* (1972) and *The KGB and Soviet Disinformation* (1985)
Sejna, *We Will Bury You* (1982) and with J. Douglass, *Decision-Making in Communist Countries: An Inside View* (1986)
Sakharov, *High Treason* (1980)
Chambers, *Witness* (1952)
Gouzenko, *The Iron Curtain* (1948)
Golitsyn, *New Lies for Old* (1984)
Khokhlov, *In the Name of Conscience* (1959)

Orlov, *The Secret History of Stalin's Crimes* (1953)
Krivitsky, *In Stalin's Secret Service* (1939)
Medvedev, *Let History Judge* (1971)
Myagkov, *Inside the KGB* (1976)
Penkovskiy, *The Penkovskiy Papers* (1965)
Solzhenitsyn, *The Gulag Archipelago* (1974-76)
Suvorov, *Inside Soviet Military Intelligence* (1984) and *Inside the Aquarium* (1986)
Shevchenko, *Breaking with Moscow* (1985)
Voslensky, *Nomenclatura* (1984)
Articles, testimony and hearings, reports of Royal Commissions, and special reports and monographs by defectors and émigrés, and so on may be added to these sample titles.
Insofar as the Trotskyites continue to be almost visceral targets of Soviet state security, the literature of certain Trotskyites and former Trotskyites offers rather special insight into the counterintelligence-active measures tradition of the KGB and its predecessors. See, for example, Georges Vereeken's *The GPU in the Trotskyist Movement* (1976).

5. **A commentary on sources in general.** While the study of closed, despotic police states poses difficulties for serious scholars, material is surprisingly accessible. Though it can protect state secrets far more efficiently than open societies, it is remarkable just how porous the USSR has proven periodically. It frequently hemorrhages or expels well-informed witnesses—hence the plea of this chapter to treat such sources seriously. The fact is that defections, which at times have occurred in clusters, were indicators of serious internal social or political traumas.

Looked at another way, the paucity of data on closed despotic systems applies to virtually *all* areas of the Soviet party-state. Do we really know how the Politburo and the Defense Council do their work and arrive at their decisions? Aren't population loss figures since 1917 still hotly debated? Don't well-informed government and private economists still aggressively disagree over military claims on the Soviet state budget? Hasn't the U.S. intelligence community evinced strong disagreement over Soviet oil reserves? And on and on. Yet serious scholars still pursue these issues.

What may be astonishing to the reader is the amazing variety of data on Soviet state security that can be mosaically fit to present a fairly coherent picture. Robert Conquest recently made the following observation about his study of the Soviet security organs:

> It is natural that the affairs of the secret police should be among the more arcane. What is surprising is the opposite: how much information there is and how generally clear the picture it makes. There are important points which can be solidly established: others which are reasonable and probable interpretations of the data.[47]

Much of this material is still largely unmined. This includes, for example, German World War II documents; defector and émigré literature and testimony; released Western official documents and the results of Freedom of Information requests; the Soviet media itself, including the provincial press, where one may glean such items as award lists, biographies, and organizational orders of battle as announced in obituaries, honorifics, and so on; Soviet heroic and hagiographic literature on state security and prominent Chekists; and *samizdat* and tolerated dissident writings (e.g., Medvedev's account of NKVD Deputy Commissar M. P. Frinovsky's fall from grace in his *On Stalin and Stalinism* (1979)).

Against this optimism must be posted another order of difficulty, which is persistent and which links back to the counterintelligence-active measures tradition of the system: tainted material. From the "Trust" materials, to the Politburo "minutes," to the Zinoviev letter, to the Litvinov diaries, and to the forgeries of the 1970s and 1980s, Western governments and researchers have had to contend with spurious materials. Coupled with this are the continuing defector controversies dating from Baajanov and Bessedovskiy of the 1920s and 1930s to the Nosenkos and Yurchenkos of the current era. But such controversies are themselves compelling tributes to the nature of the counterintelligence state.

CONCLUSIONS AND RECOMMENDATIONS

A. Soviet state security in its internal and external counterintelligence, foreign intelligence, direct action, special operations, and satellite traditions is a topic worthy of scholarly scrutiny and merits the same depth of study as the party, the economy, the military, the nationalities, and other prominent features of the Soviet system.

B. Each scholarly discipline should incorporate state security into its purview since, together with the party, state security probes and permeates all facets of the system as the party's cutting edge. A broader perspective on the service beyond mere "police" politics is essential to deepen understanding of the total system.

C. To this writer, a cross-discipline approach seems to be the most fruitful point of departure, beginning with reexamination of major issues or epochs of both Soviet domestic and foreign affairs to discern and calibrate the role and impact of state security therein. For this task it is worth revisiting Robert Slusser's pieces of 1965 and 1973.

D. Scholarly associations and collaborative efforts, such as the Intelligence Studies Section of the International Studies Association and the Consortium for the Study of Intelligence, are extremely useful in sponsoring and encouraging new initiatives in intelligence studies. Such efforts are to be encouraged.

E. Finally, there is a need to further refine the "counterintelligence state/state security" concept for application in (1) comparative intelligence and studies; (2) the study of Soviet satellites, surrogates, and clients; and (3) the study of international terrorism, indirect conflict, and low-intensity warfare.

NOTES

1. The pervasiveness of the Soviet police state renders it different from the police systems in more traditional, authoritarian societies. The police in the latter systems tend overtly to enforce the political will of a ruling group or clique, frequently allowing important margins of social, cultural, and even ideological elbow room in society. The Soviet system uses the police, among other party-state institutions, overtly *and* covertly to enforce unitary social, cultural, and ideological norms determined and articulated by a single center, the party.

2. On the issue of "Oriental" or "Asiatic despotism" and the USSR as an evocative variation of these, see Karl A. Wittfogel's *Oriental Despotism: A Comparative Study of Total Power* (New Haven, Conn.: Yale University Press, 1957).

3. Grigorii Zinoviev, *History of the Bolshevik Party: A Popular Outline*, trans. R. Chappell (London: New Park Publications Ltd., 1973), p. 158.

4. Stefan Possony, *Lenin: The Compulsive Revolutionary* (Chicago: Henry Regnery Company, 1964), p. 388.

5. *Vestnik vremmenogo pravitel'stva*, June 16, 1917, p. 3. For the full commission report see: *Padeniye tsarskogo rezhima: Stenograficheskiye otchety...* 7 vols. (Moscow: Gosizdat, 1924-1927).

6. Edward Ellis Smith, *The Young Stalin* (New York: Farrar, Straus and Giraux, 1967), p. 282.

7. V. I. Lenin, *Selected Works* Vol. 3 (New York: International Publishers, 1943), pp. 238, 260-61.

8. Ibid., Vol. 8, p. 489.

9. George Katkov, *Russia 1917: The February Revolution* (New York: Harper & Row, 1967), pp. 119-132.

10. J. F. N. Bradley, "The Russian Secret Service in the First World War," *Soviet Studies* 20, no. 2 (October 1968): 243.

11. M. D. Bonch-Bruevich, *Vsya vlast' sovetam* (Moscow: Voenizdat, 1957), pp. 55-65.

12. Katkov, *Russia 1917*, pp. 128-129. Keskula, an Estonian Bolshevik and adventurer, was part of the German-Lenin connection that included, among others, Alexander Helphand (Parvus) and Jacob Hanecki (Ganetsky). See Michael Futrell, *Northern Underground: Episodes of Russian Revolutionary Transport and Communications through Scandinavia and Finland, 1863-1917* (London: Faber and Faber, 1963), pp. 119-196; and Joel Carmichael, "German Money and Bolshevik Honor," *Encounter* 42, no. 3 (March 1974): 81-90.

13. Nicholas N. Golovine, *The Russian Campaign of 1914* (Ft. Leavenworth, Kans.: The Command and General Staff School Press, 1933), p. 40.

14. *Dekrety sovetskoy vlasti* Vol. 1 (Moscow: Voenizdat, 1957), p. 522.

15. Possony, *Lenin*, p. 167.

16. *Posledniye Novosti*, January 1, 1934, p. 3.

17. Ellis Tennant (pseud. of Edward Ellis Smith), comp. and ed., *The Department of Police 1911-1913, From the Recollections of Nikolai Vladimirovich Veselago, Manuscript* (Stanford: Hoover Institution Archives, 1962), pp. 26-29.

18. See, for instance, Anton Antonov-Ovseyenko, *The Time of Stalin: Portait of a Tyranny*, trans. George Saunders (New York: Harper & Row, 1981), p. 148. See also *Voprosy istorii KPSS* no. 11 (1965), where Beria's links to the intelligence service of the Moslem Democratic Party (*Mussavat*) are alleged.

19. Roy Medvedev, *Let History Judge: The Origins and Consequences of Stalinism*, trans. Colleen Taylor (New York: Alfred A. Knopf, 1972), pp. 312 ff.

20. Ibid., p. 312.

21. S. P. Mel'gunov and M. A. Tsyavlovskiy, eds., *Bol'sheviki: Dokumenty po istorii bol'shevizma s 1903 po 1916 god byvshego moskovskogo okhrannogo otdeleniya* (Moscow: Zadruga), p. ix.

22. Medvedev, *Let History Judge*, p. 315. For another well-informed dissident's view that gives credence to the same sources disparaged by Medvedev, see Antonov-Ovseyenko, *The Time of Stalin*, pp. 240-241.

23. Alexander Orlov, "The Sensational Secret Behind Damnation of Stalin," *Life* (April 23, 1956): 34-38, 43-45; *The Legacy of Alexander Orlov*, Committee on the Judiciary, U.S. Senate, 93rd Cong., 1st sess. (Washington, D.C.: U.S. Government Printing Office, 1973).

24. Isaac Don Levine, *Stalin's Great Secret* (New York: Coward-McCann, 1956). A facsimile of the *Okhrana* memo—also known as the Eremin Letter—was reproduced in the book as well as in the 1956 *Life* issue (pages 47-51) that carried Orlov's piece.

25. Maxim Litvinov, *Notes for a Journal*, Introduction by E. H. Carr, Preface note by General Walter Bedell Smith (New York: William Morrow & Company, 1955). Bessedovskiy, a Soviet diplomat when he defected in Paris in 1929, was the author or suspected author of a number of literary fabrications and was suspected, with cause, of being under Soviet control. On this point, see Gordon Brook-Shepherd, *The Storm Petrels* (New York: Ballantine Books, 1982), pp. 70-90.

26. Smith, *The Young Stalin*, pp. 308-309.

27. For the actual protocol, see G. A. Belov et al., eds., *Iz istorii vserossiyskoy chrezvychaynoy komissii 1917-1921 gg.: Sbornik dokumentov* (Moscow: Gospolitizdat, 1958), p. 78.

28. "From Our Moscow Correspondent," *Novaya zhizn'* (June 9, 1918): 4 of the Bertram Wolfe Collection, Hoover Archives, File 110-12.

29. V. I. Lenin, "Speech Delivered at a Meeting of Activists of the Moscow Organziation of the R.C.P. (B.), 6 December 1920," *Collected Work* Vol. 31 (Moscow: Progress Publishers, 1966), p. 444.

30. A. V. Tishkov, *Pervyi chekist* (Moscow: Voenizdat, 1968), p. 100. Agabekov, a former member of the INO in 1921 claims that it was then still called the 14th Special Section, which would suggest that there was an institutional predecessor to the INO within the *Cheka*; G. Agabekov, *G.P.U. (Zapiski chekista)* (Berlin: Izdatel'stvo "strela," 1930), pp. 43-44.

31. Leszek Kolakowski, "Marxist Roots of Stalinism," in Robert C. Tucker, ed., *Stalinism: Essays in Historical Interpretation* (New York: W. W. Norton & Co., Inc., 1977), pp. 283-298.

32. Ibid., p. 287. Emphasis added.

33. Ibid., p. 289.

34. George Leggett, *The Cheka: Lenin's Political Police* (New York: Oxford University Press, 1981), p. 359.

35. The full range of Khrushchev's solutions obviously cannot be addressed here. But the bizarre and inherently dangerous quality of some of them—from the party's perspective—contributed to the palace coup of October 1964. Some observers have detected parallels between Khrushchev's and Gorbachev's efforts to improve the efficiency of the system without altering its fundamental tenets.

36. On the organizational details of these changes, see the account of one of the participants: Anatoliy Golitsyn, *New Lies for Old* (New York: Dodd, Mead and Company, 1984), chaps. 6 and 7. See the following for separate verification on selected aspects of these changes: *Pravda*, May 18, 1959; and V. Minyailo, "The Conference of the State Security Organs," *Bulletin: Institute of the Study of the USSR* (September 1959): 21-23. For a broader discussion of Soviet political deception, see John J. Dziak, "Soviet Deception: The Organizational and Operational Tradition," in Brian Daily and Patrick Parker, eds., *Soviet Strategic Deception* (Lexington, Mass.: Lexington Books, 1987), pp. 3-20.

37. Abdurakhman Avtorkhanov, "The Soviet Triangular Dictatorship: Party, Police and Army: Formation and Situation," *Ukrainian Quarterly* 34 (Summer 1978): 135-153.

38. Peter Deriabin with T. H. Bagley, "Fedorchuk, the KGB, and the Soviet Succession," *Orbis* 26, no. 3 (Fall 1982): 611-635.

39. Robert M. Slusser, "Recent Books on the History of the Soviet Security Police," *Slavic Review* 14 (March 1965): 909-98; Part II, *Slavic Review* 22 (December 1973): 825-828.

40. An earlier and somewhat different schema of such an approach may be found in Alexander Orlov, *Handbook of Intelligence and Guerrilla Warfare* (Ann Arbor: The University of Michigan Press, 1963), chap. 2.

41. For a broader explication of the deception/active measures aspects of this tradition, see Dziak, "Soviet Deception," *Soviet Strategic Deception*.

42. For a more detailed examination of the interaction of internal and external counterintelligence, see John J. Dziak, *Chekisty: A History of the KGB* (Lexington, Mass.: Lexington Books, 1988).

43. See, for instance, "From Azeff to Agca," *Survey* 27, no. 118/119 (Autumn-Winter 1983): 1-89.

44. This writer has made some initial efforts to examine the Special Operations Tradition in the following: John J. Dziak, "Soviet Intelligence and Security Services in the 1980's: the Para-Military Dimension," in Roy Godson, ed., *Intelligence Requirements for the 1980s: Counterintelligence* (Washington, D.C.: National Strategy Information Center, 1980), pp. 95-115; "The Soviet Approach to Special Operations," in F. Barnett, H. Tovar, and R. Schultz, eds., *Special Operations in U.S. Strategy* (Washington, D.C.: National Defense University Press in cooperation with the National Strategy Information Center, 1984), pp. 95-133; "Military Doctrine and Structure," in Uri Ra'anan et al., eds., *Hydra of Carnage: The International Linkages of Terrorism and Other Low-Intensity Operations* (Lexington, Mass.: Lexington Books, 1986), pp. 77-92.

45. For excellent documentation on the recent application of this tradition, see Department of State and Department of Defense, *Grenada Documents: An Overview and Selection*, intro. by Michael Ledeen and Herbert Romerstein (Washington, D.C.: U.S. Government Printing Office, 1984).

46. Raymond G. Rocca and John J. Dziak (in collaboration with the staff of the Consortium for the Study of Intelligence), *Bibliography on Soviet Intelligence and Security Services* (Boulder, Colo.: Westview Press, 1985).

47. Robert Conquest, *Inside Stalin's Secret Police: NKVD Politics 1936-1939* (Stanford: Hoover Institution Press, 1985), p. 8.

5

Intelligence in an Arab Gulf State

DALE F. EICKELMAN

The comparative study of political intelligence provides a challenging point of departure for exploring how the specific political, social, and economic contexts of particular countries shape the production, maintenance, and reproduction of "authoritative" intelligence knowledge about these countries. The research project described here, still in progress, assesses how the informal norms, structures, cultural contexts, and management of knowledge in intelligence services affect the production and content of short- and long-term estimates of political "threats."

The ethnographic component of the project concerns a small but strategic Arab Gulf state, the Sultanate of Oman, which had a population of 1.2 million as of 1986. The period covered, for which access to former intelligence personnel, their former adversaries (nearly all granted amnesties in the 1970s), informed Omani and non-Omani observers, and extant archives has been obtained, dates from the creation of a modern intelligence service in 1957 through mid-1970, when the present ruler, Sultan Qaboos bin Said, replaced his father, Said bin Taimur (r. 1932-70), in a palace coup.

This focus upon political intelligence as it was until nearly two decades ago deliberately removes the analysis from a specific discussion of current intelligence organization and priorities. In so doing it facilitates the cooperation of participants in the events of the 1957-70 period. Nonetheless, the study addresses major current concerns.

One major similarity to the present is in how intelligence personnel perceived and analyzed shifting popular ideas of legitimate rule and political and security "threats." From 1957 to 1970, modified ideas of "just" rule were precipitated by the massive economic improvements made possible by oil revenues and Omani perceptions of political change in other Arab states.

At present, the instability of oil revenues and the coming of age of the first generation of youth in the Gulf who have benefited from mass education are two leading factors contributing to shifts in political expectations.

The fact that senior personnel were British may at first make the intelligence services of the pre-1970 period appear somewhat anomalous. Yet foreign Arab and non-Arab personnel continue to play a significant role in the security services of the states of the Arab Gulf; and the intelligence organizations of major powers continue to train and advise local personnel, thus shaping significantly, if not always directly, patterns of professional perceptions and reporting.

The first section of this chapter outlines the political threats facing Oman in the 1957-70 period, both regional and domestic, and the development of a modern intelligence organization in response to them. The sources and methods for the study of the country's political intelligence are then described and compared with those used for the study of other topics in political anthropology. Next, the research issues that form the core of this study—the delineation of "convergent data" shaping the reporting and assessment of political events and trends, the linguistic categories and key terms with which political events were reported and assessed, and the "life cycles" of intelligence officers, indicating how career patterns affected reporting and judgments—are presented. These issues are then used to indicate how a specifically anthropological contribution to the study of intelligence can complement the approaches dominant in other disciplines. The final section assesses how the study of political intelligence in one of the smaller non-Western states contributes to the comparative study of intelligence systems.

The theoretical and policy implications of such a study are closely intertwined. An awareness of the structures that shape the reports and estimates of intelligence communities can enhance an understanding of the contributions of intelligence knowledge, and the limits of these contributions, to policy formation. Intelligence analysts intend the political information that they gather and assess to be more objective and authentic than alternative bodies of knowledge. In academic and scientific settings, the "invisible colleges," or subgroups of cooperating research scholars that form the communication networks that shape and support academic thought, have been charted and related to the production of "authoritative" and "objective" knowledge.[1] For the purpose of understanding the craft of intelligence analysis, it is useful to regard the production of authoritative knowledge in analysis as analogous to work in academic disciplines and other fields of acquired, organized knowledge.

The constraints of official secrecy, however, provide political intelligence systems with sharper parameters than those present for academic "invisible colleges." Once learned, the craft of intelligence may appear natural or inevitable to its practitioners, but their sense of what is "natural" is actually acquired through apprenticeship and on-the-job training, which in most intelligence services to date have been valued more than formal courses and academic credentials.

Because intelligence communities require secrecy, they are generally less conscious than their "open," knowledge-oriented counterparts, including academic communities, of how informal norms and expectations shape and constrain what information they perceive, interpret, and report.[2] Secrecy similarly impedes policymakers, the consumers of the intelligence product, from recognizing how social and cultural factors shape the production of classified knowledge. This can lead to a downgrading of analyses based upon open sources.

If knowledge is a significant element of political authority, then effective decisionmaking can be enhanced by understanding not only how the social organization of intelligence communities shapes the knowledge they generate but also how intelligence officers are trained to perceive political activities in societies with often significantly different cultural assumptions about politics.

WHY OMAN?

Regional Politics

Intelligence collection and analysis in Oman from 1957 to 1970 involved regional, not just domestic, concerns. In 1957 a major insurgency began in the northern interior of the country, with facilities and support provided by Egypt, Saudi Arabia, and subsequently Syria, Kuwait, and Iraq. Rebel threats in the north were effectively held in check after 1962, although they intensified again in early 1970.

By 1965 a separate insurgency began in the southern province of Dhofar, sustained by contributions and support from Dhofaris working elsewhere in the Arabian Peninsula. After the Arab-Israeli War of 1967 and Britain's precipitous withdrawal from Aden, the Dhofar insurgency expanded rapidly in scope and acquired cross-border bases and sanctuary in South Yemen. By late 1968 the rebellion was under Marxist leadership and began to secure significant support from Communist bloc nations. By 1970 sultanate authority in the south barely extended beyond the barbed-wire perimeter of Salala, the southern region's capital.

The inability of Oman's former ruler to convince Omanis that he intended to apply the country's new oil wealth—the first commercial exports began only in 1967— to the country's welfare intensified resentment against his rule. Although some development projects were under way, the former ruler was perceived by key sectors of the Omani population and by some private and official British observers as moving much too slowly to satisfy changing Omani expectations of what a ruler should do. The ruler was also especially reluctant to facilitate the education and training of younger Omanis. This perception of inertia was a major contributing factor in his downfall.

Tribal leaders, the merchant community, large numbers of migrant Omani workers elsewhere in the Gulf, and even key members of the royal family had either withdrawn active support or entered the opposition. Indeed, the British-officered intelligence service was aware of the justice of some of the complaints against the sultan and the increasing anomaly of an army almost entirely officered by foreigners.

By 1970 rebel groups from both the north and south of the country had begun to coalesce, initiating major, if unsuccessful, operations. American and British analysts became concerned that Oman's collapse, especially at a time of overall British withdrawal from the region, threatened oil supplies and the stability of conservative regimes in neighboring states. This concern was shared by Iranian, Trucial States (now the United Arab Emirates), and Saudi decision-makers. After the July 1970 coup, a successful counterinsurgency and development program was implemented with both overt and unpublicized assistance from several states of the region, Britain, and the United States. The Dhofar insurgency was officially declared at an end in 1975.

The study of political intelligence in Oman from 1957 to 1970 provides an unusual opportunity to assess from its inception the growth and development of a small, region-oriented intelligence system and its strengths and limitations in determining political threats and transformations. Prior to 1957 the ruler denied any formal intelligence capability to his armed forces, preferring instead to rely upon a combination of tribal counselors and letter writers.

The foreign-backed 1957-59 insurrection caught the ruler by surprise and obliged him to call upon the British for assistance in July 1957. In June 1958, an Arabic-speaking former Royal Air Force intelligence officer serving in the Sultan's Armed Forces was sent to London for advanced training from the appropriate specialized British service. On his return to Oman in July, the country's first intelligence office was established in Nizwa, the capital of the interior and the largest town near rebel activities. As some former officers indicated, the Omani request for assistance also provided British intelligence personnel sent temporarily to Oman with practical experience in a region seen as vital to British security interests.

Relation to Other Intelligence Studies

Because of perceived status and career priorities, intelligence officers focus more upon declared hostile states than upon actions in states considered friendly or peripheral to imminent political and security concerns. When such threats are diffuse, involving long-term changes in popular understandings of authority and legitimacy in "small" states, rather than clearly delineated military and political threats, there is no clear intelligence target; the delineation of threats depends more upon an awareness of prevailing cultural perceptions of politics. Such was the case in pre-1970 Oman. The politics were Arab and Omani but were interpreted by both the ruler and his intelligence service within the framework of European and European-inspired understandings of Arab and Omani politics.

Intelligence activities and the shaping of foreign policy in modern societies has to date been a primary concern of political scientists and historians, not of anthropologists. Scholars from these other disciplines, as well as intelligence officials and policymakers themselves, have addressed the issue of how the informal norms and incentives of intelligence organizations shape ideas of objective and effective reporting. Jervis emphasizes how the preconceptions of policymakers significantly constrain their ability to use contrary intelligence assessments; this constraint, in turn, seriously limits the assessments offered.[3] Allison's seminal study of U.S. decisionmaking during the 1962 Cuban missile crisis highlights the organizational dynamics and perceptions at the upper levels of the policy process of a major power. Sick's accounts of the Iranian crisis of 1978-79 and of subsequent efforts to secure the release of the hostages seized at the U.S. Embassy in Tehran is especially effective in hinting at the informal norms and incentives shaping information and policy at all levels of personnel involved in the management of the crisis.[4]

More recently, the contributors to May's *Knowing One's Enemies* portray the strengths and weaknesses of particular individuals and factions operating within the intelligence and policy circles of various major powers prior to the Second World War.[5] Yet, as the title of May's work specifies, it is concerned with perceived *enemies*, not with situations in the countries of presumed friends or neutrals, that at various times in the last three decades for the United States and Britain have included Iran, Saudi Arabia, Oman, the Yemens, and Morocco. Actual or potential low-intensity conflicts in such nations are increasingly recognized as significant threats to international security.

Adequate intelligence reporting and analysis on such countries require substantial cultural and social understanding and a focus on long-term political change. Indeed, the analytical goals of anthropologists and other academics concerned with developments in non-Western countries partially overlap those of intelligence analysts. However, major intelligence organizations often rely upon smaller services whose officers receive advice, advanced training, and organizational assistance from larger metropolitan organizations. Such foreign training can inadvertently contribute to deflecting attention away from the structural and *cultural* constraints upon intelligence reporting and analysis, a primary focus of this study.

The Politics of Legitimacy

Oman's foreign-backed 1957-59 rebellion, the Jabal al-Akhdar War, received significant support in the northern interior for intertwined reasons involving both religion and the politics of oil exploration and development. In the eyes of many of the interior's tribal and religious leaders, Oman's Al Bu Said dynasty had become compromised since the late-nineteenth century through close identification with British interests.

Also, the northern interior of the country is exclusively Ibadi Muslim. The Ibadiyya, unlike their better known Sunni and Shi'a Muslim counterparts, hold that the community of the faithful (*umma*) should be led by a theocratic *imam*, selected for his religious and political qualities by a consensus of scholars and tribal leaders.[6] The *imamate* was successfully restored in 1913, and tribes acting on its behalf attacked Muscat itself. The surrender of Muscat was averted only with British intervention. By 1920 an agreement mediated by the British granted de facto internal autonomy to the northern Oman interior.

The Sultanate of Muscat and Oman, as the country was known until 1970, was in a state of near bankruptcy when Sultan Said bin Taimur assumed rule in 1932 at the age of twenty-one. The young ruler gradually elaborated a policy of reuniting his coastal domains with the interior. Concession payments by the Iraq Petroleum Company (a forerunner of Petroleum Development Oman) and military and financial support from Britain during the Second World War enabled him to pursue this policy with increased vigor after 1946. However, Imam Muhammad ibn 'Abd Allah al-Khalili (r. 1920-54) continued to block petroleum exploration in the interior. In the late 1940s, without the aging *imam's* authorization, several of his key supporters began to approach oil company representatives and diplomatic personnel outside of Oman.

Sultan Said's efforts to consolidate his rule over the interior paralleled a shift in British priorities that encouraged oil exploration and development. Sultan Said cautiously manipulated Oman's complex tribal, ethnic, and sectarian politics to facilitate oil exploration. A 1952 Saudi incursion into the northern oasis of Buraimi underscored the need to assert full sovereignty over the country. Indeed, the sultan's initial response to the Saudi incursion was to organize, in cooperation with the *imam* (recognized by the sultan as a distinguished man of learning, not as a ruler), tribal levies to expel the Saudis. However, the Omani military effort was blocked by the British, who feared a major regional conflict.

By 1954 Imam al-Khalili had died, and his successor failed to gain support for his selection from key tribal groups, in part due to the skillful intervention of Sultan Said. In December 1955 the sultan finally assumed direct administration of the interior, symbolized by the reoccupation of the Buraimi oasis and a royal "progress" in a convoy of Dodge pickup trucks to the region. This was to be the ruler's only visit to the interior.

Sultan Said was at first cautiously welcomed in many quarters and was actually seen as representing progress. When no major improvements or announcements of reform came about as a result of his assuming direct authority over the region, an opening was created for dissident elements to rebel against his rule. With support from Saudi Arabia and other Arab states, an *imamate*-in-exile was created in Dammam, Saudi Arabia, in 1954. The *imamate*'s Omani supporters were given arms and military training for cross-border incursions.

Britain intervened cautiously in the Jabal al-Akhdar War, in part out of concern for Arab protests at the United Nations; the "Oman question" became an annual fixture on the United Nations' agenda until 1971. The formal terms for British intervention were negotiated during a January 1958 visit to Muscat by Julian Amery, under secretary of state for war, and concluded in July during the sultan's annual London summer holiday.[7]

At the outset of the 1957-59 rebellion, the sultan agreed to detach several officers from his small British-officered armed forces to perform intelligence functions. This organization was regarded as insufficient in itself to fulfill intelligence requirements, especially as the rebels were based outside of Oman. The terms of the British-Omani accord specified a judicious combination of increased facilities for coping with "subversion" including a modernized military, an agreement to a modest development program (heavily subsidized by the British but obstructed from the outset by the sultan), the enhancement of the sultan's own intelligence service, and the secondment of career British military intelligence personnel for limited tours of duty in Oman. Several civilian intelligence officers were given military cover but were quickly identified by regular military personnel, were regarded as ineffective, and were finally withdrawn by 1959.

Intelligence Organization and Structure

An organizational peculiarity of pre-1970 Omani intelligence made it both international in scope and, in one respect, a miniature version of debates prevalent in intelligence organizations elsewhere. Approximately half of the shifting total of eight to ten officers present in the country at any given time were seconded from British military intelligence services, and all had specialized training in Arabic. In the nomenclature prevailing for most of the period, these were called Desert Intelligence Officers (DIOs). These officers reported both to Muscat and to external British commands in the neighboring sheikhdom of Sharjah, which was headquarters for the Trucial Oman Scouts, and in Bahrain, where the political resident for the Persian Gulf, the senior British diplomatic representative in the region, and a British SIS (MI6) station were located. Seconded officers had an average tour in Oman of two to three years. The other half of the officers, called Sultan's Intelligence Officers (SIOs), were on direct contract to Oman and were on indefinite periods of service. These officers were also British nationals.

The result was a parallel system of reporting. Officers working for the sultan reported only through the "Omani" hierarchy. All Omani intelligence was shared with the British; but seconded officers could, and on occasion did, report outside Omani channels directly to British headquarters in Sharjah and Bahrain and withhold some reporting from their Sultan's Armed Forces (SAF) counterparts. These complicated lines of authority sometimes created friction. In practice, however, cooperation was close so the reports, even those intended for "British Eyes Only," were routinely, if informally, shared. Similarly, some officers developed informal networks to exchange reports and analyses outside of formal, hierarchical channels.

The distinction between domestic and foreign intelligence was blurred both because of the dual nature of the intelligence organization and the nature of the "threat" facing the sultanate. Reports concerning Omani rebel activities in neighboring states, including occasional reports from non-British intelligence sources, were routinely, if unofficially, made available to sultanate intelligence personnel. In the sultanate itself, returning workers and amnestied rebels were regularly questioned concerning external developments, and these reports were made available to the British personnel. A few sources had regular access to the exiled *imamate* leadership, and several double agents were cultivated.

Most intelligence officers lived in villages in the interior, usually near military bases but independent of them. And each worked with an Omani "headman" (*muqaddam*), although Adenese were temporarily (and unsuccessfully) used at the outset. Headmen were significant figures in the intelligence system, although their lack of officer status caused them to be relegated to minor roles in official reporting. Since officers' roles and those of their headmen were universally known, intelligence personnel had to see as many people as possible to conceal the identities of their sources. Most officers enjoyed living in the interior. Many engaged in modest forms of medical and agricultural assistance, occasionally interceded successfully to get the sultan's decrepit local administration to work in favor of villagers, and secured amnesties for former rebels wanting to return to their villages.

Each category of officer possessed a set of conventional assumptions about the strengths and weaknesses of the other. Short-term personnel, for example, presumed that an intelligence officer burns out after several years because of enmeshment in local politics and personalities. The ability to achieve the proper balance between empathy and objectivity was deemed compromised by long stays. Long-term officers, for their part, felt that they possessed a more profound understanding of the country's politics. The two perspectives echo a common career concern among intelligence professionals in much larger organizations on the advantages to becoming "generalists" as opposed to "specialists" and of balancing empathy with professional detachment.

RESEARCH SOURCES AND METHODS

Kim Philby, admittedly an unreliable witness in other respects, perceptively remarks that "documentary intelligence, to be really valuable, must come as a steady stream, embellished with an awful lot of explanatory annotation" from "trustworthy" informants.[8] These conditions, difficult to meet in the study of intelligence systems, are met in this project. Significant quantities of the pre-1970 intelligence reports are available, often in the sequence in which they were originally prepared and filed. Further, intelligence officers involved in the preparation and analysis of these documents are available to discuss them and other aspects of their work.

Access

The study of Oman's pre-1970 intelligence system, a rather unusual project for an academic anthropologist, grew out of a prior, long-term study begun in 1978. This study focused on changing popular perceptions in Oman of community, authority, and political legitimacy under the impetus of massive and rapid social and economic transformations related to the development of oil resources.[9] This ethnographic research, conducted prior to being granted access to intelligence personnel and archives, provides an independent perspective for assessing pre-1970 intelligence reporting and analysis. The research involved intensive fieldwork in the northern Omani interior with tribesmen, tribal leaders, merchants, present and former government personnel, participants in the *imamate* administration, and former rebels and exiles as well as access to the pre-1970 political and tribal files of Petroleum Development (Oman) (PDO), then the sole oil company active in the country. This field research provided an understanding of the key events and experiences of Omanis of various generations and social categories in the tumultuous years prior to 1970.

Systematic attendance at tribal and governmental sessions in which disputes were mediated and adjudicated and sustained private discussions with a range of Omanis provided the background necessary to comprehend the evaluative, culturally specific terms and categories by which both economic and political conditions and opportunities were discerned and loyalties and obligations assessed.[10] This research provided sustained contact with persons possessing differential access to political knowledge and involvement in political affairs.

A key issue in anthropological research is how to get "insiders" to relate what they know to the researcher as they would to other insiders.[11] Living in the country's interior in Omani quarters, unlike even foreign

Arabs, and meeting non-Arab foreigners only infrequently, an Arabic-speaking anthropologist can soon be attributed with a knowledge of local conditions and an ability to understand local biographies.

"Insiders" in Oman, as elsewhere, often assert the inability of outsiders to share their perceptions of events. However, as a distinguished contemporary Arab historian observes, sometimes the outsider is less suspect of participating in local rivalries and is thus more likely to secure cooperation.[12] The outsider is also obliged to ask basic questions about the nature of the social world that "natives" are supposed to know and, therefore, ordinarily do not or cannot discuss with one another. At times the "outsider" anthropologist is also privileged to speak with persons from different social and political perspectives who do not regularly communicate with one another or who do so primarily only in restricted or highly stylized ways.

To the discomfiture of anthropologists, it might be added that the foreign intelligence officer as an outsider similarly aspires to speak across the board to persons representing different social and political perspectives. An important difference, of course, is that the anthropologist is less likely to be perceived as capable of influencing policy decisions or the actual course of events.

The initial impetus for requesting access in late 1982 to Omani intelligence files for the pre-1970 period was to derive relevant political and social information that would complement oral narratives obtained primarily through extensive interviews with participants in the events of the period. Informal inquiries suggested that of all government documents of the pre-1970 period, only the intelligence archives had survived intact.

The request for access to these records was an unusual one, but in many respects involved procedures no different from those necessary for obtaining research clearances for other aspects of social anthropological research. Field research in Oman had from the outset required the support of senior officials, who were kept regularly informed of its progress, although to their credit they never interfered. It should be noted that the use of political intelligence documents by scholars in other Middle Eastern contexts is not novel in itself. However, such documents have primarily been used to comprehend the political events reported by them and not to discern intelligence systems and knowledge in themselves.[13]

Documentary Records and Interviews

The overall quality and substance of pre-1970 Omani intelligence reporting, both in official and in private files, quickly suggested its potential for a separate, independent project in the anthropology of knowledge. The anthropologist's sustained prior and continuing research on Oman made present and former officers willing to discuss their pre-1970 work in detail because of a shared familiarity with Omani social and political history.

As in prior research, including studies of religious intellectuals and rural notables in Morocco and of Oman's first State Consultative Council (*al-majlis al-istishari li-l-dawla*), some initial interviews were met with caution and circumspection.[14] In a few cases present and former intelligence professionals interpreted their work as precluding discussions with an outsider; however, once the interviewer's goals became better known and understood, some insiders themselves facilitated further contacts. Other former intelligence practitioners offered that they had little time or formal professional inducement to explore the intellectual dimensions of their craft but readily acknowledged the value of such an activity. Cooperating with the research project provided some former officers an opportunity to engage in such exploration.

Many documents for the pre-1970 period did not survive in government files, a matter of embarrassment to some officials once authorization to these files had been granted. The best preliminary guides to the extant records were personnel who served in earlier periods and who had returned to active service in Oman. Some of these officers acknowledged that efforts to preserve records were at best intermittent. The transient involvement in Oman on the part of some officers, who perceived their careers as situated elsewhere, is in itself sociologically significant. Further, a major intelligence reorganization initiated in 1971 and a series of post-1970 physical moves of intelligence headquarters contributed to the apparently inadvertent loss of records. Some officers suggested that earlier bureaucratic rivalries may have caused some records to drop from view.

Many former officers, however, aware of the historical nature of their involvement with the country as some of the last Middle Eastern janissaries—professional outsiders loyal exclusively to the ruler—meticulously preserved copies of their personal reporting and, frequently, copies of reports and orders received. A provisional estimate is that 30 to 40 percent of these archives have survived.[15]

Surviving records for northern Oman include translations (but not the Arabic originals, possibly sent to the sultan in Salala) of all documents captured from rebels during the 1957-59 Jabal al-Akhdar War; reports of periodic conferences intended to coordinate the activities of intelligence personnel during the war; and the "Oman Intelligence Diary," a daily log recording all intelligence-related events, reports, and signals (telegraphic communications) initiated in August 1959 and replaced in November of that year, when activities became less intense, by weekly and monthly intelligence summaries (ISUMs). The file of ISUMs is almost complete for the 1959-62 period, for 1966 to 1968, and for 1969 through early 1970. Only scattered ISUMs are available for other periods. These detailed summaries include abstracts of reports from code-named sources, including separate evaluations of their reliability. Periodic lists of rebel suspects, circulated in mimeograph form, survive but not the card index, a central archive recording in summary form with cross-references to all information pertaining to persons of intelligence concern. Duplicates of some individual cards, however, provide insight into the nature of the missing index.

The files of particular posts are especially valuable, although only several of these files can be currently located. Post files included the routine reporting on specific incidents, weekly and monthly reports, and, as guides for incoming officers, more comprehensive introductions to local notables, regional political events, social groups, and sources. Other files include complete accounts of particular incidents and disputes, tasking instructions, periodic long-term "appreciations" of Omani politics written by various officers, interrogation reports in Arabic (prepared by headmen), summary accounts in English of events in neighboring countries meant for the guidance of post officers, and descriptions of economic conditions. Reports are candid and caustic, especially those initiated by seconded officers, who were regularly rotated out of Oman and not dependent upon the ruler's favor. Some four thousand pages of material are presently available. Sufficient quantities of "raw" intelligence data survive so that they can be traced through their distillation to higher levels of reporting.

Although the surviving Omani documents are not complete, there is every reason to believe that they are representative of the intelligence material produced for the 1957-70 period. Surviving Omani materials include uninterrupted sequences of documents and reports, so determined by the filing numbers. Related preliminary interviews have provided extensive explanations and glosses on incidents, procedures, and personalities. Because most of the officers who prepared this reporting were then in early or mid-career, they remain accessible for interviews concerning the contexts in which their reports were created.

Surviving documents for northern Oman have not been "weeded," to use the horticultural British metaphor equivalent to the "sanitization" of the hygiene conscious Americans.[16] Weeding would have required an intensive investment of scarce resources to accomplish a task for which no clear precedent existed. Further, intelligence officers recognized that anthropological reporting and analysis in itself requires safeguarding the reputations and privacy of persons being studied, and a standard convention of anthropological reporting is to withhold the names and identifiers of individuals unless their use is specifically agreed or is already public.

Omani intelligence reporting has genre limitations involving a stylized and learned rhetoric. Events are reduced to "cases" and "incidents," and forms of reporting learned in various branches of British military intelligence (at least for the 1957-70 period) are adapted to the conditions of the Arab Gulf.[17] The reports suggest subtle, shifting patterns of assumptions concerning Arab politics, loyalty, and authority and the "proper" role of the military. As new officers were initiated into the nuances of local concerns, their reporting became perceptibly more "proper" and "ordered."

Indeed, reports with "extraneous" background information were looked upon as unrelated to the tasks at hand. As officers were socialized into the requirements of local intelligence reporting, their perception of what was "extraneous" became more developed. The interpretation of these records is facilitated through intensive interviews that elicit the shared understandings of those who wrote the records. As many officers related, face-to-face discussions with fellow officers and informal exchanges of information often rivaled formal reporting in importance.

Preliminary interviews were begun in Oman in 1982, but systematic interviewing began in the summer of 1985 with ten of the forty-two surviving intelligence officers (out of a total of forty-seven) who served in Oman in the pre-1970 period. The intention was to interview the majority of surviving officers, of whom only two have so far declined to cooperate with the author. Contact has also been made with roughly half of the thirteen surviving former Omani headmen and with other Omanis and non-Omanis familiar with Omani intelligence activities in the pre-1970 period.

As in much anthropological work, interviews are conducted on a "not for attribution" basis unless specific agreement to the contrary is obtained, a convention followed by at least some scholars concerned with the study of intelligence.[18] The emphasis is upon eliciting shared assumptions and understandings and not to establish individual responsibilities for past actions, in which case attribution would have been more appropriate.

In interpreting initially unfamiliar intelligence documents and procedures, the author has proceeded as with other forms of anthropological inquiry. Preliminary conclusions and interpretations have been offered to "natives," in this case former intelligence officers and their assistants. Such discussion elicits more detailed comments and cases and reveals unintended lacunae.

RESEARCH ISSUES

The ongoing interviews and documentary analysis are intended to explore several complementary issues: (1) the delineation of "convergent data" related to political intelligence as a social activity, (2) the linguistic categories or key terms used by persons in the intelligence community to conduct their métier and taken for granted by them as natural or inevitable, and (3) the life cycle or career patterns of participants in the intelligence community.[19]

Convergent Data

In most fields of knowledge—the art world, international banking, professional associations, and key governmental activities, including the fields of intelligence and foreign policy—the community of significant persons rarely exceeds the size of a small village and the ways of doing things within each of these "worlds" can be just as ingrown and conventional.[20] Larger organizations often break down into work groups of similar size. The task of the anthropologist is to elicit the shared understandings of these social worlds and how they are related to one another.

Such data for Oman focus upon what tribesmen, tribal leaders, Omani officials, and merchants saw at the time as political realities and the efforts of intelligence officers and their Omani headmen to report selectively on these perceptions and activities. A central issue is how these events were perceived over time by intelligence personnel, how the "real world" activities of career and institutional loyalties shaped their perceptions and reports, and how Omanis in contact with intelligence personnel sought to manipulate intelligence perceptions and reporting. Among the influences on the style and substance of reporting were daily work routines, working "background" notions of Omani social structure and social categories, formal and informal channels of written and face-to-face communication, the definition and shifting importance of intelligence targets, "tasking," and the latitude of initiative and discretion available to individual officers and headmen.

The academic anthropologist lacks direct, sustained access to current intelligence operations and concerns. This inability to conduct direct "field" research presents less of an obstacle than may first appear to be the case. Anthropologists occasionally assert an advantage over historians in their ability to observe contemporary societies. Yet large sectors of contemporary activity are routinely closed off to direct anthropological scrutiny. The reluctance of persons and institutions in many societies to discuss current disputes with outsiders impedes lines of inquiry, which for earlier periods can be explored with ease and for which memories remain sharp. The seminal point of reference for political anthropology is often a point just behind the horizon of the present. Attitudes toward such events not only shape current activities, but also are often discussed with less reserve than contemporary events. The point just behind the horizon of the present is equally appropriate to the study of political intelligence. Properly interpreted, analyses of past events and organizational frameworks provide significant insight into current conceptual and organizational issues.

Several main themes emerge from an analysis of the convergent data available for the study of pre-1970 Omani political intelligence. There is a gradual, almost imperceptible, shift in the nature of intelligence reports from the late 1950s through the end of the 1960s that mirrors transformations in popular political sentiments elsewhere in the Middle East. In the late 1950s, when the service was still in its formative stages, most reporting was directly related to imminent military operations and defined targets such as shipments of arms and explosives. Reports were often delayed by days because of primitive communications. By the early 1960s, there were more sustained accounts of rebel organization and objectives, appreciations of the susceptibility of specific tribal notables and others to support the rebel cause, and suggestions of administrative reforms and possible "hearts and minds" developmental measures that could be pursued by the sultan, who consistently showed a singular lack of interest in such measures.

In part because of the small scale of the intelligence organization, the lines of what U.S. professionals call "tasking"—the definition of intelligence priorities and targets—are often more implicit than explicit. Only rarely are orders defining intelligence priorities transmitted from the sultan down through the military hierarchy, although like senior consumers elsewhere the ruler often expressed an interest in seeing "raw" intelligence data, such as captured rebel documents. The desk officer at SAF headquarters, Bait al-Falaj, ordered specific inquiries to be pursued, but because officers had a shared knowledge of overall objectives, tasking was generally conveyed in informal instructions.

Several times a year, Oman intelligence officers convened at Bait al-Falaj for all-day meetings. These sessions provided a major opportunity to share information informally and to specify goals. At other times, promising lines of inquiry from intelligence officers in the interior were disseminated intact to other posts with no more than a cover note from the desk officer.

Once a month either the desk officer, or in his absence the ranking SIO, would attend a meeting in either Sharjah or Bahrain to meet with the British serving in similar capacities in other Gulf countries. These meetings, which never occurred in Muscat, served as a means of disseminating regional intelligence information and provided opportunities for sustained lateral communication irrespective of formal hierarchies or responsibilities. The heads of the S.I.S. station in Bahrain paid regular visits to Muscat, but these visits were fully known to the sultan and to local intelligence personnel. Contact with other "friendly" intelligence organizations in the Arab Gulf and Indian Ocean region in the late 1960s was limited to cooperation over specific incidents.[21]

In the aggregate, intelligence reporting suggests patterned omissions due less to the skills of particular officers than to the organizational framework through which political information was collected, assessed, and disseminated. By the late 1960s, the "old threat" of the nominal theocracy in exile became replaced by the growing attraction of younger Omanis, especially the large numbers working abroad, to Pan-Arab nationalist movements.[22] Adherents to these movements were labeled the "new threat" in intelligence reports. Out of deference to the ruler, who regularly scrutinized intelligence reports, nationalists were termed "subversive nationalists."

Despite the changing attitudes of younger Omanis and their growing dissatisfaction, the intelligence organization in the late 1960s continued to work primarily with the same informants it had recruited over a decade earlier. Some officers recognized the disenchantment of politically active young Omanis with Sultan Said but did not go beyond recommending that younger Omanis be trained for intelligence work. None were. Even the older Omani personnel and sources were increasingly equivocal in providing information, preferring ambivalently to "sit out" what was seen as the coming debacle. After all, the British could leave Oman, but the Omanis would remain.

In November 1967, the same month that the last of the British left Aden, Goronwy Roberts, minister of state at the Foreign and Commonwealth Office, affirmed to Gulf rulers that Britain would support them militarily at least through the end of the 1970s. In January 1968, faced with the devaluation of sterling and domestic political pressures, Britain reneged on this commitment. In a new round of visits to Gulf rulers, Roberts informed them that the British would support them only through 1971. Thus the international climate was ideal for fostering alternative and radical political movements and ideologies.

The French scholar Xavier Raufer suggests in a thoughtful essay that the neglect by political analysts of the ideologies of contemporary groups advocating violence and terrorism, as opposed to the names of participants and their organizational structure, has hampered the ability to distinguish among them and to identify their sources of indirect support.[23] Former intelligence officers in Oman acknowledge that they paid minimal attention to dissident ideologies and their potential for creating, or at least indicating, new loyalties and organizational forms capable of attracting support beyond the small nucleus of core members. Not until 1968 did officers begin to attach importance to the activities of dissident "discussion groups" in Muscat and the capital area. These groups were belatedly recognized as linked to rebel organizations elsewhere in Oman and the Gulf and as sources of recruits for armed attacks. An important smuggled arms cache was discovered in one cell in Mutrah in June 1970. Capital-area political activities were noted but were not followed with the same intensity and skill that were devoted to tribal areas.

Part of the problem faced by intelligence officers in monitoring these movements was organizational. The sultan directly assumed responsibility for security in the capital area; the intelligence organization, operating within the framework of the military, was primarily oriented toward outlying regions. Although the ruler claimed to monitor the capital through his own resources, his ability to evelute and act upon intelligence information proved to be as deficient as it was for the 1957 rebellion, for which he disregarded ample and specific warnings.

The capital area possessed a small police force, the only one in the country except for a poorly trained "Oil Installation Police" meant to guard oil installations against sabotage. From the 1940s until 1968, it was commanded by a Baluchi officer formerly with the Muscat Infantry. In 1968 a British major from the Oman Gendarmerie was charged with reorganizing the Muscat Police. He brought in a Sri Lankan formerly with the colonial Tanganyika Police.

There was no intelligence or Special Branch office, although another ex-Tanganyika Sri Lankan was brought in to head a small Criminal Investigation Department. This officer opened some intelligence files and performed Special Branch tasks when required, but lacked the resources, languages, and local knowledge needed to perform intelligence tasks adequately.

Capital area surveillance was increased in the months prior to the 1970 coup, but suffered from significant constraints. Thus when the presence of opposition "discussion" groups was reported to the sultan, he ordered the immediate arrest of their members. Only with difficulty was he convinced to allow the "penetrated" groups to continue so that their contacts, networks, and goals could be discerned.

Similarly, the ruler initially prohibited the posting of an intelligence officer to Dhofar. When rebel activities began in earnest in 1965, the army was compelled to "smuggle" an intelligence officer into the region without the ruler's specific consent. A blind spot more attributable to the intelligence organization itself was counterintelligence. Only in the last months prior to the coup did intelligence officers, who, like other British officers in Oman, prided themselves on their relations with their subordinates, seriously consider the possibility of dissidents in the armed forces themselves.

As elsewhere, the interests of commercial and government intelligence were at times markedly distinct. For its purposes, PDO regularly monitored events both in the interior and in the capital. Unlike Omani government intelligence, PDO regularly stayed in contact with the merchant community and members of the royal family. Oil company "local relations" managers also occasionally made contact with exiles outside of the country and with senior British officials in the region outside of Oman. The manager of PDO also had regular access to the sultan but never shared his reports of these discussions with government personnel. Government intelligence officers had minimal direct access to the ruler, with the partial exception of the officer assigned to Salala to monitor the Dhofari rebel movement. Most intelligence reporting was filtered through nonintelligence military superiors, some of whom shared the ruler's disdain for intelligence reporting.

As the ruler increasingly confined himself to his palace in Salala, insulating himself even from direct contact with his intelligence officers, the loyalty of many officers incrementally shifted to the population of ordinary Omanis among whom they worked and to the army. The relation between the intelligence organization and the communities in which they served was necessarily political, moral, and personal, involving a delicate balance between empathy and detachment. Many officers retained contact with key Omanis long after their departure from the country. Living in Omani towns that were deprived of schools, adequate medical facilities, and other basic necessities and encumbered by multiple petty restrictions imposed by the ruler, intelligence officers had few illusions concerning the quality of the regime they served.

In such a small intelligence community, much secrecy was "counterfeit."[24] Especially in the final months prior to the 1970 coup, persons were often obliged to act as if they were unaware of incidents and patterns of activity that were widely known. There was general knowledge that the British were preparing to "make things happen," but the cost of publicly affirming such knowledge outweighed silence and feigned ignorance, both among Omani notables and intelligence officers aware of the deteriorating political and military situation. At times, operational necessity compelled efforts at secrecy, but in general these efforts were successful only at ensuring subsequent deniability.

Linguistic Categories and Key Terms

Professions, crafts, and academic disciplines develop a matrix of key terms and ways of formulating events and experience that express shared implicit perceptions, expectations, and understandings.[25] Since the research described here is still in a preliminary stage, it is possible only to describe the general importance of such terms. Evaluative terms in Arabic or direct quotations from informants indicating the ideological contours of loyalties or political beliefs are rarely introduced into pre-1970 intelligence reporting. In longer reports and appreciations, officers often present their own general understandings of Arab politics, such as the claim that monarchy is the most "suitable" form of government for Arab societies (from a 1968 "appreciation").

Of equal significance is the evaluative language used by officers among themselves to describe events and evaluate one another's skills. The evaluation of sources is standardized in categories such as "highly reliable," "often correct," and "unreliable" in formal reporting. Much more nuanced categories emerge from interviews and from written "appreciations" intended for local use, especially the written briefings made by officers to orient their successors. Especially valuable is the intelligence vocabulary appropriated by headmen, which often appears to be used in equally stylized ways, adapted to local working conditions, and often used in ways different from those for which the vocabulary, exclusively English, was initially intended. Indeed, headman understandings of operations and situations offer an interesting complement to those of their superiors.

One important key term emerges from how former officers evaluated one another and were evaluated in personnel reports. The label of "good operator" or "highly reliable operator" evoked the implicit criteria of good field technique, versatility, and, above all, the ability to achieve consistent results. A "good operator" ran an effective team of headmen and agents and maintained a steady flow of reliable information. The reports of a good operator were clear and concise and focused upon implicitly agreed intelligence priorities. A good operator did not have to be reminded of priorities or pushed to pursue certain topics. The best operators and headmen were said to possess an empathy with their sources but at the same time maintained a professional detachment from the "target" population.

The Life Cycle of Intelligence Officers

All DIOs and SIOs, both seconded and contract, had prior military training. All DIOs had prior military intelligence training and some had intelligence backgrounds. Some SIOs had similar backgrounds, although some locally hired contract officers were selected solely because of a prior command of Arabic. Some officers saw intelligence as a career in itself; others saw it as an interlude in their military careers, as a stepping stone to other government careers, or as a prelude to commercial activities.

Motivation within the British military intelligence community to be posted to Oman was high. Because of the active insurgency in the 1960s, it was one of the few places in the world where a British officer could get "active" intelligence experience in the British army.

Seconded officers underwent short, intensive courses in Arabic in addition to a three-month intelligence course. In retrospect many stated that classroom intelligence had minimal relevance to what they had to accomplish once in the country. As one former DIO caustically remarked, there is little point in mastering the mechanics of dead letter drops when dealing with illiterates or running safe houses when intelligence officers were almost the only foreigners in the interior and all of their movements were conspicuous.

SIOs served for indeterminate periods, and some were former DIOs who had resigned their British commissions in order to remain in the Gulf. Oman was one of the last places in the 1950s and 1960s where officers could pursue careers in an Arab country; and it attracted highly talented but sometimes idiosyncratic personnel who possessed a mixture of affinity for living under hardship conditions in a "primitive" Arab country, disillusion with postwar Britain and its empire, and a perceived lack of opportunity or challenge in the British services. A major achievement of several SIOs was to spot and deflect a major rebel initiative reportedly financed and organized in 1969 by Iraqi intelligence in Kuwait.

For DIOs, service in Oman was a passing moment in a British army career, offering possibilities for gradual promotion. For SIOs in the direct service of the sultanate, the rhythm of promotion was glacial and irregular.

With the exception of some additional training arranged by British services when the SAF was reorganized in 1959, SIOs received no additional formal training during the 1960s. However, specialist units were loaned to them by the British for interrogations and informal training after the June 1970 attack upon a military base in northern Oman.

Headmen were the third category of intelligence professionals, although usually not considered as such by members of the first two categories because they lacked officer status. Their roles were very much tied to their immediate superiors, to the point that some were praised as "brilliant extensions" of the particular officers with whom they worked. They were occasionally transferred from post to post but in general were less mobile than officers because of their irreplaceable local knowledge of politics and personalities. Headmen were often persons marginal in political importance or social standing at the time of recruitment but who rose in influence because of their role in "filtering" information to influential non-Arab superiors. Some headmen spoke English fluently; all mastered the ability to communicate in an Arabic unadorned with local dialect and thus more comprehensible to their British counterparts, all of whom had prior training in Arabic but never in its spoken Omani variants. Some headmen initiated reports in English on their own that were forwarded intact by their officers. Although some files and sources were supposed to be held "secure" from them, headmen were generally aware of the full range of activities of each post. Headmen often ran their own agents, and their personalities directly influenced the quality and nature of the information they collected. They lacked career mobility and were trained only through informal apprenticeship. Their careers were necessarily limited to Oman itself, a fact that sharply influenced the substance and scope of their activities in the late 1960s when the future of existing political institutions was very much in doubt.

TOWARD A COMPARATIVE ANALYSIS
OF POLITICAL INTELLIGENCE

As with most ethnographic studies, discerning the salient characteristics of an intelligence organization is facilitated by comparison with counterpart organizations. Although studies exist of the formation, development, and functioning of major European and Soviet intelligence organizations and of U.S. intelligence requirements,[26] few systematic studies exist of smaller, Third World intelligence organizations or their colonial predecessors. There are massive differences of scale between the intelligence organizations of the major powers, even the major regional powers, and smaller services. Such differences preclude the direct comparison of some aspects of political intelligence in a small organization with similar issues in larger ones. Likewise, differences of scale preclude the comfortable inference that the intelligence process in smaller organizations represents a microcosm of what occurs in larger ones. Yet differences of scale do not in themselves preclude properly constructed comparisons.

One possible dimension of comparison is to speculate upon what happens when the transition is made from a foreign-trained and supervised intelligence organization to a "national" one. For nonnationals in the service of foreign countries, there is more organizational loyalty. Officers with careers in external metropolitan organizations or under direct contract to a foreign government are less likely to become involved in local political maneuvers. There is more incentive to perform their roles with primary loyalty to the intelligence bureaucracy.

Once a transition to local control takes place, other factors come into play. Where promotion and advanced training require bilingualism among locally recruited individuals, there is an initial tendency to favor those minorities or privileged families that by accident of history have had greater contact and experience with foreigners. In small states the problem of competing loyalties is pervasive. The pool of potential personnel becomes restricted after "indigenization." Even when intelligence personnel are supposedly covert, there is widespread knowledge of confidential roles. Where the pool of available cadres is limited to begin with and often is drawn from extended families of notables, secrecy becomes difficult to maintain.

The compartmentalization of knowledge is also more difficult than is the case with major services in which personnel ideally identify with their service and their organizational roles. The need to balance loyalty to the state, especially to its intelligence organization, must be carefully balanced against competing personal, family, and regional interests. Information on improper activities by senior officials, for example, is unlikely to be reported if such an action would threaten career prospects. Appointments are perceived as being less dependent upon merit and loyalty to the system than loyalty to particular individuals and their interests, especially in the case of autocracies. Stated more positively, cultural factors other than primary loyalty to a bureaucratic organization come to the fore. Hence the informal, though actual, functioning of intelligence organizations begins to acquire significantly different characteristics as the transition is made to local direction and control.

A useful comparison can also be made between intelligence in terms of scale and of how information is handled in other knowledge-based organizations, including academic ones. Preliminary discussions with former U.S. intelligence analysts and scholars interested in the study of intelligence suggest that useful comparisons can be made with mid-level intelligence reporting in the U.S. intelligence community, where except in times of crisis it is unusual to have more than a handful of analysts responsible for regularly following events in Third World countries. Moreover, there are often career disincentives for acquiring the sort of cultural and sociological expertise necessary to make sense of long-term political trends in specific Third World contexts. Much pressure appears directed to reporting political activities in terms of personalities in such a manner as to diminish the need to explain cultural and sociological factors. There are clear differences of substance and scale between Omani intelligence reporting and analysis and that of large-scale intelligence organizations, but both organizational frameworks share the similarity of being closed systems in which certain types of information and interpretation tend to be undervalued, disregarded, and overlooked for organizational and cultural reasons.

In terms of the social organization of knowledge, academic research and decisions to support it are based, at least ideally, upon an extensive system of peer review, open discussion, and the exchange of ideas. It is a system particularly suited to the analysis of long-term trends, where there is a necessary uncertainty as to the range of relevant factors. Promotion is based principally upon the quality of research as evaluated by peers engaged in similar activities and generally results in enhanced opportunities to conduct similar research.

The organizational environment within which political intelligence is organized, evaluated, and reported, at least within governmental organizations, differs significantly from its academic counterpart. Government systems appear contrived to elicit clearly defined "facts," even when available information is sparse and tentative. Moreover, intelligence knowledge by its nature is secret and compartmentalized. It flows primarily through hierarchical, separated channels.[27] There are possibilities for debate, but mostly in the form of often heated and competitive "positions" between agencies. Within any given agency there is often a tendency to overcontrol, either for institutional reasons or to safeguard the reputation of superiors. The possibilities for long-term research without immediate policy implications remain the exception, not the rule. The professional rewards go to those involved in day-to-day reporting and briefing, with the successful promoted up and out to management and administrative positions.

As a former CIA officer states, "Analysts learn early in their careers to be wary of doing longer-range or in-depth studies. The task of writing such estimates and think pieces, according to the culture, is to be avoided. In fact, these studies are largely turned out by members of a special staff, who have made their peace with the system and who do not expect or require further promotion."[28]

The "community" places higher value on so-called "facts," preferably derived from classified channels, rather than upon the search for alternative, "speculative" interpretations. Indeed, the preferred government product is short reports, which the busy superior or policymaker has time to read or hear. Brief reports are not always sufficient for "thinking the unthinkable" or challenging accepted ways of doing things. They can accommodate dissent but do little to alter basic assumptions or established ways of doing things. Nor do they encourage an awareness of how the systems in which information is gathered and decisions are made themselves contain major unexamined constraints and assumptions.

As in all anthropological accounts, the value of a study of political intelligence in Oman prior to 1970 must be assessed in terms of the general insights derived from it. Three salient areas of interest can be specified here. First, this project explores a sensitive aspect of British involvement in the Arabian Peninsula, easy to categorize as "colonial" from a distance, but more complex and nuanced from both British and Arab Gulf perspectives when considered at closer range. Understanding the attitudes and assumptions of the cadre of highly talented and motivated British officers and Arab officials involved in the events of this period and discerning what they perceived and what they missed, and why, contributes directly to an understanding both of the events of the period and to the strengths and limitations of knowledge derived from political intelligence.

Second, and more generally, this project is intended as a first step toward developing insight into the sociological and cultural factors involved in the collection, interpretation, and dissemination of knowledge in the intelligence process. The intelligence apparatus in Oman was sufficiently limited in size and historically recent enough to permit intensive assessment of how operations, collection, and analysis were articulated and of the implicit peer pressures and informal understandings that led to the shaping of raw reporting, analysis, and contributions to policy throughout the entire intelligence "cycle." The small scale of the intelligence apparatus and its lack of insulation from external career and political pressures provide insight into the constraints of intelligence systems of comparable size elsewhere.

Finally, the research described here is intended as a first step toward evaluating the strengths and limitations of how other, larger intelligence communities, especially that of the U.S., perceive and interpret long-term shifts in political attitudes and expectations in non-Western cultural contexts and how such reporting and analysis can be made to contribute more effectively to the shaping of policy options. Likewise, social theory can be significantly enhanced through a renewed concern with the strengths and limitations of intelligence knowledge as a form of "authoritative" knowledge. The issues explored here primarily concern the influence of "objective" intelligence knowledge upon policy; how perceived policy and career patterns implicitly influence the production and dissemination of intelligence knowledge; and the "enclosure"[29] of valued concepts and operations, encouraging short-term "factual" questions to be raised and leaving other issues and approaches to be undervalued or even unconceived. Of course, differences of scale, organization, goals, and context preclude direct comparison beyond the countries of the Arab Gulf. Nonetheless, the issues explored here in the context of political intelligence in Oman can also be explored within other intelligence organizations and other contexts in which "authoritative" knowledge is produced.

NOTES

A key sign of the strength and confidence of any polity is the ability of those involved in it to engage in a critical discussion of political events in the immediate past and their implications for subsequent developments. I wish to thank the official and nonofficial Omanis who supported my work at various stages and those former military and intelligence officers who found sufficient intellectual interest in the present project to contribute to it. I also wish to thank Roy Godson, Jon Anderson, and two readers who prefer anonymity for comments upon an earlier draft. All intepretations and opinions expressed in this chapter remain the author's sole responsibility. The author received a summer 1986 grant from New York University's Research Challenge Fund, which facilitated the interviews and preliminary analysis of archival materials. Continued support for 1987-88 has been provided by the MacArthur Foundation Program for Research and Writing in International Security.

1. See Pierre Bourdieu, "Systems of Education and Systems of Thought," *International Social Science Journal* 19 (1967): 338-58; and Diana Crane, *Invisible Colleges: Diffusion of Knowledge in Scientific Communities* (Chicago and London: University of Chicago Press, 1972).

2. Concern with such issues within the intelligence community is usually framed in terms of how analysts should adapt to bureaucratic systems for the reporting and communication of knowledge. See, for example, Dennis C. Howley, "Intelligence, Bureaucracy, and the Country Analysts," *The American Intelligence Journal* 6, no. 4 (February 1985): 1-4.

3. Robert Jervis, "What's Wrong with the Intelligence Process?" *International Journal of Intelligence and Counterintelligence* 1, no. 1 (Spring 1986): 28-41.

4. Graham T. Allison, *Essence of Decision: Explaining the Cuban Missile Crisis* (Boston: Little, Brown and Company, 1971); Gary Sick, *All Fall Down: America's Tragic Encounter with Iran* (New York: Random House, 1985).

5. Ernest R. May, ed., *Knowing One's Enemies: Intelligence Assessment Before the Two World Wars* (Princeton, N.J.: Princeton University Press, 1984).

6. Although the formal language of the *Ibadi* theocracy implied no territorial limits to its domains, it was in practice confined to specified tribal groups in the interior with no expansion through the conversion of neighboring groups. See Dale F. Eickelman, "Religious Knowledge in Inner Oman," *The Journal of Oman Studies* 6 (1983): 163-72; and "From Theocracy to Monarchy: Authority and Legitimacy in Inner Oman, 1935-1957," *International Journal of Middle East Studies* 17, no. 1 (February 1985): 3-24.

7. John E. Peterson, *Oman in the Twentieth Century: Political Foundation of an Emerging State* (London: Croom Helm, 1978), p. 184.

8. Kim Philby, *My Silent War* (London: Granada, 1969), p. 230.

9. Field research in June and July 1978 was sponsored by a postdoctoral fellowship from the American Council of Learned Societies/Social Science Research Council Joint Committee on the Near and Middle East. Work from August 1979 through January 1981 was supported by National Science Foundation grant BNS 79/07127; and from September through December 1982, by a Fulbright-Hayes Faculty Research Abroad Award.

10. For a complementary account of some aspects of this field research, see Christine Eickelman, *Woman and Community in Oman* (New York and London: New York University Press, 1984).

11. Dale F. Eickelman, *Knowledge and Power in Morocco* (Princeton, N.J., and London: Princeton University Press, 1985), pp. 14-36.

12. Abdallah Laroui, *The History of the Maghrib: An Interpretive Essay*, trans. Ralph Mannheim (Princeton, N.J.: Princeton University Press, 1977), p. 15. On the "insider" versus "outsider" perspectives in the study of intelligence, see Walter Lacqueur, *A World of Secrets: The Uses and Limits of Intelligence* (New York: Basic Books, 1985), pp. ix-xi.

13. Among these studies are Hanna Batatu's *The Old Social Classes and the Revolutionary Movements of Iraq* (Princeton, N.J., and London: Princeton University Press, 1978), on the Iraqi Communist Party; Amnon Cohn's *Political Parties in the West Bank Under the Jordanian Regime, 1949-1967* (Ithaca, N.Y.: Cornell University Press, 1972), using captured Jordanian documents; Gilles Kepel's *The Prophet and Pharoah: Muslim Extremism in Egypt*, trans. Jon Rothschild (London: Al Saqi Books, 1985); Benny Morris's "Operation Dani and the Palestinian Exodus from Lydda and Ramle in 1948," *The Middle East Journal* 40, no. 1 (Winter 1986): 82-109, utilizing Israel Defense Force intelligence reports; and Dale F. Eickelman's *Moroccan Islam: Tradition and Society in a Pilgrimage Center* (Austin, Texas, and London: University of Texas Press, 1976), pp. 239-54, on French operations in Morocco just prior to imposition of the 1912 protectorate. Robin Bidwell's *Morocco Under Colonial Rule* (London: Frank Cass, 1973), esp. pp. 155-98, is one of the rare studies that pays direct attention to a colonial intelligence system.

14. Dale F. Eickelman, "Kings and People: Oman's State Consultative Council," *The Middle East Journal* 38, no. 1 (Winter 1984): 51-71.

15. Surviving official files were located at the Office of the Adviser on National Security Affairs, Muscat, until that office was eliminated through an administrative reorganization in 1983. Copies of other files were obtained from former officers. Plans are under way for records pertaining to the pre-1970 period to be housed in the Bait al-Falaj Military Museum, Ruwi. The author has encouraged all former officers to provide copies of their private records once this facility is opened or to deposit them with the Middle East Centre, the University of Cambridge, which has an archive collection of manuscript materials related to the Arabian Peninsula.

16. Christopher Andrew, *Secret Service: The Making of the British Intelligence Community* (London: Heinemann, 1985), p. xvi.

17. See P. S. Allfree, *Warlords of Oman* (London: Robert Hale, 1967). This book describes Allfree's experiences as a contract intelligence officer.

18. See, for example, John Prados, *The Soviet Estimate: U.S. Intelligence Analysis and Soviet Strategic Forces*, new ed. (Princeton, N.J., and London: Princeton University Press, 1986), p. xiv.

19. These categories are derived from Clifford Geertz, *Local Knowledge* (New York: Basic Books, 1983), pp. 156-60; Jervis's "What's Wrong with the Intelligence Process?" is a study based upon an in-house analysis of an intelligence organization, and deals independently with analogous issues.

20. Geertz, *Local Knowledge*, p. 156.

21. For example, Iranian intelligence intercepted a vessel carrying Dhofari rebels and arms in 1968. According to a former SIO (interview, Muscat, December 4, 1982), they were presumed at first to be Arabic-speaking Iranian subjects. Once their identity was established, Omani intelligence was invited through an intermediary organization to send a representative. In Tehran the SIO prepared written questions for the Iranians to pose to the detainees but was not allowed to meet directly with them. The Dhofaris were eventually handed over to authorities in Muscat.

22. Fifty thousand Omanis, mostly young males, out of the country's estimated population of four hundred fifty thousand in 1971, were working in neighboring states. See John Townsend, *Oman: The Making of the Modern State* (London: Croom Helm, 1977), p. 18; and Peterson, *Oman in the Twentieth Century*, p. 207.

23. Xavier Raufer, *Térrorisme, violence* (Paris: Editions Carrère, 1984).

24. Stanton K. Teft, "Secrecy, Disclosure and Social Theory," in *Secrecy: A Cross-Cultural Perspective* (New York: Human Sciences Press, 1980), pp. 39-40.

25. For extended examples of such key terms, see Eickelman, *Moroccan Islam*, pp. 123-54; and

Octave Marais and John Waterbury, "Thèmes et vocabulaire de la propagande des élites politiques au Maroc," *Annuaire de l'Alfrique du Nord* Vol. 7 (1964): 57-78.

26. Useful relevant studies and sources include Andrew, *Secret Service*; May, *Knowing One's Enemies*; Roy Godson, ed., *Intelligence Requirements for the 1980's* (7 vols.) (New York: National Strategy Information Center; Lexington, Mass.: Lexington Books, 1979-1986); Jonathan Bloch and Patrick Fitzgerald, *British Intelligence and Covert Action* (London: Junction Books, 1983); and Alfred C. Maurer, Marion D. Tunstall, and James M. Keagle, eds., *Intelligence Policy and Process* (Boulder, Colo., and London: Westview Press, 1985).

27. See Jervis, "What's Wrong with the Intelligence Process?"

28. Allan E. Goodman, "Dateline Langley: Fixing the Intelligence Mess," *Foreign Policy* no. 57 (Winter 1984-1985): 173-74. For a CIA riposte to Goodman, see George V. Lauder, "Letter," *Foreign Policy* no. 68 (Spring 1985): 171-73; and Goodman's reply on pp. 173-77 of the same issue.

29. Michel Foucault, *The Order of Things* (New York: Random House, 1970), pp. 30-34.

6

Political Intelligence in Non-Western Societies: Suggestions for Comparative Research

ADDA BOZEMAN

KNOWING THE SELF AND THE OTHER. "COMPARISON" AS CONCEPT, METHOD, AND AS PREREQUISITE FOR STATECRAFT AND POLITICAL INTELLIGENCE

Every comparison carries the assumption (1) that the phenomena up for juxtaposition are comparable and (2) that they are probably dissimilar. Further, all comparisons are initiated and guided by the researcher's explicit or implicit choice of norms for measuring relations among phenomena A, B, C, and so forth. And in that phase of the intellectual process it stands to reason that the measure of comparison will be provided by the society or culture that the scholar knows best. In fact, no comparison—whether in the context of philosophy, theology, history, economics, the social sciences, or the arts—can get off the ground unless this kind of extended self-understanding is firmly in place.

Next, it is axiomatic that one cannot proceed to comparisons without having reached an understanding of "the other" on its own terms—be it a social institution, a mindset, a nation, a language, a form of government, a way of war, or the totality of a foreign civilization. This intellectual and political challenge was often met successfully in the politically divided but morally unified European world. For example, Hugo Grotius knew that

115

he had to compare the laws, ethics, and customs of the continent's diverse peoples before he could single out affinities and accords that could be trusted to sustain order in relations between Europe's newly independent states. Indeed, the truth bequeathed by the "Father of International Law" is the effect that good international law is a function of good comparative law.[1] (Little heed has been paid to this thesis in our times.)

Also, and as illustrated by the Federalist Papers and other historical documentation, the founding fathers of the United States were not ready to draft a federal constitution until they had conducted comparative studies of European forms of constitutionalism, the English common law, and classical jurisprudence, specifically of the Roman law.

The demands implicit in cross-cultural comparisons are obviously more complex than those related to intracultural comparisons if only because the scholar cannot expect to find innate affinities such as shared religious, linguistic, ethnic, or historical legacies. Here the task of understanding "the other" usually calls for starting from scratch as the following allusions to the West's early relations with non-Western societies suggest.

Herodotus reminds us forcefully in *The Histories* that Greece was not Persia and that both knew the measure of that "otherness" throughout the protracted conflict during which neither tired of holding out for the integrity of its self-view.[2] Likewise, we know from the well-kept records of classical Rome that generations of jurists were as committed to preserving Rome's cultural integrity as they were to understanding the beliefs and institutions of multiple other human groups with which Rome had come to coexist. The main purpose of the comparison here was to distinguish, and then to link, the *ius civile* and the *ius gentium*.

It is important to bear in mind that these precedents in comparative research had not been set in academic enclaves by scholars concerned with theory building but by learned elites serving the internal and external needs of statecraft. Further, and not surprisingly, it was recognized in precisely this context that close studies of other societies were prerequisites for strategic thinking and the conduct of political and cultural relations and, therefore, that it was imperative to develop systematic methods of collecting and analyzing foreign data—in short, to ground diplomacy in what we have come to call "foreign intelligence."

The archival records of three cosmopolitan Christian power centers— the Byzantine Empire, the Papacy, and the Republic of Venice—show convincingly that these goals were concretized impressively during medieval and early modern times. Also, one learns much about what has come to be called "methodology" from this literature as well as from the biographies and narrative accounts of a host of scholarly European explorers, missionaries, diplomats, and agents of influence who were committed by choice or mandate to the cause of understanding societies in the Orient and in Africa.

Whether one follows the two ninth-century Byzantine apostles to the Slavs, who invented an alphabet for native languages, translated the Holy Scriptures for their use, and preached in Slavic; or the two sixteenth-century Dominicans, Bartolomé de Las Casas and Francisco de Vitoria, and the seventeenth-century Quaker William Penn—all three equally determined to comprehend the nature of American Indians; or Marco Polo, Matteo Ricci, and Sir William Jones who pioneered in intellectual explorations of China, India, Central Asia, and Abyssinia; or La Cerda e Almeida, Robert Moffat, David Livingstone, Richard F. Burton, Mary Kingsley, Johann L. Krapf, Henry Barth, Robert S. Rattray, and Leo Frobenius who worked ceaselessly to map Africa's human panorama, one finds an overwhelming concensus on the need to identify the foreign springs of thought and mental processes that might account for institutions, customs, beliefs, and modes of comportment that were found to differ radically from European "home" norms.

The particular purposes or reasons for these European journeys of discovery were infinitely various, whether self-set or assigned by European governments, churches, religious orders, geographic societies, medical associations, trading companies, or philanthropic enterprises. But whatever the auspices, the quests for foreign intelligence were generally uniform in aiming at opening lines of human as well as technical communication with non-Western regions; identifying politically cohesive entities—be they tribes, nations, or empires—in terms of location, language, and form of administration; gaining insight into the character traits of ruling personalities and elites; and uncovering basic values, social customs, and orientations toward the outside world.

Specific objectives ranged from propagating Christianity to improving health and education; introducing writing and literacy (as, for example, in the Slavic regions north of the Byzantine Empire and in later centuries throughout black Africa); stimulating commerce and economic reform; abolishing the Arab and European slave trade (specifically as it related to black Africa); inducing compliance with Western-type laws and modes of treatymaking; settling regional disputes at the behest of local non-Western principals; winning friends, surrogates, or clients; and extending spheres of influence or control.

Knowing the self, knowing the other, and knowing how to measure the distance between the two were prerequisites in all ventures of this kind. The relevant questions in the present inquiry are, therefore, the following: How did early Western collectors and analysts of foreign intelligence go about their business? Where and how did they find the information they were looking for? What can be said about research methods in both collection and analysis throughout the centuries that preceded the advent in the mid-nineteenth century of the modern European university with its dense variety of separate academic disciplines and methodologies and its well-stocked libraries? A reading of biographies and histories suggests convincingly that Alexander P. Martin, an American Protestant missionary in nineteenth-century China, actually spoke for many generations of Western diplomats, agents, and scholars when he noted simply, "With no book or vocabulary to guide me, I was left to form my own system."[3]

Collecting, Analyzing, and Using Information: Case Studies in China and Africa

China

In regard to China, the majority of these "personalized systems" converged on the ultimate aim of Christianizing the Chinese people. However, each emissary seems to have realized soon after his arrival that first, he could not possibly reach the people's minds unless and until he had succeeded in penetrating those of the emperor's bureaucratic elites, and, second, he would not even reach this subsidiary goal if he would openly speak about the superior qualities of a non-Chinese faith and culture.

Prolonged observation and study persuaded all Jesuit and most other Christian missionaries that indirect approaches would have to be designed in order to win confidence, respect, and official status in the empire's ruling circles. And this was indeed achieved after Matteo Ricci and his successor, Adam Schall, concluded that they would have to overwhelm the educated Chinese imagination with the wonder and precision of Western science and technology if they wanted to condition it for the reception of the most sublime of Europe's gifts. And indeed, the Jesuits' learning in mathematics, cartography, and such mechanical skills as repairing clocks, spinets, and cannons convinced the Chinese that they were dealing here with men of unrivaled learning and expertise.

But, and as Ricci had rightly fathomed, it was the impact of Occidental astronomy that convinced Ming elites and China's Manchu conquerors that they were dealing here with the sources also of unrivaled power. Ricci's correction of the Chinese calendar thus had great psycho-political importance, for almost all facets of life including political decisions ran to the rhythm of the lunar months, auspicious days, and authoritative predictions as recorded in Peking. And since the emperor was the mediator between heaven and earth in Chinese belief as well as the paramount father figure in the Sinocentric family of nations, Chinese calendars were followed unswervingly also in the tributary border states.[4]

Success in these respects earned Ricci and later Jesuits admission to the highest ranks of the bureaucracy.[5] But Ricci realized early that more was required if he was ever to attain his ultimate goal. And since he knew that his ideas would only be taken seriously if he was able to present them in Chinese and do so with literary elegance, he learned to master the language in just that measure. More important, he immersed himself in China's culture, history, and literature, specifically the Buddhist and Confucian classics, so that he could understand the Chinese mentality, communicate with the learned on an equal footing, and qualify as an instructor for their sons.

The following episode illustrates Ricci's phenomenal learning and the uses to which he put it in cross-cultural research and diplomacy. Drawing on Chinese conceptions of the past and traditions of memorization and on his own highly developed theories of memory training, Ricci wrote a short book in Chinese on how to foster advanced skills in remembrance. The purpose of this "Memory Palace"[6] was probably dual. He presented the work to a powerful Chinese governor whose sons were candidates for important government-sponsored examinations in the evident hope that success in passing the tests would enhance official interest in Christianity—the manual's ultimate mental and moral source. But this worldly calculation is offset by the substance of the work, which consists of intricate designs for fixing the meanings of Christian symbols, images, and ideas "permanently" on Chinese minds.

Hopes for permanent achievement were difficult to sustain. Both Ricci and Schall had discovered in the course of acquiring knowledge of Chinese matters that in order to convert China to Christianity they would first have to convert themselves to China. And this they had accomplished not only by reaching great depths in penetrating the foreign civilization but also by adopting the surface appearance and comportment of Chinese-ness as represented by the literati. Indeed, in the judgment of some of the latter, the two Jesuits had come to look and even think like them—an impression also relayed by Ricci when he chose the Buddhist attire while absorbed in studying that faith. It is noteworthy, however, that Ricci failed to gain the identity as a Confucian that he had ardently sought.

Disappointment deepened when the Jesuits realized that Christianity itself would have to be Sinofied to a degree and that they would have to be satisfied with winning only an "accepted place" for their religion. Further, anti-Christian and generally xenophobic reactions developed in late Ming and early Qing time—to gain momentum in subsequent centuries. In 1664 Schall was accused by his Chinese adversaries of high treason. The charge as memorialized was that he had come to Peking secretly and had posed as a calendar maker in order to engage in spying out the secrets of the imperial court.[7] The original penalty of death by dismemberment was modified to flogging and banishment, and this again was eventually muted to house arrest until death—a destiny earlier assigned also to Ricci. (Twentieth-century equivalents of this penalty probably include "hostage status" and the communist practice of "internal exile.")

I chose Matteo Ricci and his immediate successors as proponents of early modern European designs for that process of getting to know China, which is commonly called "the opening up of China," because they were pioneers in the art of examining a complex foreign literate society systematically (and sympathetically), and because they left records that tell us reliably just what they did in that business of collecting and assessing foreign data and just how and why they ultimately failed.

These records introduce the Jesuits as intelligence officers working for an ulterior ideological cause under the ultimate direction of distant principals. Yet they also, even primarily, establish them as self-directed, self-reliant scholars and personalities. Indeed, had it been otherwise, Ricci and Schall could not possibly have penetrated to the deep recesses of China's cultural and political identity while at the same time withstanding "acculturation" without morally and psychologically cracking up.

Parallels with modern Soviet and Western techniques of training and running intelligence agents abroad suggest themselves but cannot be sustained readily. In regard to "acculturation," for example, operatives today—whether native or foreign-born—also assume "new" identities and professional associations when serving abroad. But these are programmed covers and acts of dissimulation, all closely monitored by political superiors. In short, they are not open expressions of a scholar's individually felt need to know what Confucianism is all about; why Western-type law is irrelevant; why the calendar is so important; how China profits from technical assistance; or when and why a mission had to be deemed a failure.

Ricci and Schall found the answers to questions such as these. Both were thus aware of China's deep-seated hostility toward foreigners and the creeds they brought even as they valued Chinese friendship in interpersonal relations, and both came to realize that Christian missionaries were actually being appreciated mainly for their technical skills. Insights and experiences such as these were confirmed by the biography of the Belgian Jesuit Ferdinand Verbiest (seventeenth century) who ended up serving China by tutoring the K'ang-hsi emperor in astronomy, the *Elements of Euclid* (which Ricci had translated into Chinese), and spherical trigonometry, besides executing an imperial order to cast "light but effective cannons. ..."[8]

It is relevant for the particular purposes of this discussion to note that the Jesuits were also asked to act as technical advisers in matters of law and foreign affairs. Some served as multilingual interpreters in relations with the Dutch and other European governments. Others played a decisive role—thus qualifying as agents of influence in the "intelligence" meaning of that term—in negotiating border conflicts with Russia and drafting the Treaty of Nerchinsk in 1689, which purported to settle the vexing disputes "forever." However, neither this pact nor subsequent Sino-Russian accords were instrumental in narrowing existing disputes—a reality that Matteo Ricci had accurately foreseen.

There are no ancient laws in China under which the republic is governed in perpetuum, such as our laws of the twelve tables and the code of Caesar. Whoever succeeds in getting possession of the throne, regardless of ancestry, makes new laws according to his own way of thinking. . . . The extent of their kingdom is so vast, its borders so distant, and their utter lack of knowledge of a trans-maritime world is so complete that the Chinese imagine the whole world as included in their kingdom. Even now, as from time beyond recording, they call their Emperor ... the Son of Heaven.[9]

This was written when Hugo Grotius, Ricci's contemporary, composed a European code of international law by relying on the same scholarly disciplines and comparative techniques. Neither text was remembered or fully understood in the mid-nineteenth century when Alexander P. Martin, a Protestant American missionary, took time off from religious concerns to translate Henry Wheaton's *Elements of International Law* (originally published in Boston in 1836) into Chinese to help bring Chinese education and Chinese ways of conducting international relations into line with Western norms.[10] These lofty purposes were not achieved. Rather, China's imperial officials made it incontrovertibly clear that they would not follow the principles set out in the Wheaton volume even though they attached tactical usefulness to the work in their traditional scheme of planning "border defense," specifically as this related to controlling the red-haired barbarians from the West. In this context, foreign affairs administrators were able, for example, to force the Prussians to relinquish a Danish ship that they had captured in China's territorial waters.

By the end of the nineteenth century it was rather clear that Westerners had ceased trying to understand China on its own terms and were no longer able to function effectively as political agents of influence and gatherers of intelligence. Instead, they were as content to serve China as agents dispensing technical assistance as they were prepared to endure China's open and often violent persecution of the Christian faith that had brought them to the Orient in the first place. In short, they had forgotten the major purpose of the mission.

Africa

The foregoing case study illustrates orientations to the collection, analysis, and usage of information about "other," or foreign, societies that I have found to be typical of all groups of European explorers. (Constraints of time and space prevent the inclusion of additional case studies in this chapter.) But the most productive and innovative among them—at least in the context of comparative studies of intelligence—may well have been the men and women who uncovered Africa in its full geographic and human diversity. Their collective accomplishment is of singular and lasting importance—whether recorded between the fourteenth and eighteenth centuries by the Portuguese, the Dutch, and the Order of the Capuchins or in the eighteenth and nineteenth centuries by French, German, Scottish, and English nationals—for one main reason: it was carried out in a world in which writing was unknown. This meant that European explorers had to make their particular, usually lonely ways in the uncharted continental vastness without meeting people who could read or write. Further, it meant that they had to learn how to compensate for the absence of written literary and historical records by cultivating oral sources and by learning local languages through reliance only on speech. Lastly and mainly, it meant that they could not hope to master the standing task of identifying, understanding, and assessing scores of linguistically distinct communities without knowing how to gain insight into nonliterate modes of thought and communication.

Our libraries today are dense with well-kept journals and other original source materials that attest to the attainment of these objectives and to the efficacy of near-countless "personalized systems" (see *supra*, this chapter) of interpreting, projecting, and organizing the information so assembled.

Further, we learn from the data banks left by these early Occidental Africanists what we also learn from the legacies of the early Occidental Orientalists, namely, that explorers had a way of intuitively upping the stakes of their self-set or mandated tasks and of embarking on revolutionary causes. In the case of Africa, this disposition found paramount expression in determined attempts to bring writing to approximately one thousand linguistically discreet communities that had resisted literacy as represented by Egyptian, Arabic, and Coptic influences for the preceding millennia.

This revolutionary program[11] was predicated on finding and accurately assessing information about the mental, social, and political implications of orality on the one hand and writing, on the other, which was not required for the task of tracing the course of rivers like the Niger, the Nile, the Congo, or the Zambezi. Close cooperation with centers of administration, both indigenous and European, was needed, especially when it was realized by governing authorities that self-government and modern statehood were absolutely dependent upon the firm installation of writing.

The following illustrations must suffice. The first relates to the Christian Kingdom of the Kongo where the Christian sovereigns of the African Kingdom and of Portugal, the Capuchins, and the Papacy had decided in the fifteenth century to embark on a program that would introduce literacy and education and strengthen Christianity, thereby establishing the African Kingdom as a member of the international Christian society of states.

It is relevant to note that the kings of Portugal and Kongo were equals in the sense that both were subservient to the universal church; that Kongo was drawn into diplomatic relations with other European powers; and that "acculturation" between the Portuguese and the Kongolese was openly promoted by intermarriage, dispatches of diplomatic missions, exchanges of persons, and programs of technical assistance. Yet, sizable segments of the populations became resentful of the inroads made by Christianity and literacy, and anti-Christian movements arose with increasing frequency. By 1700 the Kongo had lost its status as an Afro-European state and had been reabsorbed into the African nonliterate, non-Christian scheme of things. Indeed, a twentieth-century review of this extraordinary international relationship led a leading African historian to conclude that the European presence had not left any significant traces, even though it had been experienced for four hundred years.[12]

Commitments to implant the written word so as to further such causes as education, historiography, national consciousness, statehood, and pacification were carried through in record numbers throughout the nineteenth and early-twentieth centuries. One of the most productive English scholars was Robert S. Rattray, a British colonial administrator who engaged in tireless linguistic research before he was able to give written renditions and assessments of the proverbs, folk tales, religious beliefs and rituals, and laws and constitutions that together represented the formidable Ashanti Kingdom in what is Ghana today. Another was Dr. Henry (Heinrich) Barth who spent years studying the composite societies of tributary systems that had evolved in Islamized central Africa on the basis of conquest, slavery, slave raiding, and the exaction of tribute. In regard to the role of writing in these essentially nonliterate areas, Barth concluded in the course of his explorations and negotiations that he was dealing with zones of "restricted literacy" where Arabic had been drawn into the Negro host culture in which the written word was esteemed more or less exclusively for its magical qualities.[13]

Conclusions such as these were obviously of great importance for such requirements in the conduct of Euro-African relations as the selection of allies and agents, the interpretation of incoming information, and the structuring of agreements. It is not surprising, therefore, that most European colonial administrators discriminated carefully between literate and nonliterate, Muslim and native African customs when they initiated bargaining procedures and between verbal assurances and written pacts when it came to concluding accords.[14]

Early Multidisciplinary Approaches to the Collection and Analysis of Information

The Europeans who pioneered in Africa and Asia as collectors of intelligence on behalf of the West converged on the following dispositions and ground rules for research and operation.

Most were self-directed individuals whose commitment to learn about foreign lands and peoples was basically personal and voluntary, far exceeding the needs of governments in whose services they often stood.

The ultimate source of their steadfast interest to understand the "others" they encountered was humanism in its classical and Christian connotations. This explains why comparisons with "the self" did not automatically establish "the other" as the "enemy"; why information was collected and assessed in accordance with observations of reality rather than by following preconceived theories; why the explorers were after original sources; why cross-cultural communications in matters of both collection and analysis were preferably cast in terms of interpersonal relations; and why the quests for intelligence invariably centered on the need to understand the workings of individual foreign minds and the mindsets identified with their societies.

Reflections on the work done by this innovative breed of men lead to the conclusion that the explorers reached this central target of their intellectual activities by developing what we are now accustomed to calling multidisciplinary research. The disciplines that disengage themselves from the maze of these early operations as indispensable guides for the penetration of foreign societies and their ways of thought are language studies and literature; religion, theology, philosophy, and ethics; ethnography and general anthropology; geography and history.

An overview of recorded achievements shows a consensus also on two other points: first, the humanities were deemed the most valued sources of insight for an understanding of Asian and African societies (quite contrary to what contemporary Chinese surmised, namely, that the West's inventiveness and learning were rooted in mathematics); and second, no discipline in the humanities was cultivated as assiduously and profitably as history.

Several reasons explain this focus. It was recognized by scholarly European explorers in the last five hundred years as it had been by their classical forebears that non-Western perspectives in time differed radically from their own inasmuch as time's weight was supposed to lie heavily on the past. To preserve traditional thoughtways and institutions, not to change them, has, therefore, been the standing orientation in both literate and nonliterate cultures. This meant that serious European researchers could neither assess nor deal effectively with an Asian or African society unless they had succeeded in reconstructing its past and in identifying the constant or unwobbling principles that made it "tick."

This way of digging for intelligence explains the successful identification of certain semi-covert yet effective non-Western forms of political organization and decisionmaking that would have eluded research in pure political science because they were not sufficiently concrete or adaptable to norms known in the West. The Jesuits in China could thus come to terms with the intricacies of Peking's celestial statecraft, while European Africanists had no trouble "reading" the historical and political meanings of mythical and symbolic "constitutions," understanding the past as relayed by the dreams of their informants, and assessing the actual relevance of such magical commonwealths as the conglomerate of "spirit provinces" that some Shona peoples had called into being on the Zambezi.[15]

Last but not least it should be noted in this summation of early European designs for the collection and analysis of information about foreign peoples that those in quest of intelligence were not working in academic enclosures and that they were not adverse to close cooperation with policy-making officials and institutions in their own society. Rather, the opposite seems to have been the norm. After all, and as mentioned earlier, the modern European university—upon which later American, Asian, and African universities were modeled—did not emerge before the middle of the nineteenth century. This meant that learning was not the monopoloy of the academically educated but a shared legacy on which all could draw and to which all could contribute, whether they were explorers, missionaries, government officials, envoys, agents of influence, or traveling citizens.

Nowhere in Europe were the themes sketched here more persuasively exemplified than in the long history of the Venetian intelligence system.[16] At the core of this establishment were erudite, highly disciplined envoys and secret agents who knew how to evaluate the long-range significance of events, whether recorded in Europe or Asia; how to recruit reliable informants; and how to size up the character traits and political dispositions of influential personages, whether in the Papal court in Rome, the Byzantine Christian empire, the capitals of Europe, or the far-flung domains of Mongols, Turks, Persians, and Arabs. The information thus collected was regularly submitted to the Venetian government in the form of official ambassadorial reports (*relazioni*). These were carefully preserved over the centuries in well-organized, readily accessible archives that had the ultimate function of conditioning successive generations to understand foreign societies realistically on their own terms and to develop unifying time-transcendent perspectives on the republic's national interests in world affairs.

This unusual conception of statecraft and intelligence could be concretized successfully even in the most stressful periods of any type of conflict or war because the Venetian data banks did not simply contain summaries of recent developments, biographical profiles, accounts of a given area's geography, local laws, and governmental institutions. Rather, and most importantly, they were replete with precise references to historical precedents for each of the phenomena to which an envoy had drawn the senate's attention so as to establish politically significant continuities.

History, then, was deliberately used here as the primary tool of political analysis both at home and abroad because it "contributed to the reputation of states" and because it instructed rulers "in the management of their daily business," thus assisting them "to foresee with greater prudence the things to come...." Such was the main reasoning in a decree of 1530 that stipulated the appointment of an official historian who would guard the abiding values and traditions that sustained the identity of the republic in both time and space.[17] It also persuaded the Florentine historian Guicciardini to take note of the conviction shared by "certain of the oldest and most reputable members of the Venetian Senate that Venice enjoyed a particular advantage in her ability to wait for the opportunity of times and the maturity of occasions."[18]

This judgment was essentially confirmed in the early nineteenth century by Leopold von Ranke, probably Europe's greatest historical analyst of foreign affairs and a pioneer in modern comparative studies. The theme in international history that preoccupied him throughout his life was the seemingly endless counterplay between Occident and Orient, specifically Europe and the Islamic Middle East, which was at that time dominated by the Turkish Empire. It was in this context that Ranke had occasion to reaffirm the time-transcendent function of the Venetian *relazioni* as the only reliable data bank of intelligence about critical developments in sixteenth- and seventeenth-century Turkey; and its contents presaged decadence.[19]

POLITICAL INTELLIGENCE IN AMERICAN THOUGHT AND POLICY

The United States is historically and culturally an offshoot of Europe. Two centuries ago it ceased being a European dependency and began evolving a mindset of its own. Today it is clear on the one hand that the United States is politically the lead power in that concert of states that links the Western half of Europe to North America and, on the other, that American thoughtways in the domain of statecraft and intelligence diverge significantly from those identified with all of Europe in the preceding twenty-five hundred years.

What are the determining factors in this development? Which new norms or concepts have been shaped in American scholarship and statemanship? How do they "play" in today's world environment, specifically in relations with non-Western non-Communist societies? And how effective is the U.S. political intelligence system in coping with foreign ways of conceptualizing, organizing, and using this complex matter called "intelligence"?[20]

Questions such as these should be addressed by scholars and government officials since the evidence indicates that the United States has not been as successful as it is expected to be in dealing with nations in the so-called Third World.

The point was thus often made in the course of the American Consortium for the Study of Intelligence's colloquia that the United States does not really know how today's non-Western nations "tick." And indeed, a stocktaking of intelligence and policy failures directly attributable to misperceptions and wrong assessments suggests strongly that something is askew in the nation's thoughtways when different administrations and successive generations of congressional representatives, public policy elites, and officers in the intelligence community continue to be unprepared for such developments as the Leninization of Cuba and Ethiopia, the Yom Kippur War, the Arab oil embargo, the North Vietnamese offensives of 1968 and 1975, the Shiite transformation of Iran, the Soviet Union's operations in Central America and Africa, and the Soviets' open military takeover of Afghanistan.[21] The chief underlying reasons for U.S. intelligence failures in such contexts seem to be the following:

1. Carried away by the inspiring language of the Declaration of Independence, the nation as a whole has come to commit itself to a simplistic or reductionist version of the noble message, namely, that mankind is essentially undifferentiated and that the world society is meant to be unified both morally and politically.

2. In this spirit Americans have gradually come to believe that *their* main political values, norms, and institutions—among them democracy, civil liberties ("human rights" in present-day rendition), peace, and the rule of law in national and international affairs—are the birthrights and choices of men everywhere. In accordance with this fundamentally ethnocentric self-view, the United States is a "lesson" and a guide for mankind. In that capacity it is presumed to have a missionary mandate to help democratize those who are still stuck with traditions of statecraft deviating from what are deemed to be universally valid norms of political organization and behavior.[22] In short, U.S. views of the world and of the national self appear to converge today in the certainty that culture is a nonconcept or nonreality when statecraft is the issue[23] and that, since people are meant to be essentially alike, there really are no "others." The need to assess an African, Asian, or Latin American society does not really arise in such premises. Comparisons become pointless and "political intelligence" evaporates as a concept, a process, and a set of institutions.

3. Next, modern American thought about relations between "the other" and "the self" is confounded by a neglectful disposition toward the human experience of the past. This orientation deviates from the legacy of Western civilization but is congruent with an indigenous American persuasion that all relevant history begins in 1776 and that it is actually only with the future and the very recent past that policymakers need to be concerned.

   It goes without saying in light of these assumptions that present-day Americans know little about Europe's history and its organic linkage with that of the United States and even less about the millennial past of Asian and African peoples and its extraordinary hold upon the thoughtways of present generations. True, the case of the "missing historian" is officially recognized today by the United States's schoolmasters as a grave calamity for its educational system. But the fact remains that he was not on the job in critical times to help direct the work of collecting and analyzing intelligence data on behalf of the government's foreign affairs establishment.[24]

The records thus show indisputably already in the nineteenth century that American dealings with non-Western societies are marked by great weariness with others' dispositions to respect the past. American missionaries in nineteenth- and twentieth-century China are a case in point. Martin was thus decidedly irritated by that "constant harking back to the past" in which the Chinese engaged during negotiations pertaining to one or the other plan for improving or changing a customary life-style, institution, or set of beliefs, and so were most of his countrymen.[25] All were concerned with fashioning China's future by "doing good" in terms of supplying technical assistance and modern educational facilities including medical schools; and all were destined for disappointment because the imports were resisted and at times brutally dismantled.

4. Not much had been learned from the accumulation of such experiences when the United States embarked on extensive world-wide economic aid policies after the end of World War II. The standing expectation continues to be that material improvements in living conditions will automatically spark political developments favorable to U.S. versions of freedom, democracy, and peace. Even these goals are being conceived rather mechanistically today for the United States is obviously satisfied when the foreign governments—be they non-Communist, non-Western, or Communist—provide their nations with constitutions modeled on Western norms and when they sign UN charters, resolutions, and declarations. How else can one explain the State Department's assessment that scores of long-established African and Asian societies had actually put away their past and acquired a new identity in 1948 when they affixed their signatures to the Universal Declaration of Human Rights?

The stress on materialism, economic determinism, and current events in this projection of "development" in times-to-come explains why the collection of foreign intelligence has been generally confined to recording recent economic, social, and, in some instances, military data. Altogether missing are commitments to identify the foreign nation's *own* values and idea systems; to find out how its people feel, think, and reason; and to determine whether or how the preexisting cultural infrastructure can accommodate the American norms pressed upon them now.

In short, the fourth and, in my view, most critical aspect of American dispositions toward non-Western societies—and it is obviously closely related to the preceding three—is a pronounced inability or unwillingness to come to terms with religions, philosophies, ideologies, and other bodies of belief that have decisively shaped the foreign mindsets that baffle Americans so much. As I had occasion to point out in earlier papers on comparative studies and non-Western cultures,[26] numerous strategically significant intelligence and policy failures could have been averted if we had assessed the psychological, intellectual, and political relevance of Confucianism, Legalism (also known as Realism), Buddhism, Shinto, Hinduism, Sikhism, Islam, Judaism, Africa's diverse renditions of Christianity, Islam, and Animism, and South East Asia's complex syncretisms of a variety of creeds.

A few references will serve to illustrate this issue. The United States's zeal to transform defeated Japan into a docile, nonwarring political democracy was so obsessive that the victor chose to strike at Shintoism, Japan's ancient state-sustaining religion. The program's administrator thus announced that since Shintoism had too long been used "as a tool for militarism," Japan's history texts on the subject would have to be reduced to pulp, while all "early" history would have to be assigned to the category of folklore.[27]

The same ahistorical and anticultural bias has pervaded American attitudes toward embattled non-Western allies whose independent statehood the U.S. government had vowed to preserve, for their sake as well as for that of the United States. Just as the United States never tired of calling South Vietnam to task for abiding by its own Buddhist and Confucian rules of ethics rather than by U.S. ethics—thus rendering that nation's government and people insecure even on their home ground—so has the United States been relentlessly disposed to knock the cultural infrastructure of South Korea,[28] another strategically vital ally whose inner strength is also rooted in Confucianism. Deep intelligence gaps of this kind were also at the core of U.S. failures in dealing with Iran, one of the United States's geopolitically most valued assets in the Middle East. As Americans have learned from authoritative sources, the U.S. government did not know much about either the Achaemenid-Zoroastrian traditions that the Pahlavi dynasty had activated deliberately in the twentieth century so as to support a modern secular state on Western models or the nature of the Shiite persuasion and its special role in Iran's history.[29] Americans in policy-making circles were, therefore, unprepared for the discovery, first, that the Khomeini regime was set in the mold of a totalitarian Islamic theocracy and, second, that it would be possessed by implacable hatred for the West in general and the United States in particular. Further, but in the same context, it was obviously being assumed in Washington during the United States's brief effort to halt Khomeini's violations of international laws and established diplomatic codes that Iran's laws were of the American kind. Members of the foreign service and the intelligence community were thus instructed by the Carter administration that they should under no circumstances "offend the laws of Iran" during their operations in the hostage crisis. In this as in numerous other instances, one could only conclude that area specialists in government service had not studied Islam seriously or had not been concerned with the general matter of comparative law, for it is surely common knowledge— judging by the profusion of scholarly texts on the subject—that Islamic law stands in stark contrast to U.S. law since it is an integral part of the religious faith and therewith also of Islamic statecraft.

A survey of non-Western societies in this era reveals incontrovertibly that all had acceded voluntarily to the European states' system and to the West's law of nations and that all had freely accepted Western forms of constitutionalism as core principles of administration. None of this should have been taken to mean, however, that non-Western states had suddenly become Western states. It is thus one of many puzzling blind spots in U.S. diplomacy and intelligence that scant, if any, attention was being paid on the one hand to the gradual waning of trust in panaceas offered by the West and, on the other, to the steady resurgence of confidence, even pride, in traditional ways of coping with life's insecurities on political, moral, and mental levels. Overlooked altogether, therefore, was the fact that the legacies of the past were being reactivated without discarding the new protective umbrella of modern Western-type statehood. Indeed, comparative studies show that non-Western peoples exist consciously in two different worlds and that their political representatives operate equally effectively within two conflicting frames of reference and in accordance with two disparate codes of thought and conduct.

This was confirmed and illustrated by an African judge during a collo- quium at The Hague Academy of International Law on "The Future of International Law in the Multicultural World."[30] African states, he explained, play two separate games: one on the international level of the UN and in relations specifically with the West in which they draw deliber- ately on Western norms, and another on the level of their own society and culture zone, which in counterpoint to the former, is openly atuned to local or regional values, interests, and problems.

The other self-inflicted impediment in U.S. relations with non-Western peoples is the proven U.S. incompetence to predict, contain, and assess the impact of Marxism-Leninism and totalitarian statecraft upon their destinies.[31] This failure is partly due to faulty readings of Communist strategies, but it is a function also of the United States's stubborn disposition to identify non-Western states in terms of their nominal Western appearance rather than in those of their authentic substance. Yet it is the latter, not the former, that supplied the countervailing forces to the intruding alien power, and these differ greatly from one case to the next as do the tactics of Leninist principals and surrogates. Since Americans do not know the basic or sub- stratal configurations of non-Western mindsets, they are obviously not equipped in intelligence terms either to isolate these "contra" forces or to anti- cipate, preclude, and actually cope with Communist-controlled insurgencies.

By programmatically dissimulating the true identities of just about all non-Communist non-Western states, the U.S. government has deluded itself so thoroughly that the United States has so far lost the cold war of ideas and of nerves, the twentieth-century war that really counts. For since it has been obvious for several decades that the so-called Third World is the stage on which the Soviet Union has chosen to fight and defeat the United States and the West, it should have been equally obvious that the United States cannot even hope to deal effectively with the Soviet Union's global strategy unless it understands the basic configuration of each non-Communist non-Western country.

5. My last comments on present-day American orientations to comparative intelligence studies in regard to the non-Western world bear on the state of the art in U.S. academic institutions and on the relationship between these institutions and the nation's policy-making agencies. These relations have often been described as decidedly adversarial (they seem to be warming up right now), but a juxtaposition of intelligence-related policies and intelligence-related academic research shows a near total convergence of views on major issues. The question whether this is so because the professoriate's input in terms of personnel and therewith of information has been so great as to be decisive or because it is so small as to be inconsequential may therefore be irrelevant.

Not irrelevant are the following facts: 1) academic programs made scant, if any, allowance for national security studies; they made their appearance slowly in the 1970s under the auspices of such private research centers as the National Strategy Information Center, Inc.; 2) political intelligence was conspicuously missing in the curricula until the Consortium for the Study of Intelligence succeeded in making a convincing case for honoring this age-old phenomenon of statecraft; 3) multidisciplinary approaches have been strongly advocated by the International Studies Association in earlier years, but they remain anchored, by and large, in political science, the behavioral sciences, and economic theory; and 4) comparative studies on the level of world affairs are wanting in depth and significance. As I suggest in an earlier part of this chapter, this is so for a variety of reasons, among them neglect of the humanities and therewith absence of vital data from non-Western societies.

Where, then, is the academic—and therewith the educational—focus in comparative research? Professional literature indicates that it continues to be on theory building. True, some excitement seems to have been "lost," as relayed in the proceedings of a recent conference,[32] but the consensus was that comparative political analysts are more rigorous and scientifically sophisticated than their predecessors. Little was made of the undeniable fact that non-Western cultures and societies have not brought forth academic establishments, disciplines, and theories of the kind the United States takes for granted[33] and that the United States allowed its theories to take off as universal givens even though they had evolved almost exclusively from working Western data. In short, much needs to be done by way of understanding the real world before U.S. analysts are ready to formulate internationally tenable theories.

The modern professoriate's commitment to the primacy of theory in international relations research is the counterpart of the U.S. government's present-day commitment to uphold at all costs the universal validity of some internationally untested American ideals of human life on earth. This correspondence is not surprising, since most government officials, congressmen, and senators received their education in the nation's colleges and universities. In recent times, therefore, there has been a striking convergence of inclinations not to perceive new realities, especially when these are inimical to the national interest. Indeed, the very notion of the national interest has been eroding in the last critical decades during which academic institutions cast themselves in the role of value-neutral, quasi-supernational monitors of their country's behavior in foreign affairs.

When the president of the University of Minnesota was asked by the State Department in 1981 to cooperate with its policy of imposing security restrictions on the research activities of mainland Chinese scholars (then guests on the campus), he replied curtly:

> Our mission is teaching, research, and public service, and neither our faculty nor our administrators were hired to implement security policies.[34]

Likewise, and in a similar vein, the University of California refused to allow the Department of Defense to use fifty beds at each of its five hospitals for the treatment of military casualties in the event of a war.[35] As Alvin H. Bernstein concludes in his illuminating essay,[36] there is a good deal of evidence that this kind of pronouncement is echoed approvingly throughout the groves of academe and that the assumptions underlying such rebuffs represent a wide consensus among the professoriate.

The targets singled out consistently for the deepest antagonism have been on the one hand "the military" and its "fascist mindset," and, on the other, the intelligence community, specifically the Central Intelligence Agency. Some of this ire in the ranks of our educated elites may well be due to an inadequate understanding of modern species of irregular, protracted, and political warfare and of the nullifying effect they have had on traditional American conceptions of war and its relation to peace.[37] However, the public case against political intelligence in general and its covert dimensions in particular, as it was steadfastly made in classrooms until recently and as it continues to be made in Congress and the media, appears to stem from an unresearched but culturally congenial assumption that "intelligence"—a word that had come to stand for plain old espionage and dirty tricks in the ivy halls of academe—is incompatible with an open democratic society. This, too, was poignantly illustrated when over one hundred law professors protested a bill proposed in 1981 by the Senate subcommittee on terrorism (S.2216) that was designed to ban the publication of the names of U.S. intelligence officers. Unmoved by the knowledge that such publishing would gravely imperil the lives of U.S. government agents, they stuck to their objection that the legislation in question would limit the freedom of speech and press guarantees of the First Amendment.[38]

In the vacuum of civic ethics and concern for national security that resulted from academic actions such as these, it is no wonder that leaking state secrets and classified information is today not generally viewed as treason but rather as its opposite, an exercise in true democracy. This metamorphosis of norms and values definitely conduced not only to a breakdown of security—here viewed as concept and reality—but also to a breakdown of the concept and reality of national consensus policy. In this respect, then, I agree with James A. Schlesinger who observed during a discussion of the uneasy relationship between freedom and security that "to preserve secrecy, especially in a democracy, security must be part of an accepted pattern of behavior outside of government and inside."[39]

Americans may have come closer to a national consensus on these grave matters of state in the last few years and may even have started to do something about the depleted state of U.S. intelligence capabilities. But I doubt that the United States's achievements to date would meet the standards set by George Washington—the founding father personally supervised intelligence operations during the Revolutionary War—when he insisted in a speech in 1777 on "the necessity of procuring good intelligence" and on "secrecy" as its indispensable requirement.[40] In fact, I think this nation-state has steadily regressed in the art of statecraft, mainly because it could not count on the civic support and scholarly contributions of its most highly educated elites and because its principal foreign policy-making institutions—Congress, the State Department, and the Central Intelligence Agency—have gradually become too close extensions of these elites.[41]

Robert A. McCaughey has taken a sharp look at all this in a recent volume on *International Studies and Academic Enterprise: a Chapter in the Enclosure of American Learning.*[42] There he defines "international studies" as a specific collectivity of intellectual pursuits through which Americans have sought greater knowledge and wider understanding of the world beyond their national boundaries and those of culturally akin Western Europe—those parts of the world, namely, that they have traditionally regarded as having histories, cultures, and social arrangements distinctly different from their own. Quite in contrast to other intellectual enterprises that were "academized" soon after the emergence of the university in the United States in the last third of the nineteenth century, the study of foreign cultures and societies was not monopolized or "bounded" in this fashion until 1940 when it, too, became an academic enterprise.

Among many central questions raised in this illuminating volume, the following as presented by McCaughey are particularly pertinent to the themes here under discussion:

> Could the achievements that characterized international studies as an academic enterprise have come except at the relative if not actual expense of international studies as an intellectual enterprise?
> Might not the talent and energies that academic enclosure concentrated within the university have had a more beneficial impact on American society had they been more widely dispersed?
> Did enclosure advance or hinder the formulation of an enlightened American foreign policy and the education of an internationally informed electorate?
> Need the flourishing of international studies within the university in the 1950s and 1960s have been attended by the withering of non-university components of the enterprise that seemed so vital as late as the 1930s?
> Should international studies be viewed today as "a saturated activity"?[43]

Whether U.S. intelligence studies stay within the academic enclosure or take distance from it by following in the footsteps of earlier explorers, it is probably evident to many that the nation's intelligence arteries are seriously clogged today. This challenge implies the following tasks: to refine or correct public conceptions of the meaning and function of intelligence, to reassess the curricular base for studying intelligence in all its segments, and to evaluate existing techniques of research. Unless these needs are met expeditiously, comparative studies of intelligence will not be developed since "comparison" cannot get off the ground as long as the home norms are defective.[44]

POLITICAL INTELLIGENCE STUDIES IN NON-WESTERN SOCIETIES

The coauthors of this book were asked to address the following central question: "What are the unique problems and prospects posed by the nature of your subject (intelligence in your country or region)?"

One unique problem in my case is that my subject is intelligence not in one country and not in one region but in all regions and countries commonly encompassed under the term *the non-Western world*. Communist non-Western countries are usually excluded from the non-Western category (but they are not in the purview of my assignment), either because they have been officially extinguished as sovereign states or because they have voluntarily opted to be Communist rather than non-Western, or because Western scholars and statesmen are as yet unsure of their actual identity. However, the point needs to be made that it is not possible in *our* time to understand non-Western systems—those taken over by Communist regimes and those still free to isolate differences between Western and non-Western systems of statecraft, and avoid failure in policy and intelligence contexts, unless one has Marxist-Leninist ideology and statecraft firmly in mind. Also, and specifically in the context of comparative studies, it should be mandatory to compare Communist and non-Western thoughtways to be able to estimate the impact of the former on the latter on political, mental, and psychological levels and identify linkages, affinities, and deviations.

The Question of What Is a State

A second problem in my undertaking—and I actually think it affects all of us who study intelligence—relates to the unit of comparison. We speak today either of "the non-Western world"—even though we know that it consists of hundreds of very different political entities—or of "non-Western societies"—even though we know that the word *society* may stand for village, state, city, tribe, clan, secret fraternity, bazaar, empire, a group of assassins, or the world entire. This set of uncertainties may explain why we are reluctant to let go of that tidy Occidental concept of the territorially defined nation-state that has long served as the globally valid norm or measure of political identification and comparison. But this unifying principle, too, is shaky and embattled today, nowhere more so than in non-Western and Communist regions of the world.

For example, most states in black and Islamized Africa consist of pluralities of ethnic, religious, or linguistic folk societies that have not been able to evolve into unified nations held together by shared convictions and commitments. Almost all have become fields of "foreign relations" between contending parties, and none comes to mind in which tribally induced apartheid is not the general norm of coexistence outside urban centers. Nor can one think of a new African state that has not been beset by internal tribal conflicts and warfare.

In the culturally unified Arab-Islamic Middle East, the Western model of the state is precariously grounded for different reasons. In the Islamic context, it is refuted as categorically today as was that of the Persian/Turkic power *mulkh* in the early Islamic centuries because it is absolutely incompatible with the prophet's idea of the universal *umma* of all believers. In the Arab context, meanwhile, long-established theory continues to insist on one all-Arab commonwealth, not on separate Arab nation-states. Needless to say, none of these are reliably defined in territorial terms. Further, here as elsewhere in the non-Western world, one also finds that the state has degenerated into a protective cover for the dissemination of contra-state ideologies. Internationally relevant decision making thus emanates increasingly from scattered, often dissimulated command posts of liberation fronts, terrorist brigades, provisional governments, or international Communist parties. All of these operate across state boundaries, and none is recognized in international law as an equivalent of the state.

Next, the integrity of the concept "state" is critically impaired also because it is applied to political establishments that are too different to be comparable or equal in terms of either international law or power politics.

Today the term is allowed to cover new types of vast multinational empires such as those of the Soviet Union, Communist China, and Communist Vietnam where strategic and ideological doctrines of expansion insist that existing boundaries are provisional only. At the same time, however, the word *state* continues to be the unchallenged appellation also for nations whose independence has been canceled through Communist conquest or military occupation. The Soviet Union's satellites are thus not classified as protectorates or dominions in the manner customary, for example, in the former British empire. Rather, each ranks as a sovereign state and, therefore, rates a full vote under charter provisions of the UN and other international agencies, even though it was officially deprived of its sovereignty in domestic and foreign affairs by the Brezhnev Doctrine (1968) and a reinforcing sequel enunciated by Brezhnev in the wake of the Soviet invasion of Afghanistan.

The state, then, is not the decisive working unit for intelligence studies, comparative or otherwise.[45] And the same holds mutatis mutandis for Western understandings of war and its relation to peace as incorporated in international law because the rights of war and peace were conceived from Grotian times onward as functions of the territorially defined sovereign state.[46] In short, we do not have a globally meaningful international system. Therefore, we cannot count with a precise or bounded political framework capable of hallowing all of our comparisons; to put it differently, we cannot systematize studies of intelligence in terms of a state system that is defunct.

This realization has served to confirm my view that the world society consists today as it did before the nineteenth century of a plurality of diverse political systems, and that each of these in the final analysis is the product of culture-specific ideas and modes of thinking rather than of particular political and economic arrangements. The challenge in my view of comparative studies is, therefore, to identify the structuring concepts and values that lend uniqueness or distinction to "the other" society, region, or culture—namely those that provide moral and mental security because they stubbornly resist compromise under the impact of international and intercultural relations.[47]

The Widened Field of Inquiry

Another major question to which we were asked to respond relates to the function of academic disciplines and research techniques in comparative intelligence studies, more specifically to the conceptual and/or methodological problems and prospects they might present.

On the assumption that I am proposing a somewhat different, perhaps an "alternative" approach to intelligence research, I should begin by saying that the general study of cultures, belief systems, and modes of thinking—most of them transterritorial in conception and reality—is more time-consuming and comprehensive in scope than that of territorially bounded states or political systems. In my experience, it cannot be undertaken in the narrow context of social or political science but simply requires multidisciplinary work. Further, and as explained earlier,[48] the humanities are the best guides in these endeavors, foremost among them language, literature, history, religion, philosophy, and philosophical anthropology.

For example, I could not come to intellectually satisfactory terms with the nature and incidence of war and conflict in black Africa or with African ways of absorbing or managing these phenomena until I had immersed myself in the belief systems and historical traditions of about one hundred separate African communities. Most Sinologists feel the same way about the task of understanding China in its own terms. Simon Leys explained this recently in the following passage:

> Specialization is impossible. China is an organic entity, in which every element can be understood only when put under the light of other elements; these other elements can be fairly remote from the one that is under consideration—sometimes they do not even present any apparent connection with it. If he is not guided by a global intuition, the specialist remains forever condemned to the fate described in the well-known Buddhist parable: as they wanted to figure out what an elephant really looked like they groped, one for the trunk, one for the foot, one for the tail, and respectively concluded that an elephant was a kind of snake, was a kind of pillar, was a kind of broom.[49]

The Chinese case is a particularly instructive example of the need to study particular phenomena in the extended general framework of culture. Thus it is noteworthy that the Chinese themselves have traditionally conceptualized the Middle Kingdom not as one bounded state in the company of others, but as a civilization so uniquely superior that it cannot be presumed to have frontiers. This self-view spawned China's insistently Sinocentric world view; sanctioned imperial schemes of military and political expansion; and sustained several politically and culturally potent ideas of imperial administration, chief among them the notion of the emperor's "heavenly mandate" and the concept of a family of unequal and inferior nations held together by the "Imperial Father"—images persuasively concretized throughout the centuries by the tribute system and the well-organized dependence on hedgeguarding satellites and surrogates.

The advantages of a widened field of inquiry for issue identification (in our case "intelligence") are illustrated also by studies of China's greatly various schools of thought, philosophies, and religions, which have been contending with each other from about the sixth century B.C. onward. I do not think it is possible to understand any norm, institution, or policy, either in traditional or in modern China, without both being at least on speaking terms with Confucianism and Legalism (and their often contentious interactions), Taoism, and Buddhism and remaining keenly aware in particular of the decisive impact that Legalism has had on dynastic as well as on Maoist and post-Maoist statecraft.[50] Further, it goes without saying that knowledge of these idea systems and their different syncretisms is required for any intelligence-centered research in the rest of the Orient, perhaps specifically in the Sinofied societies of northeast, southeast, and central Asia.[51]

In sum, cross-cultural comparative studies of such topics as time perspectives and history; philosophy, religion, and ideology; law, ethics, and jurisprudence; political organization, government, and statecraft; international law, diplomacy, and intelligence; conflict and conflict management; and of the relation between peace and war have persuaded me that the whole of a given society or culture must be explored before one can reach tenable conclusions about the meaning/content of one particular manifestation of "the whole."

The first segment in my scheme for the comparative study of intelligence in the non-Western world consists, therefore, of extended examinations and comparisons of non-Western cultures and societies. Since I obviously cannot append my published work on this matter to the present chapter, I decided to extrapolate the main findings in an "Inventory of General Propositions" (A) upon which I find non-Western cultures to converge. This is designed as background for the second segment dealing specifically with non-Western orientations to intelligence, which are abstracted in an "Inventory of Propositions" (B) that focuses on concordance or affinity—thus justifying our summary reference to "The Non-Western World." (Most divergences are explicitly marked under each of the two headings.)

A. Inventory of General Propositions that Determine the Meaning and Function of Intelligence in Non-Western Societies

1.   In non-Western as in Western societies, "understanding" means insight into the workings of the human mind. However, conceptions of mind differ and so do the purposes of gaining insight into it.

    Asian and African pronouncements on this subject as recorded in millennia of history and explicated in religions and philosophies of timeless significance are at one in taking a dim view of human nature. The task incumbent upon government and education, therefore, has been to know how to mold and socialize the human mind so that people would stay pliant and subservient in the stations to which they are assigned, whether by religion and birth as in India's caste system, by the Confucian dogma of the five classic human relationships as in China and most Sinofied societies, by tribal and intertribal customs as in black Africa, or by simple fiat of a ruling establishment. Nowhere are individuals presumed free and equal, destined to develop independently on their own. Rather, what one detects in all non-Western records is mistrust of the individual human being and fear of the moral, social, and political implications of individualism as this concept has been understood in the West in the last millennia.

These factors, often in conjunction with the religious requirement to eliminate the ego altogether—as in Hindu and Buddhist societies—help explain the paramountcy of authoritarian rule in the diverse provinces of the non-Western world and that striking stress on harsh punishment and internal espionage or surveillance commonly found in traditional Asian and African empires, kingdoms, caliphates, sultanates, chiefdoms, and folk societies as well as in most of their present-day successor states.

The same set of basic persuasions and ruling norms provides the reason why "the other"—namely the one who does not "belong"—is almost automatically regarded as an enemy. The following additional circumstances help explain the orientation.

2.   Non-Western societies and political systems were not designed either as nations of equal citizens or as melting pots of people. Rather, order was maintained by keeping classes, factions, and racially different groups in conditions of apartheid.

This is well illustrated in traditional China by dense catalogs of gradations in the class system—the role of regulations regarding "the mean people" (slaves, entertainers, beggars) and "the good people" and elaborate prohibitions attending relationships between members of these different categories.[52] Further, the logic of the Chinese self-view demands uncompromising hostility against non-Chinese. These were, therefore, routinely regarded and described as "devil slaves," "ghosts," "inhabitants of the nether world," "animals" or "issue of union with animals," and, of course, "barbarians"—epithets also heaped upon Europeans and Americans in the nineteenth century as in modern Communist times.[53]

African cultures differ in numerous significant respects from those associated with the Orient, but homogeneity is society's commitment here as there. Indeed, here it is an absolute requirement. For contrary to the situation in ancient literate civilizations where it was always possible, with the aid of writing and adjunct intellectual skills of communication, to extend the boundaries of the politically unified or unifiable groups, nonliterate societies had to be small and self-sufficient if they were to be effective and enduring. Furthermore, each had to be composed exclusively of people who spoke the same language, actually and figuratively, since cohesion and order cannot be assured in conditions of orality unless all people think in terms of the same symbols, identify with the same ancestral spirits, and obey the same taboos.

The order of the folk society, upon which modern Africa continues to rest, has ensured this type of closely knit, kinship-centered solidarity and conformity for millennia. The man who did not belong simply could not have a standing here (unless he became a fictitious relative through adoption). Outside such exceptional circumstances, the stranger has invariably been a calamity and an object of extreme suspicion. Frequently cast in the ritual role of scapegoat, or "carrier," he was saddled with all the evil that had accumulated in the community and driven out or killed so as to allow the in-group to survive in its authenticity.[54]

In sum, literate and nonliterate non-Western societies originated as closed, tightly controlled societies, and most have continued to be just that. Most are also conflicted societies where mistrust and hostility mark the coexistence of diverse religious, linguistic, racial, social, or ideological groups today as they did in the past, while relations between the central government and all it governs are chronically informed by reciprocal antagonisms and fears.

3.   Dissidence, subversion, internecine feuding, and conspiracy have been endemic occurrences according to the records, as are harsh responses by ruling establishments. How to discover and control conspiracies; guard against treason, overthrow, and assassination; and ferret out fifth columns within and trace their connections with enemies outside the realm have, therefore, been paramount preoccupations by rulers everywhere. A comparison of the modalities upon which pros and contras in all categories of association—whether governmental or nongovernmental—relied, shows conclusively that covert thought and covert action constituted the indispensable essence of political existence throughout the non-Western world.

A pronounced predilection for clandestine political action and organization; secrecy in decisionmaking, communication, and negotiation; and insistence on absolute confidentiality among the like-minded emerges in this context as yet another theme upon which non-Western societies have converged for centuries. Indeed, none of the scores of modern coups, plots, counterplots, insurgencies, counterinsurgencies, revolts, and civil wars could have taken place in Asia and Africa had it not been for these deeply rooted predispositions and their foremost manifestations: secret societies and secret systems of internal intelligence or espionage.

As I had occasion to note in earlier publications, Islamic empires were layered societies, composed of numerous essentially self-sufficient corporations, guilds, bazaars, sects, and religious brotherhoods. These, too, were closed societies in the sense that they were beholden to their own social codes and customs. And since they were usually hostile to state authority as well as to other non-state associations, they often engaged in clandestine and covert operations. Further, and more to the point of this discussion, flights into subversive association were so commonplace between the seventh and twentieth centuries that "the secret dissimulated society" became the normative organizational model for religious and political activism, especially in Persia and the Arab lands.[55]

Analogous patterns emerge from the histories of East Asian civilizations. China was honeycombed with secret societies, and many of them came to constitute states within the state. Some were conceived as benevolent associations, others as expressions of the criminal underworld. However, most existed for the purpose of opposing existing authorities in the ranks of the imperial administration, the mandarinate, the army, religious circles, and merchant classes and were active also in stirring up revolts or spearheading xenophobic movements. Highly disciplined as covert martial orders, which could maintain their identity and cohesiveness through reliance on a system of passwords, magic rituals, oathing, and so forth, they have been functioning effectively for centuries, often in clandestine cooperation with other revolutionary elements and aspirants to power. Secret society leaders thus became pioneers in China's Communist party and were held in considerable esteem by Sun Yat-sen, the Kuomintang, and Mao Zedong.

A related, yet somewhat different secret-society syndrome evolved in culturally homogeneous Japan. Here it was patriotism, not its opposite, that motivated Japanese citizens in the nineteenth century and thereafter to form secret associations to support the cause of imperial expansion. The precedent for this kind of service was set in the context of preparing the war against China when *Genyosha* (the "Black Ocean Society") was founded in 1881 for the purpose of gathering intelligence through undercover espionage. Described by Richard Storry (a noted English historian of Japan) as a terrorist organization and school for spies, it yet contributed greatly to Japan's dramatic victory over China. Also, it spawned another ultranationalist secret society—"The Black Dragon Society," or, more correctly, the "Society of the River Amur" (founded in 1901)—that prepared the equally successful war against Russia by collecting intelligence in Manchuria and Siberia and relaying it to the Foreign Office and the military, by organizing Chinese guerrillas to harass the Russians, and by establishing links with Muslim secret societies in the Tsarist realm.[56]

Lastly, the following are a few general observations on the place of secrecy, dissimulation, and deception in African approaches to communication and administration.[57] Here, where the communal unity of greater societies was traditionally symbolized by kings or paramount chiefs, effective power usually emanated from occult organizations. These included such secret societies as the far-flung Poro in Liberia, Sierra Leone, the Ivory Coast, and other West African regions; the Egba society in southern Nigeria; and the intricately organized "spirit" provinces linking different Shona peoples (see *supra*, this chapter).

The majority of these organisms issue from religious or metaphysical convictions. Based on the belief that the dead continue to live and take an active interest in the affairs of the living and that nature is peopled by spirits and ghosts, the secret societies exist in order to control human behavior by maintaining links with the invisible commanding principals and by exercising their right to apply ultimate sacred sanctions. Their statecraft is thus essentially magical, for it relies on a body of esoteric knowledge communicated in conditions of secrecy through the medium of masks, occult words, signs, and rites. It also depends on disciplines—usually including the taking of oaths—that are designed to rally the membership into absolute obedience to the purposes of the society as interpreted by a hidden government.

Furthermore, the case of dissimulation and covert organization is enhanced in many instances by the belief that the human realm is related inextricably to that of the animal realm. To imitate the habits, particularly the modes of killing peculiar to a locally prominent beast—as, for example, the leopard, the panther, the lion, the crocodile, or the python—and in so doing increase the sense of awe and mystery by disguising the human will or action, became the constitutional source, as it were, for such secret societies as the leopard men and, in more recent times, as, e.g., during the UN Congo War, the *Simbas* (lion men).

Further, but in the same context, attention should be drawn to the highly developed art of dissimulating human identities and intentions as this is illustrated by Africa's near-countless comprehensive agency patterns in terms of which principals can be shaded or altogether hidden by surrogates or intermediaries.

The following general trends are noteworthy today in light of the fact that modern state structures are particularly fragile in Africa. First, interactions between covert and overt regimes have been and continue to be more pronounced here than in West and East Asia. And second, many of Africa's secret societies have been degenerating steadily into unprincipled and often terrorist bands, thus further destabilizing intergroup relations and processes of administration.

The chief underlying reason for this set of developments is no doubt the spontaneous activation, in the stressful circumstances of postindependence insecurity, of traditional beliefs in such supernatural forces as witchcraft and sorcery and in the efficacy of such magical proceedings as the casting of spells and death-inducing curses. What is new today, however, is the ruthless exploitation of these beliefs by scores of modern Africa's absolutist leaders.

4. The foregoing survey of concordances among non-Western cultures and societies also provides some explanation for the common incidence of internal, or domestic, intelligence. The classical case for the necessity of keeping subjects under surveillance and of "learning the secrets of the people" was developed between the fifth century B.C. and the eleventh century A.D. by two great Asian empires.

In West Asia the practice was initiated by Persia's Achaemenid dynasty when "the King's Eyes and Ears" were institutionalized in an exemplary manner. As discerned from Hindu texts, the precedent was followed by India's Hindu kingdoms (many of them had been included in the original Persian empire). As elaborated by Persia's Sassanian dynasty, it was accepted by all Islamic caliphates, albeit in versions strictly inferior to the original model.[58] The theater of most intelligence operations, including covert actions, was everywhere in the immediate entourage of the governing personality since it was he who personified the state in the past as he does now.

In East Asia it was China that set the example beginning with the period of the Warring States. In fact China may well be *hors concours* in comparative studies of intelligence because it is the only politically unified region in the world in which policy-making has always been closely and consciously aligned with political theory. It is, therefore, difficult to imagine how the period of the Warring States could have come to an end had it not been for the impact on statecraft of that Realist (Legalist) science that began evolving in the seventh century B.C. to reach its apogee in the writings of Lord Shang, Han Fei Tzu, and Sun Tzu—works that have decisively molded military strategies and domestic policies in both dynastic and Communist China. In regard to matters of internal intelligence, it is thus noteworthy that Mao Zedung chose to follow carefully in the footsteps of the First and Second Ch'in emperors.

For example, the Communist system of grouping families or households in city dwellings and rural communes in such a way that reliable cadres can assure close surveillance of their thoughts, words, and actions recalls the precedent of a Ch'in decree on "Household Registration System." This provided that people had to be organized into groups of five and ten households that would spy on each other and expose "evil persons" so that they could be made to share in each other's crimes and penalties. Further, the parallels are close between the Maoist tactic of allowing a hundred schools of thought to bloom in order then to have them wilt and the Ch'in policy of "surveillance and castigation," which provided that all books of poetry and history had to be burnt and Confucian scholars buried alive.[59]

According to my findings in studies of Asian systems of intelligence or espionage, it is the human mind in its totality that is targeted rather than the actual evidence of willed wrongdoing. However, the studies also indicate that methods of tracking and punishing the movements of the mind differ considerably, even in the East Asian context. This is illustrated by a juxtaposition of China and Japan.

As the records of the cultural revolution show, the Chinese regime is not satisfied unless it succeeds by means of tightly organized mass "struggle sessions," extreme humiliation and physical aggression to decompose or liquidate the minds of those it has identified as traitors.[60] Their counterparts in Japan, by contrast, were usually confined to prison during the stressful 1930s. There they were pressured to think about the aberrations of their thoughts; to de-convert from positions taken earlier; and to compose a detailed, well-reasoned, and sincere *tenkosho* (recantation), even when execution was a foregone conclusion of the case. Also, they, like all other Japanese for that matter, were watched routinely in those times by the "Thought Police" (*Tokko*), which had been created in 1911 as an instrument of the government for the purpose of coping with left-wing thought and enforcing national security laws.[61]

Japanese deviations from Chinese norms are of special interest for scholars of comparative intelligence because they combined, in the course of many centuries, to constitute a unique "system," not just in non-Western but in global terms. What is noteworthy here is that Japan's system had indeed been shaped decisively by Sun Tzu in military as in civilian terms. The records not only tell of battles and protracted military campaigns, which were planned and executed in conformity with Sun Tzu's guidelines, but also are replete with accounts of teams of officially appointed spies who were constantly on the move in the country, watching and listening for any signs of revolt or criticism of the government, of experts in "divination"—a skill regarded throughout Asia (and Africa) as indispensable for intelligence work on human minds—and of an elite corps of samurai who had mastered techniques of dissimulation so completely that they could make themselves invisible.

However, and in counterpoint to Chinese conceptions and practices of internal and external intelligence, spying was acclaimed openly in Japan as a noble and patriotic duty that was doing honor to Japan. In this respect, then, Japan resembles Venice rather than China. Both were island states and empires, and it is unlikely that either could have survived had it not been for a national dread of treason and a confidence in intelligence. It is in this sense that one should probably understand the following boast attributed to Major General Fukushima after Japan's victory over Russia at the opening of the century:

> Sun Tzu would have been proud of this operation. He would have said we had followed his text-book to the very last sentence. But we know that we did better than that. We started a new book where he left off.[62]

The striking convergence of non-Western societies upon the need to know and control the human mind has numerous interlocking causes. In the context of this inventory of propositions, it also has a few interesting if somewhat discomfiting connotations for the West that deserve mention. Paradoxical as it may appear to be, one learns from a comparison of non-Western and modern Western intelligence systems that the former—which are culturally not conditioned to subscribe to individualism—pay far greater heed to the workings of the mind than the latter, which pride themselves on their commitment to the cause of the individual and are renowned for their know-how in psychology and psychiatry, yet often fail conspicuously when challenged to deal wisely with treacherous operatives of their own or defectors from an enemy camp.

The chief source of this focal non-Western concern is the deeply ingrained disposition to perceive "the other"—be he at home or abroad—as an actual or potential enemy. For whether contenders are active or dormant, non-Western common sense suggests that one cannot cope with their existence unless one always knows just what and how they think. To discover, thwart, or retool the "other's" intentions; guess or forestall his likely moves; and neutralize, trick, or turn— and, if necessary, entirely undo—his intellectual processes is thus obviously a greater, more serious challenge than *understanding* the "other" whom one does not identify in this way.

Further, but in the same context of comparative psychology, Asian biographies and histories of ideas teach that individuals in educated circles do not strive for that total integrity in commitments to causes and beliefs with which moral and mental achievements are commonly associated in the West. Rather, they tend to be at ease belonging to different schools of thought, which would be viewed as mutually exclusive in the West and representing a plurality of identities that individuals in the West would find confusing, to say the least. Yet in the perspective of intelligence concerns, there are definite merits in such dispositions. For example, the enigmatic Japanese traitor Ozaki was at one and the same time a Marxist-Leninist, a Communist internationalist, a Japanese nationalist, a member of the government's Showa Research Association, a serious scholar, a spy serving the Soviet Union, and a journalist. He, not unlike other intellectuals known in East Asian history, was a covert personality whose "true" identity was usually disguised.

Studies of Islamic patterns of thought and communication reveal closely similar variations on the theme of dissimulation. For instance and as William S. Haas points out in a pioneering analysis of the Persian mind,[63] the Shiites countered the Sunni faith of Persia's Arab conquerors by making allowance for faith by "mental reservation" (*ketman*). Under the protective cover of this religious dispensation, a Shiite was allowed to pretend that he was a Sunni, or even a Christian or a Jew, whenever he felt he was in danger of being found out by his mortal enemy. This custom gradually came to dominate other life contexts as well. In that of statecraft, *ketman* thus supplied techniques of cunning, simulation, and ruse that generations of Shiites within and outside of Persia/Iran have deployed successfully in the management of both domestic and foreign affairs.

As Americans and Europeans have had occasion to discover in recent times, it is difficult for the West's open societies to contend with this particular dimension of psycho-political warfare in the Middle East.[64] Here as throughout the Orient, rulers and ruled have traditionally recognized that deception and dissimulation are the essence of statecraft and that, as the ancient Hindus put it, a kingdom has its roots in espionage. A tightly organized network of agents and informants (the *barid*)—all masters in the art of disguise—thus spanned each caliphate or empire in the domains of the Islamic Persians, Turks, and Mongols. The ruling principle in these counterintelligence establishments was a total commitment to confidentiality and secrecy. And, as comparative historical studies of this Asian ethic show, it was honored almost two thousand years ago in India's *artha* world, where he who divulged a secret as by talking in his sleep "was to be torn to pieces,"[65] just as in this century's Near East, where the highly influential Bairut Society—which had begun as a whispering campaign of like-minded opponents to the Turkish regime—was dissolved voluntarily when it was discovered that its secret had not been kept.[66]

In short, communication throughout Asia calls not for openness but for allusiveness, indirection, and a host of secret modalities in speech and behavior. In explaining his rejection of interviews with American journalists, an Arab OPEC official said simply:

> What you have here are two different cultures. In the United States, communication is a virtue. You come home and can't wait to discuss the day's events with your wife. People who communicate well are respected. But in the Arab world, the opposite is true. Communication is a vice. Secrecy is a virtue.[67]

The West has only fragmentary knowledge of explicit intelligence arrangements in Africa's traditional nonliterate societies. One of them relates to Mzilikazi, an early nineteenth-century warrior king in the tradition of the Zulu chief Shaka, whose conquests established a far-flung Ndebele empire south of the Limpopo River in that area, then part of Southern Rhodesia, now of Zimbabwe. Since intelligence was of the utmost importance for Mzilikazi's military campaigns, diplomatic exploits, and scheme of administration, the chief relied heavily not just on usual go-betweens and scouts but on specially selected spies charged with collecting information about the movements of all enemies.

Further, Mzilikazi made extensive use of literate white traders and hunters and established unusual personal relationships with the celebrated explorer and missionary Robert Moffat and several other missionaries (among them three Americans). The major compelling motive behind these contacts seems to have been Mzilikazi's speculation that missionaries would be ideal mediators in his relations not only with other white men but also, perhaps mainly, with his native enemies.[68] However, all categories of agents were supplemented and outclassed by the ruler's wives. Stationed at every major kraal, they shared power with the district commanders and provided the king with continuous information on local developments.

More relevant for an appreciation of typically African methods of collecting information, communicating with others, and exerting influence are both the structured palaver, in which talk is meant to be protracted, discursive, and roundabout, and the vast array of overt and covert intermediaries, deputies, and ritual agents. These traditional intelligence operatives include the bards (*griots*) who are highly esteemed as masters of the spoken word; such "outcasts" as the smith whose potent curses are among the most feared sanctions; and the prophets, diviners, rainmakers, medicine men, witch doctors, and other parties with connections to the domain of the occult who are not presumed to operate on the side of order, peace, goodwill, and mutual under-standing and who occupy their positions of trust precisely because they are capable of operating beyond good and evil. What is considered active measures today was certainly an accomplished skill throughout nonliterate traditional Africa.[69]

The foregoing survey of shared culture traits suggests that non-Western societies are complex covert, not open, societies and that they are culturally and politically comfortable being just that. None of the modern non-Western states can be understood on its own terms unless one fully assesses both the present officially overt identity and the traditional covert identity and unless one finds the key to this combination.

Next, comparative studies make it clear that non-Western societies are internally conflicted by virtue of basic culture-sustaining belief systems and that relations between government and the governed are marked by standing mistrust. Cold wars of minds and nerves are thus integral aspects of the social order here; and this explains why they tend to be protracted, even endless, quite in contrast to the common American assumption that a "Cold War" has somehow been "declared" and can, therefore, also be "de-established" by an act of will.

This difference between non-Western and modern American orientations explains why internal intelligence and espionage is accepted as a must in the former and as a deviation from the Declaration of Independence and the Constitution in the latter, permissible only in a national emergency.

It also explains, in conjunction with the absence or irrelevance of the principle of territoriality in political jurisdiction, why it is at times difficult in non-Western societies to distinguish clearly between wars against individual minds and social mindsets on the one hand and irregular, indirect political warfare—including such so-called "low-intensity" conflicts as terrorism, highjacking, and assassination—on the other. Indeed, since the concept of "the enemy" transcends all boundaries, and since war and peace interpenetrate in non-Western thought, it is even difficult to draw reliable lines of distinction between any of these war-related species and outright formal military war.[70]

Whatever the captions that Western theorists have supplied for non-Western modes of waging internal and external warfare, the actual non-Western rules of engagement are essentially the same for all types of war and conflict. They were set out clearly over two thousand years ago by Sun Tzu in the context of Chinese culture and politics, but comparative studies strongly suggest that the following maxims are in fact valid summations of all non-Western practices:

> All warfare is based on deception.
> Thus, those skilled at making the enemy move do so by creating a situation to which he must conform.
> He who knows the art of the direct and indirect approach will be victorious.

The philosophy underlying these and numerous other instructions as presented in the section on "offensive strategy" centers in the norm: "Know the enemy and know yourself; in a hundred battles you will never be in peril."[71]

The Chinese and other Asian peoples learned early that only double knowing of this kind can assure successful strategic deception. However, and as Scott A. Boorman reminds us,[72] the art of attacking by stratagem is not merely outwitting an enemy—whether in internal or external statecraft. Rather, it aims at breaking his will without fighting by manipulating his view of the world and inducing him to contribute to his own encirclement. Accounts from the long period of China's Warring States thus relate in great detail how to create false impressions, use divination as a ploy in psychological warfare, exploit the vanity of opponents, and disrupt alliances in the enemy camp. Further, the records of all Oriental despotisms tell what it takes to recruit surrogate societies that would be fit to manage other "inferior" polities, how to find reliable individual agents while avoiding security risks, and when to entrust defectors with the task of collecting intelligence. In regard to the all-important matter of inducing and sustaining loyalty, one notes a remarkable concordance on favoring eunuchs and slaves.

B. I. Findings: Inventory of Propositions on Concordance of Non-Western Orientations to Intelligence

This comparative study of orientations to intelligence in the non-Western world allows for the following conclusions or propositions:

(a) Intelligence pervades and dominates statecraft.

Internal and external (or political) intelligence interpenetrate.

All intelligence stands for "knowing the enemy." Since knowing the enemy is tantamount to fighting him, the conclusion is tenable that intelligence stands for warfare of one kind or another.

(b) These circumstances, together with the absence of a politically independent academic establishment, explain why definitions of intelligence are not provided explicitly.

Those who want definitions must extrapolate them from the facts.

(c) Western definitions and classifications of the separate elements of intelligence are not readily applicable; they require adjustment.

Collection and analysis are institutionalized processes in most literate societies, but it should be borne in mind that perception and estimate are usually near-instant mental operations.

Counterintelligence is subsumed in all statecraft, and covert action is the name of the game in domestic and international affairs. Neither is adequately covered by our distinctions and definitions, which derive from premises not acknowledged in Africa and Asia.

B. II. Summary: The Relevance of Non-Western Concordances on Approaches to Intelligence for Western Scholarship

The following notations are abstracted from the foregoing analyses because they bear directly on the standing task to further the scholarly development of intelligence in the United States:

Comparative culture studies of the West, the Communist realms, and the non-Western non-Communist regions show incontrovertibly that norms and values dominant in a society's inner order are inevitably operational also in that society's relations with the outside world. This organic linkage explains why orientations to foreign or strategic intelligence are everywhere reflections of a culture's disposition to domestic government and surveillance.

Today's political systems as associated, respectively, with the West, the Communist realms, and the non-Western regions are too diverse to constitute a meaningful international system. This factor, in conjunction with other data assembled in this chapter, makes it unlikely that there can be one theory that would do justice to the world's varieties of intelligence.

An African scholar observed not long ago: "If you systematize in Africa, you lose." This cautionary advice applies in my view also to most literate, non-Western non-Communist nations. As matters stand today, U.S. intelligence is far removed from the goal of understanding the latter on their own terms. To systematize and internationalize present U.S. versions of "the truth" would, therefore, be irresponsible in the context of both scholarship and statesmanship, since it would mean simplifying or misconstruing the very ideas that make the difference in foreign affairs. (Just look at the damage done in recent years to such strategically vital Western words and concepts as *democracy, law, individual rights,* and *peace.*) What the agenda calls for in the present era is restraint in internationalizing the little we know and determined efforts to revitalize comparative multi-disciplinary studies on behalf of all that we do not yet know.

NOTES

1. This theme is developed in A. Bozeman, "On the Relevance of Hugo Grotius and *De Jure Belli Ac Pacis* for our Times," *Grotiana* Vol. 1 (1980), pp. 65-124; and in "Does International Law Have A Future?," banquet address at the annual meeting of alumni from the New York Law School, March 1984, as published in the *New York Law School Journal of International and Comparative Law* 6, no. 2 (Winter 1985): 289-299.

2. For an extended discussion of this theme, see Bozeman, "Understanding 'The Other': The Missing Link in U.S. Foreign Policy," Marshall Hayes, ed., *Book Forum* VII, no. 1 (1984): 21-24.

3. Jonathan D. Spence, *To Change China: Western Advisers in China 1620-1960* (Penguin Books, 1980; reprint of the 1969 ed. publ. by New York: Little, Brown and Company, 1980, 1984), p. 129.

4. Ibid., pp. 5-22. Also Simon Leys, *The Burning Forest* (1st American ed., New York: New Republic Books, 1985), pp. 35-46, on "Madness of the Wise: Ricci in China."

5. For example, Jesuits were regularly appointed to direct the Bureau of Astronomy.

6. See Jonathan D. Spence, *The Memory Palace of Matteo Ricci* (New York: Viking/Penguin, 1984), particularly chaps. 1-4.

7. Spence, *To Change China*, pp. 20 ff.

8. Ibid., p. 41.

9. *China in the Sixteenth Century: The Journals of Matthew Ricci, 1583-1610*, trans. Louis J. Gallagher, S. J. (New York: Random House, 1953), p. 43. On this general subject, see also Vincent Chen, *Sino-Russian Relations in the Seventeenth Century* (The Hague, Boston, London: Martinus Nijhoff Publishers, 1966); John E. Wills, Jr., "Ch'ing Relations with the Dutch, 1662-1690" in John K. Fairbank, ed., *The Chinese World Order: Traditional China's Foreign Relations* (Cambridge: Harvard University Press, 1968); *A Documentary Chronicle of Sino-Western Relations (1644-1820)*, comp., trans. and annotated by Lo-Shu-Fu, 2 vols., publ. for the Assoc. for Asian Studies (Tucson: University of Arizona Press, 1966). Adda B. Bozeman, "On the Relevance of Hugo Grotius and *De Jure Belli ac Pacis* for our Times," *Grotiana* Vol. 1 (1980), pp. 74-80, for a juxtaposition of the European and Chinese international systems. And see *infra* this chapter, section III.

10. Spence notes in *To Change China*, p. 134, that Martin had studied Ricci's skills. See *supra* and *infra* this chapter.

11. Nothing like this was attempted by the Arab-Islamic imperialisms in Africa. As Sir Henry Maine and others have pointed out, Oriental empires were tax-taking, not legislating empires of the European kind. For this comparison, see also Adda B. Bozeman, "The International Order in a Multicultural World" in Hedley Bull and Adam Watson, eds., *The Expansion of International Society* (Oxford: Clarendon Press; New York: Oxford University Press, 1984), pp. 392-396.

12. Diedrich H. Westermann, *Geschichte Afrika's: Staatenbildungen suedlich der Sahara* (Cologne: GreVen-Verlag, 1952), p. 390. For other historical accounts and analyses, see Jan Vansina, *Kingdoms of the Savanna: A History of Central African States until European Occupation* (Madison, Wis.: University of Wisconsin Press, 1966); Ian George Cunnison, *The Luapula Peoples of Northern Rhodesia: Custom and History in Tribal Politics* (Manchester: n.p., 1959); and by the same author, "Kazembe and the Portuguese 1798-1832," *Journal of African History* 2, no. 1 (1961): 61-76. For a general assessment of the relationship, see Adda B. Bozeman, "Transcultural Diplomacy: The Case of Portugal" and authorities there cited in *Conflict in Africa: Concepts and Realities* (Princeton, N.J.: Princeton University Press, 1976), pp. 334-346.

13. Henry Barth, *Travels and Discoveries in North and Central Africa, being a Journal of an Expedition Undertaken under the Auspices of H. B. M.'s Government in the Years 1849-1855* 3 vols. (New York: Harper and Brothers, 1857-1859). For excerpts and other references from this work that are relevant to the present chapter, see Bozeman *Conflict in Africa*, pp. 194 ff; 328 ff; 347; 360 ff.

14. Barth's conviction that European forms of treaty-making evoked suspicion everywhere was shared by traders, travelers, missionaries, and other explorers (among them Matthews, Moffat, Livingstone, Kingsley, and Bishop Tucker). For an overview of English responses to this problem, see Bozeman, "Transcultural Law: The Case of England," in *Conflict in Africa*, pp. 346-368.

15. For case illustrations and references to source materials, see Bozeman, chap. 6, "Mythical Vision, History and Society," pp. 100 ff, and chap. 7, "States, Empires, and Society," pp. 118 ff, in *Conflict in Africa*.

16. The Eastern Christian Byzantine Empire rates first place in a comparative study of European intelligence systems. It is not discussed here even though it apprenticed Venice because its influence on Western European statecraft was negligible. But see Bozeman, "Political Warfare in Totalitarian and Traditional Societies: A Comparison," in Uri Ra'anan, Robert Pfaltzgraff, Richard Shultz, Ernst Halperin, Igor Lukes, eds., *Hydra of Carnage: International Linkages of Terrorism—The Witnesses Speak* (Lexington, Mass.: Lexington Books, 1985), chap. 2, pp. 19-48; Bozeman, "The Byzantine Realm," in *Politics and Culture in International History* (Princeton, N.J.: Princeton University Press, 1960), pp. 298-357; and "Covert Action and Foreign Policy" in Roy Godson, ed., *Intelligence Requirements for the 1980's: Covert Action* (Washington, D.C.: National Strategy Information Center, 1981), pp. 63 ff on Venice and the United States.

17. For the text of the decree, see *Nuovo Archivio Veneto*, 3rd series, vol. 19 (1905): 332 ff.

18. See Francesco Guicciardini, *History of Italy* (Florence, Italy: n.p., 1561), bk. 3, chap. 4. For a full analysis of Venetian diplomacy, see Adda B. Bozeman, *Politics and Culture in International History*, pp. 464-498; and "Covert Action and Foreign Policy" in Roy Godson, ed., *Covert Action*, pp. 15-78, in particular, pp. 63-73, "Venice and the United States," and authorities cited in these two works.

19. For an interesting commentary on this issue, see Hans Heinrich Schaeder, *Der Mensch in Orient und Okzident, Grundzuege einer eurasiatischen Geschichte* (Munich: R. Piper & Co., 1960), pp. 407 ff.

20. As a faithful member of the founding directorate of the Consortium for the Study of Intelligence, I accept the latter's definitions of "intelligence" as a complex of ideas, a process, and a set of institutions as well as its distinctions between components of intelligence—each the subject matter of specialized publications. See Roy Godson, ed., *Intelligence Requirements for the 1980's* (1979-1986). Yet I confess to being pleased to find a note in the seventh volume of the Godson series entitled *Intelligence and Policy* (Lexington, Mass.: Lexington Books, 1986), p. 106, that tells us that, in practice, covert action and counterintelligence are intimately connected with collection, since the human infrastructure for covert action is often scarcely distinguishable from that of collection, while collection is intimately involved in counterintelligence.

   In the context of political operation, I find great merit in Sherman Kent's thought that intelligence work remains the simple, natural endeavor to get the sort of knowledge upon which a successful course of action can be rested. "Strategic Intelligence," Kent continues, "is the knowledge upon which our nation's foreign relations, in war and peace, must rest." See his *Strategic Intelligence for American World Policy* (Hamden, Conn.: Archon Books, 1965), preface, p. xxii.

In the context of the present chapter, this comes close to saying that political or strategic intelligence is knowledge of "the other."

21. See Malcolm Wallop, "Speech to the Veterans of O.S.S.," September 25, 1979. Also B. Hugh Tovar, "Covert Action," in Roy Godson, ed., *Intelligence Requirements for the 1980's: Elements of Intelligence* (Washington, D.C.: National Strategy Information Center, rev. ed. 1983), pp. 72-79.

22. This orientation marked policy pronouncements in the Carter administration, notably in respect of "human rights," and it has become prominent also in the Reagan administration where the stress is on "democracy." For a recent expression of this policy commitment, see Secretary of State George P. Shultz, "New Realities and New Ways of Thinking," *Foreign Affairs* 63, no. 4 (Spring 1985): 718, 709, 710, 705. The ambiguities of "the new thinking" appear clearly when these pages are read in the sequence indicated. The core meanings of "democracy," for which worldwide accord is claimed, are nowhere clearly stated in policy statements. And the same holds for the "human rights" references during the Carter administration.

   For extended examinations of these matters, see Adda B. Bozeman, "American Policy and the Illusion of Congruent Values," *Strategic Review* (Winter 1987): 11-23; "U.S. Foreign Policy and the Prospects for Democracy, National Security, and World Peace," *Comparative Strategy* 5, no. 3 (1985): 223-267; "The Roots of the American Commitment to the Rights of Man," *Rights and Responsibilities*, copyrighted proceedings of a November 1978 conference sponsored by the Center for Study of the American Experience, the Annenberg School of Communications, University of Southern California, 1980, pp. 51-102; and "Human Rights and National Security," *The Yale Journal of World Public Order* 9, no. 1 (Fall 1982): 40-78.

23. What is odd about all this is that Americans generally continue to be avid students of foreign religions, philosophies, ideologies, art styles, social institutions, and literary forms and that they have no difficulty acknowledging each of these foreign expressions of life as unique and, therefore, as different from equivalent phenomena in the United States.

24. For distressing evidence of bungled historical facts and misunderstandings of political developments, see, e.g., *Country Reports on Human Rights Practices* for 1983 and 1982 as issued by the State Department's Bureau of Human Rights and Humanitarian Affairs. These publications were officially distributed as background for a colloquium on "Human Rights in Asia."

25. See part I of this chapter and Spence, *To Change China*, pp. 129 ff; 161-183, for an illuminating account of Dr. Edward Hume's service and the "Yale for China" complex.

26. Among them Adda Bozeman, "The Nuclear Freeze Movement: Conflicting Moral and Political Perspectives on War and Its Relations to Peace," George Tanham, ed., *Conflict: All Warfare Short of War* 5, no. 4 (1985): 271-305; "Statecraft and Intelligence in the Non-Western World," Ibid., 6, no. 1 (1985): 1-35; "Political Warfare in Totalitarian and Traditional Societies: A Comparison," chap. 2 in *Hydra of Carnage*; "U.S. Foreign Policy and the Prospects for Democracy, National Security, and World Peace," in *Comparative Strategy*; "Covert Action and Foreign Policy," in *Covert Action*, pp. 15-79; "War and the Clash of Ideas," *Orbis* 20, no. 1 (Spring 1976): 60-103; and *The Future of Law in the Multicultural World* (Princeton, N.J.: Princeton University Press, 1971).

27. Obituary of General Dyke, *New York Times*, January 18, 1980.

28. For some poignant illustrations in intelligence-related contexts, see William Colby and Peter Forbath, *Honorable Men: My Life in the CIA* (New York: Simon and Schuster, 1978), pp. 270-298.

29. Adda B. Bozeman, "Iran: U.S. Foreign Policy and the Tradition of Persian Statecraft," *Orbis* 23, no. 2 (Summer 1979): 387-402.

30. René-Jean Dupuy, ed., *The Future of International Law in a Multicultural World*, Proceedings of a Colloquium November 17-19, 1983 (The Hague, Boston, London: Martinus Nijhoff Publishers, 1984), for these and other comparisons, among them Bozeman, "A Preliminary Assessment of the Future of International Law," pp. 85-104.

31. For a brief but lucid reminder of this record, see Professor Marvin Alisky's letter to the *Wall Street Journal*, January 10, 1986, "Chiang Kai-shek had to go and China got Mao Tse-tung. ... Batista had to go and Cuba got Castro. ... Diem had to go and Vietnam got enslaved. ... Somoza had to go and Nicaragua got Ortega. ... Ian Smith had to go and

Rhodesia-Zimbabwe got Robert Mugabe. . . . The Shah had to go and Iran got the Ayatollah.
. . . Marcos must go. But awaiting power are Filipinos antagonistic to long-range US
interests." For Southeast Asian reactions to U.S. interferences in the Philippine elections,
see Barbara Crossette, "Asian Nations Alarmed," *New York Times*, February 15, 1986.

32. See James A. Bill, "Area Studies and Theory-Building in Comparative Politics: A
Stocktaking," *PS* (Fall 1985): 810 ff, for an interesting account of academic views.

33. But see Victor LeVine's reservations, Ibid., p. 811; also Herbert Simon, *Models of Man:
Social and National* (New York: Wiley Publishers, 1957), as noted by Richard J. Heuer,
Jr., "Strategic Deception and Counterdeception: A Cognitive Process Approach," *International
Studies Quarterly* 25, no. 2 (June 1981): 294-327, see p. 295: "We behave rationally within
the confines of our mental model, but this model is generally not well adapted to the
requirements of the real world."

34. *New York Times*, November 27, 1981, Barbara Crossette reporting. See Alvin H. Bernstein,
"The Academic Researcher and the Intelligence Analyst: How and Where the Twain Might
Meet," in Bruce W. Watson and Peter M. Dunn, eds., *Military Intelligence and the Universities:
A Study of an Ambivalent Relationship* (Boulder, Colo., and London: Westview Press, 1984),
pp. 37 ff for references and interpretations of the evidence.

35. *Chronicle of Higher Education*, January 16, 1982, p. 3.

36. Watson and Dunn, eds., *Military Intelligence*, pp. 37 ff.

37. This issue is analyzed in Adda B. Bozeman, "The Nuclear Freeze Movement: Conflicting
Moral and Political Perspectives on War and Its Relation to Peace," *Conflict: All Warfare
Short of War* 5, no. 4 (1985): 1-35.

38. W. Jackson Stenger, "The Perspective from Academe," in Watson and Dunn, eds., *Military
Intelligence*, pp. 1 ff, notes on p. 10 that academic opposition to a military connection is
now deeply imbedded in the universities.

39. *New York Times*, December 22, 1984. See Senator Barry Goldwater to the effect that "(we)
have the fourth-best intelligence system in the world—behind Israel, England, and Russia.
We could do better. . . ." *US News and World Report*, December 17, 1984.

40. These reminders were made by former Attorney General William French Smith in a speech
(December 18, 1981) that dealt with the depleted state of U.S. intelligence capabilities before
the advent of the Reagan administration.

41. For the most constructive critical analysis of this dilemma, see two papers by Senator Malcolm
Wallop, "The Role of Congress," in *Hydra of Carnage*, pp. 251-257, and "U.S. Covert Action:
Policy Tool or Policy Hedge?" *Strategic Review* (Summer 1984): 9-16.

42. *International Studies and Academic Enterprise: a Chapter in the Enclosure of American Learning*
(New York: Columbia University Press, 1984).

43. For references see Ibid., preface, p. xvi. For the definition of "enclosure," see preface, p.
xiv, and part I, "In the Land of the Blind, 1810-1940." The section on the founders of
American East Asian studies (pp. 82 ff) relates directly to section I of the present chapter
where nineteenth-century American emissaries to China are discussed.

44. Robert Rossow addressed a similar challenge in the 1960s when he examined the needs of
"the new diplomacy" that was evolving at that time. The agenda for recasting the training
of diplomats (he likens them to cross-cultural interpreters), which he submits in a paper
on "The Professionalization of the New Diplomacy," *World Politics* XIV, no. 4 (July 1982):
561-575, is of great relevance also for us today. Rossow warns against overdoing "pure"
social science because it would lead to disciplinary parochialism, to the conversion of
methodologies into ideologies, and to the widening of the gulf that exists between the world
of science and scholarship and the world of affairs of state. The main objects of study in
his view are culture patterns, social processes, and value systems. The culture concept should
be the starting point of professional training, and the needed disciplines here are anthropology,
history, psychology, and linguistics. A subgroup of methods comprises those that deal with
the comparative analysis of value systems and ideologies—a field (he notes) that is aptly called
"philosophical anthropology" but is not being adequately covered by the standard disciplines.

45. This was recognized by William F. Casey in regard to Central America and the Caribbean.
He noted in the summer of 1982 when he dealt with the Central American situation that
the estimates program was "way down" when he took charge of the Central Intelligence
Agency: "I asked for an estimate on the Cubans and their activities. I got it after two

months—and it neglected to mention Cuba's relationship with the Soviet Union." Suzanne Garment, "Capital Chronicle" on "Casey's Shadows: A Greater Emphasis on CIA Analysis," *Wall Street Journal*, July 16, 1982. For a comprehensive analysis of the present world's main war-torn regions and of U.S. strategy in Central America and the Middle East, see an interview with Mr. Casey in *US News and World Report*, April 23, 1984, pp. 27-29.

46. I have developed these conclusions in several earlier books and papers, among them *The Future of Law in the Multicultural World* (Princeton, N.J.: Princeton University Press, 1971); "The Future of International Law," Dupuy, ed., *The Future of International Law in a Multicultural World*; "The Nuclear Freeze Movement: Conflicting Moral and Political Perspectives on War and Its Relation to Peace" in *Conflict: All Warfare Short of War* 5, no. 4 (1985): 1-35; "Statecraft and Intelligence in the Non-Western World," *Conflict: All Warfare Short of War* 6, no. 1 (1985): 271-305; and "The International Order in a Multicultural World," in Hedley Bull and Adam Watson, eds., *The Expansion of International Society* (Oxford: Clarendon Press; New York: Oxford University Press, 1984).

47. For an extended version of this theme, see Adda B. Bozeman, "Civilizations under Stress: Reflections on Cultural Borrowing and Survival," *The Virginia Quarterly Review* 51, no. 1 (Winter 1975): 1-18.

48. Cp. *supra* this chapter, parts I & II.

49. Simon Leys, *The Burning Forest*, p. 4.

50. This has been overlooked by many Western Sinologists who chose to focus on Confucianism as the molding force.

51. The same general case for the analysis of belief systems is here made, albeit by implication, in respect of Christianity and Islam.

52. See T'ung-tsu Ch'u, *Law and Society in Traditional China* (Paris and The Hague: Mouton, 1961), pp. 128; also the "Penal Codes" identified with the T'ang and other dynasties. Cp. *supra* this chapter, part I, with observations by early European researchers, including Ricci.

53. See H. R. Issacs, "Group Identity and Political Change: The Role of Color and Physical Characteristics," *Daedalus* (Spring, 1967); and other references in Adda Bozeman, *The Future of Law*, pp. 140-160. For a recent exposition of this type of bias in the rest of Asia see Barbara Crossette, "Prejudice is One of Asia's More Common Afflictions," *New York Times*, December 29, 1985, The Week in Review.

54. See Bozeman, *Conflict in Africa*, pp. 95-99 and notes 69-76 for references and illustrations. The pronounced hostility for all things Western that pervades African rhetoric and policy today can be understood as a modern enactment of this stubborn old theme.

55. Bozeman, "Covert Action and Foreign Policy," in Roy Godson, ed., *Covert Action*, pp. 35-56; for the organization of secret societies and their role in politics, see specifically pp. 53 ff. Also "Statecraft and Intelligence in the Non-Western World" in *Conflict: All Warfare Short of War* 6, no. 1 (1985): 271-305.

56. See Richard Storry, *A History of Modern Japan* (Ontario: Penguin Books, 1979), pp. 145 ff, and *The Double Patriots: A Study of Japanese Nationalism* (Boston: Houghton Mifflin, 1957). Also, Richard Deacon, *A History of the Japanese Secret Service: Kempei Tai* (New York: Berkley Books, 1985), especially chap. 4 and chap. 7.

57. These themes are developed in Bozeman, *Conflict in Africa*, chaps. 5, 6, 7, 9, and 18.

58. I have presented the Persian, Islamic, and Indian intelligence systems in considerable detail in "Covert Action and Foreign Policy" in *Covert Action* and *Politics and Culture in International History*. The best explication and rationalization of the system is found in Nizam al-Mulk, *The Book of Government or Rules for Kings*, trans. Hubert Darke (London: Routledge & Kegan, first publ. 1960, 2nd ed. 1978), under such titles as "On Intelligence Agents and Reporters" and "On Sending Spies for the Good of the Country" and, in regard to India, in the *arthasastras* and other original literature.

59. Li Yu-ning, ed., *Shang Yang's Reforms and State Control in China* (White Plains, N.Y.: M. E. Sharpe, Inc., 1977), pp. 35 ff, 42, 48, 91.

60. See also Ti Chiang-Hua, "The Physical and Mental Destruction of the Ping-Pong Team—A Sports Horror," trans. Emily Wang, *Free China Review*, January 1986, pp. 29 ff. The champion athletes who had made great contributions to Chou En-lai's "ping pong" diplomacy were subsequently persecuted as traitors in so relentless a manner that one after the other was driven to commit suicide. This experience, the author notes, recalls the old Chinese

saying: "Once the birds are gone, the bow can be cast away; once the hares are bagged, the hounds can be killed for food."

61. Chalmers Johnson, *An Instance of Treason: Ozaki Hotsumi and the Sorge Spy Ring* (Stanford, Calif.: Stanford University Press, 1964). Richard Storry and F. W. Deakin, *The Case of Richard Sorge*, (1966); and Richard Deacon, *Kempei Tai*, for close analyses of the Japanese system and some internationally significant modern cases of treason, espionage, and retribution.

62. Deacon, *Kempei Tai*, p. 79. For other instructive information in regard to these psychopolitical issues, see Truong Nhu Tang, *A Vietcong Memoir*, with David Chanoff and Doan van Toai, (San Diego, New York, London: Harcourt Brace Jovanovich, 1985).

63. See William S. Haas, *Iran* (New York: AMS Press, 1966), and Ann K. S. Lambton, "The Spiritual Influence of Islam in Persia" in A. J. Arberry and Rom Landau, *Islam Today* (London: n.p., 1943), pp. 163-177, on the doctrine of *taqiya*, a dispensation from the requirements of religion under compulsion or threat of injury.

64. Cp. Angelo Codevilla and Roy Godson, "Intelligence (Covert Action and Counterintelligence) as an Instrument of Policy" in Roy Godson, ed., *Intelligence Requirements for the 1980's: Intelligence and Policy* (Lexington, Mass.: Lexington Books, 1986), p. 102, for a searching discussion of the problems that the United States faces in this area of statecraft.

65. Heinrich Zimmer, *The Philosophies of India*, Joseph Campbell, ed., Bollingen series xxvi (New York: Pantheon Books, 1951), p. 83; also Bozeman "Covert Action and Foreign Policy," in *Covert Action*, pp. 56-63 and notes 52-62.

66. Bozeman, "Covert Action and Foreign Policy," in *Covert Action*, pp. 51-55.

67. *New York Times*, November 3, 1984.

68. Bozeman, *Conflict in Africa*, p. 290 ff.

69. Ibid., chap. 18; pp. 259-303; also pp. 9 ff, 366 ff, and notes.

70. Cp. Ernest R. May, ed., *Knowing One's Enemies: Intelligence Assessment before the Two World Wars* (Princeton, N.J.: Princeton University Press, 1984).

71. Sun Tzu, *The Art of War*, trans. Samuel B. Griffith (London: Oxford University Press, 1981), p. 84.

72. Scott A. Boorman, "Deception in Chinese Strategy: Some Theoretical Notes on the Sun-Tzu and Game Theory," in W. Whitson, ed., *The Military and Political Power in China* (New York: Praeger, 1972), pp. 313-337; also his important volume on *The Protracted Game: A wei-ch'i Interpretation of Maoist Revolutionary Strategy* (New York: Oxford University Press, 1969).

About the Contributors

Christopher Andrew is a senior tutor at Corpus Christi College, University of Cambridge. He is vice chairman of the British Study Group on Intelligence and a member of the Executive Committee of the International Studies Association's Intelligence Studies Section. Dr. Andrew is the author of *Her Majesty's Secret Service: The Making of the British Intelligence Community* and a coeditor of the journal *Intelligence and National Security*.

Adda Bozeman is professor emeritus of international relations at Sarah Lawrence College, Bronxville, New York. She has studied and written extensively on the interrelationship of culture and statecraft. Among her major works are *Politics and Culture in International History* and *Conflict in Africa: Concepts and Realities*. She is a founding member of the Consortium for the Study of Intelligence and a member of the Executive Committee of the International Studies Association's Intelligence Studies Section.

John J. Dziak is a defense intelligence officer at the Defense Intelligence Agency, Washington, D.C. In 1970 he received his PhD in Russian history and currently is an adjunct professor in Georgetown University's National Security Studies Program, where he teaches about Soviet intelligence. His most recent book is *Chekisty: A History of the KGB*.

Dale F. Eickelman is a professor of anthropology at New York University and a member of the board of directors of the Middle East Studies Association and the editorial board of *The International Journal of Middle East Studies*. He has conducted extensive anthropological field research in North Africa and the Sultanate of Oman. His most recent book is *Knowledge and Power: Religious Intellectuals in Rural Morocco*.

Kenneth G. Robertson is director of studies at the graduate school of European and international studies at the University of Reading. He is also a secretary of the British Study Group on Intelligence. He is the author of *Public Secrets: A Study in the Development of Government Secrecy*. Recently he edited *British and American Approaches to Intelligence*.

About the Editor

Roy Godson is associate professor of government at Georgetown University, coordinator of the Consortium for the Study of Intelligence, and program coordinator of the Intelligence Studies Section of the International Studies Association.

For eighteen years Dr. Godson has taught courses at Georgetown University on international relations, national security and foreign policy, and U.S. and Soviet intelligence. In 1979 he helped establish the Consortium for the Study of Intelligence to promote teaching and analysis of intelligence policy under the auspices of the National Strategy Information Center. He is the editor of the consortium's seven-volume series *Intelligence Requirements for the 1980's* and coauthor of *Dezinformatsia: Active Measures in Soviet Strategy*.